SERIES ON

ISSUES IN

SECOND

LANGUAGE

RESEARCH

under the editorship of

Stephen D. Krashen and **Robin C. Scarcella**

ISSUES IN SECOND LANGUAGE RESEARCH is a series of volumes dealing with empirical issues in second language acquisition research. Each volume gathers significant papers dealing with questions and hypotheses in areas central to second language theory and practice. Papers will be selected from the previously published professional literature as well as from current sources. The first book in the series is *Research in Second Language Acquisition*. Subsequent books will each focus on one issue, including communicative competence (edited by Scarcella, Andersen, and Krashen).

CHILD-ADULT DIFFERENCES
IN
SECOND LANGUAGE ACQUISITION

Stephen D. Krashen
*University of
Southern California*

Robin C. Scarcella
*University of
Southern California*

Michael H. Long
*University of
Pennsylvania*

EDITORS

Newbury House Publishers, Inc.   Rowley, Massachusetts 01969
ROWLEY • LONDON • TOKYO

1982

Library of Congress Cataloging in Publication Data
Main entry under title:

Child-adult differences in second language
    acquisition.

    1. Language and languages--Study and teaching--
Addresses, essays, lectures.   2. Language
acquisition--Addresses, essays, lectures.   3. Child-
ren and adults--Addresses, essays, lectures.
I. Krashen, Stephen D.   II.   Scarcella, Robin C.
III. Long, Michael H.
P53.C48   401'.9   81-11323
ISBN 0-88377-206-X   AACR2

NEWBURY HOUSE PUBLISHERS, INC.

Language Science
Language Teaching
Language Learning

ROWLEY, MASSACHUSETTS 01969
ROWLEY ● LONDON ● TOKYO

First printing: April 1982

Printed in the U.S.A.   5   4   3   2

ACKNOWLEDGMENTS AND COPYRIGHTS

The editors are grateful to the contributors to this volume for allowing us to reprint their material. We also thank the publishers of the journals and volumes listed below for their permission to reprint the articles contained in this volume.

Asher, J., and Garcia, G. The optimal age to learn a foreign language. *Modern Language Journal.* 1969, 38, 334–341.

Seliger, H., Krashen, S., and Ladefoged, P. Maturational constraints in the acquisition of second languages. *Language Sciences.* 1975, 38, 20–22.

Oyama, S. A sensitive period for the acquisition of a nonnative phonological system. *Journal of Psycholinguistic Research.* 1976, 5, 261–285.

Oyama, S. The sensitive period and comprehension of speech. *Working Papers on Bilingualism.* 1978, 16, 1–17.

Patkowski, M. The sensitive period for the acquisition of syntax in a second language. *Language Learning.* 1980, 30, 449–472.

Olson, L., and Samuels, S. J. The relationship between age and accuracy of foreign language pronunciation. *Journal of Educational Research.* 1973, 66, 263–267.

Asher, J., and Price, B. The learning strategy of total physical response: some age differences. *Child Development.* 1967, 38, 1219–1227.

Snow, C., and Hoefnagel-Höhle, M. The critical period for language acquisition: evidence from second language learning. *Child Development.* 1978, 49, 1114–1128.

Snow, C., and Hoefnagel-Höhle, M. Age differences in the pronunciation of foreign sounds. *Language and Speech.* 1977, 20, 357–365.

Fathman, A. The relationship between age and second language productive ability. *Language Learning.* 1975, 25, 245–253.

Ekstrand, L. Age and length of residence as variables related to the adjustment of migrant children, with special reference to second language learning. In G. Nickel (ed.), *Proceedings of the Fourth International Congress of Applied Linguistics,* Stuttgart: Hochschulverlag, 1976, 3, 179–197.

Ekstrand, L. English without a book revisited: The effect of age on second language acquisition in a formal setting. *Didakometry* (Department of Educational and Psychological Research, School of Education, Malmo, Sweden), no. 60, October 1978.

Krashen, S., Long, M., and Scarcella, R. Accounting for child-adult differences in second language rate and attainment. *TESOL Quarterly.* 1979, 13, 573–582.

CONTENTS

Introduction   ix

I   Long-term studies of children and adults   1

1   J. Asher and R. García   The optimal age
to learn a foreign language   3

2   H. Seliger, S. Krashen, and P. Ladefoged   Maturational
constraints in the acquisition of second languages   13

3   S. Oyama   A sensitive period
for the acquisition of a nonnative phonological system   20

4   S. Oyama   The sensitive period
and comprehension of speech   39

5   M. Patkowski   The sensitive period for the acquisition
of syntax in a second language   52

II   Short-term studies of children and adults   65

6   L. Olson and S. J. Samuels   The relationship between age
and accuracy of foreign language pronunciation   67

7   J. Asher and B. Price   The learning strategy of the total
physical response: some age differences   76

8   C. Snow and M. Hoefnagel-Höhle   Age differences
in the pronunciation of foreign sounds   84

9   C. Snow and M. Hoefnagel-Höhle   The critical period
for language acquisition: evidence from second language
learning   93

III   Short-term studies of older and younger children   113

10   A. Fathman   The relationship between age and second
language productive ability   115

11   L. Ekstrand   Age and length of residence as variables
related to the adjustment of migrant children, with special
reference to second language learning   123

12 L. Ekstrand   English without a book revisited: The effect of age on second language acquisition in a formal setting   136

IV Some generalizations   159

   13 S. Krashen, M. Long, and R. Scarcella   Age, rate, and   161
       eventual attainment in second language acquisition

V Some explanations   173

   14 R. Scarcella and C. Higa   Input and age differences in second language acquisition   175

   15 S. Krashen   Accounting for child-adult differences in second language rate and attainment   202

INTRODUCTION

The papers in this volume focus on what is perhaps the most controversial issue in second language research: Who is "better" in second languages, children or adults? One popular belief is that "younger is better," that younger acquirers will always outperform older acquirers in second language acquisition. In recent years, this claim has been disputed, with several studies apparently showing that older students are "better." The aims of this volume are, first, to present some of the important empirical research on this issue, in the hope of demonstrating that some clear generalizations about age differences in second language acquisition can be made and supported; second, to present some possible theoretical accounts for the research; and finally to suggest future research to settle issues that are, at this time, unresolved.

The question of age differences has clear theoretical and practical significance: Educators are interested in knowing the "optimal age" to begin instruction in second languages, and want to know just how far the older student can progress. Another important practical question is whether students of different ages need different methods or approaches in studying foreign and second languages. The question of age differences is also theoretical, in that any successful theory of second language acquisition must be able to account for observed differences in second language development in children and adults.

The first three sections of this book are devoted to studies that provide empirical evidence, that compare acquirers of different ages in different sorts of linguistic environments using different measures of linguistic progress. These sections are organized according to our interpretations of the literature, according to the generalizations the data lead to. Thus, we have divided the research not according to methodology, author, or date of publication but according to the hypotheses it supports. Section IV is our attempt to state these generalizations explicitly, generalizations based on the empirical research reported in Sections I to III, as well as other studies.

Our goal in presenting research studies on age and second language acquisition is not simply to show that the available literature supports one particular set of generalizations but also to emphasize that the issue is an empirical one and that a wide variety of research studies already exist. While these studies utilize different methodologies, different techniques, different subjects, and different languages, all contribute to our understanding of age differences in second language acquisition.

Taken one at a time, each of the studies presented and discussed here is "imperfect." (There is a real sense in which all experiments are imperfect.) Each can be criticized; each leaves some questions unanswered. Taken as a group, however, they complement each other and allow a fairly complete picture to emerge. In other words, our view is that enough data are available now to form hypotheses and make generalizations about child-adult differences in second language acquisition.

Section V is devoted to explanations for observed age differences. While several of the studies in Sections I to III present interesting theoretical discussions of their results, Section V deals with explanation only, explanation in terms of current second language acquisition theory.

We do not expect, of course, that this collection will be the final word on age differences in second language acquisition. Counterexamples nearly always arise when hypotheses are presented, and ideally these counterexamples lead to new, deeper generalizations and theories that account for the data even better than previous ones. We hope this volume will contribute to the process of growth.

CHILD-ADULT DIFFERENCES
IN
SECOND LANGUAGE ACQUISITION

I

LONG-TERM STUDIES OF CHILDREN AND ADULTS

The five studies included in this section, despite some differences in research methodology, all examine *ultimate attainment* in second language acquisition, that is, how proficient second language performers can become, given a fairly long period of time.

These studies have a similar design; they compare second language performers who began second languages as children with performers whose initial exposure was during adulthood. The reader will note that the duration of the second language exposure varies from study to study, but in our interpretation it can always be considered "long-term." In every case, performers are exposed to the second language for several years. (In the next section, we present "short-term" studies, in which the duration of exposure to the second language is, in nearly all cases, less than one year and occasionally as short as a few sessions.)

Despite the methodological differences, and despite the lack of variation in target language (in all studies, with the exception of Seliger et al., the target language is English), the studies presented here are fully consistent with the hypothesis that over the long run, those who begin second languages during childhood achieve higher levels of linguistic competence. Whether it is simply a case of "the younger the better," as suggested by the linear correlations between age of arrival and proficiency found in Oyama's studies, or whether children as a group attain higher levels of proficiency than adults as a group remains a question to be settled by future research.

1

THE OPTIMAL AGE
TO LEARN A FOREIGN LANGUAGE

James J. Asher
San Jose State College

Ramiro García
Prospect High School, Saratoga, California

What is the optimal age to begin studying a second language? Theories have been created from which optimal ages have been inferred. Examples are the brain plasticity theory,[1] the biological predisposition theory,[2] and an imprinting theory.[3] All these theories share a common theme, which is that something in the early development of the child maximizes the probability that the younger the human organism when exposed to a language, the greater the probability that the individual will acquire a native pronunciation.

The brain plasticity theory suggests that the young child's brain has a cellular receptivity to language acquisition. This receptivity may be a function of cellular plasticity or elasticity which is controlled by a sort of biological clock. With age, the biological clock changes the cellular plasticity, which reduces the organism's capacity to learn language.

There is clinical evidence for a theory of brain plasticity which is controlled by a biological clock. For instance, Penfield has observed in accident cases that if the left hemisphere of the brain is damaged and speech is lost, children but not adults will tend to enjoy a recovery in the power of speech. Furthermore, for those children who regain speech, it can be demonstrated that the speech function somehow shifted from the left to the right hemisphere of the brain. This was shown by injecting sodium amytal into the child's carotid artery, producing hemiplegia for the right hemisphere of the brain. Then with aphasia tests it was observed that speech temporarily disappeared as long as the right hemisphere was paralyzed with the drug. The shift of speech from the left to right hemisphere in children but not adults suggested a greater cellular elasticity for children.

The biological predisposition theory states that the human organism is born with a unique capacity to learn language. The theory does not explain why this special ability should diminish with age. An intriguing explanation is possible if the imprinting theory is linked with a theory of biological predisposition. If, for example, there is a "critical period" early in the child's development when imprinting occurs for language acquisition, then this could account for the superiority of children.

Imprinting has been demonstrated with birds, fish, insects, and some mammals. The classic study with ducklings showed that there is a critical period of short duration in which the infant bird learns to follow its mother. The behavior of following its mother is not an instinctive response which automatically occurs just because the bird is a duckling. Rather, during a certain critical period the response of following is learned. If during this critical time the mother is absent and other objects or persons are present, then the infant bird may "imprint" and thereafter follow the object such as a toy or human in preference to the mother. By analogy, the capacity to learn a language may be keenly operative during some yet to be discovered critical period in the early development of humans.

As attractive as these theories are, there is no direct evidence that the child has a special language learning capacity which is absent in the adult. The superiority of children over adults in second language learning is a strong belief that probably results from the common observation that children living in a foreign country seem rapidly to achieve nativelike fluency in the alien language while their parents may lag far behind. In language acquisition, the implication is that children have a biological predisposition for language learning which is perhaps related to brain plasticity or imprinting.

This belief in the superiority of children for second language acquisition may be an illusion, however. Children may learn the new language in play situations when utterances are synchronized with physical movement (i.e., "Come on, Billy, let's run to the corner!"). It may also be that adults learn the new language in static, nonplay situations in which their kinesthetic system is not active and not synchronized with speech transmission or reception (i.e., "Hello, it's a beautiful day, isn't it?").

If the difference in language acquisition between children and adults is play versus nonplay, action versus nonaction, and physical involvement versus nonphysical involvement, these variables may partially explain the accelerated learning of the child. When this idea was tested in a controlled situation by Asher and Price,[4] the results showed a surprising inverse relationship between age and learning listening comprehension of Russian. When adults and children (ages 7, 11, and 14) all learned to understand Russian in situations in which the Russian utterances were synchronized with physical movement, the adults were vastly superior to the children in any age group ($p < .0005$ using two-tail t tests), and the older children outperformed the youngest children.

The superiority of adults to children may hold only for listening comprehension. Children may indeed have a prepuberty biological predisposition which enables them to achieve fidelity in pronunciation. The data to be presented next are a direct test of the biological predisposition hypothesis.

PROCEDURE

Subjects: The experimental group was Cuban immigrants ($N = 71$) between the ages of 7 and 19, most of whom had been in the United States about 5 years. This group had 26 boys and 45 girls. In the control group were 30 American children, of whom 13 were boys and 17 were girls. All the children, American and Cuban, learned their English in the San Francisco Bay Area of California.

Design: The intent was to compare the Cuban children with the American children in their pronunciation of English sentences. From the comparison we wanted to develop answers to the following questions: Is our measure of pronunciation reliable and valid? What is the optimal age for Cuban children to enter the United States if they are to achieve a nativelike pronunciation? Is there an interaction between the age of the individual when entering the country and years of residence in the United States? Is there a difference between male and female Cuban children in the fidelity of English pronunciation?

In collaboration with several linguists,[5] the measure of English pronunciation was four sentences containing a sample of English sounds which speakers of Spanish are most apt to find difficult. Each Cuban and American child was asked to utter the following sentences:

1. I had two hot dogs and a glass of orange juice for lunch yesterday.
2. The girls were jealous because we had a better party.
3. Pat and Shirley are measuring the rug to see if it shrank.
4. It started to snow when we were about to leave for the mountains.

Before a child's pronunciation of a sentence was tape-recorded, the child read and rehearsed that sentence many times until he or she felt ready to make the utterance on tape. With this procedure, the subject was able to concentrate on one sentence at a time. The pronunciation of Ss was grouped according to age with all 7-year-old children together, all 8-year-old children together, and so forth. The Cuban and American children were randomly placed in an age group.

Then each member of a class of American high school students ($N = 19$) most of whom were juniors and seniors, sat in a booth located in the language laboratory at the Blackford High School in San Jose, California, and listened to a replay of the sentences uttered by the Cubans and Americans. After hearing a set of four sentences uttered by a subject, the judges made a decision about the fidelity of pronunciation by checking one of the following categories:

A indicated a native speaker
B indicated a near native speaker
C indicated a slight foreign accent
D indicated a definite foreign accent

The judges, all of whom learned their English in the San Francisco Bay area, were instructed that a voice would utter four sentences, after which each judge would classify the pronunciation into one of these four categories: A, B, C, or D. Immediately following this, the judges matched their response with the preferred classification. The judges listened to an illustration for each of the four categories into which pronunciation could be classified.

Then the judges listened to the subjects (Ss) grouped according to age with the 19-year-old Ss first, then the 18-year-old Ss, and so forth down to the 6-year-old children. In each age group, one to three American children were randomly positioned. Each S was identified on tape by initials only.

RESULTS

The first question we asked was: "Is our measure of pronunciation reliable and valid?" Without reliability and validity, all conclusions based on the measure would be in serious error.

For each S we had a decision from 19 judges. The mode was used to represent the collective decision by the judges because the mode yielded high interjudge reliability. For example, the judges made 1919 independent decisions on the pronunciations of the subjects and in 70 percent of those decisions the judges had perfect agreement among themselves.

The mode also resulted in high validity as measured by how accurately the pronunciation measure differentiated native from nonnative speakers in English. For instance, there was near perfect discrimination because 23 out of 30 American children[6] were identified as native speakers while all 71 of the Cuban children, no matter how long they had been in the United States, were identified as nonnative speakers.

The second question asked was this: "What is the optimal age for a Cuban child to enter the United States if he or she is to achieve a nativelike pronunciation?" From Figure 1, it can be seen that 68 percent of the children between 1 and 6 achieved a near-native pronunciation while this was accomplished by 7 percent of the children between the ages of 13 or older. For those between the ages of 7 and 12, 41 percent had a near-native pronunciation.

No child 6 or under had a definite foreign accent, but 32 percent of this group had a slight accent; for children 13 or older 66 percent had a definite foreign accent and 27 percent had a slight accent. Of the children between 7 and 12, 16 percent had a definite accent and 43 percent had a slight accent.

The implication is that children who were under 6 when they came to the United States had the highest probability of acquiring a near-native pronunciation of English and children older than 13 had the lowest chance of near-native speech.

The third question was this: "Is length of time in the Unites States important in acquiring a nativelike pronunciation of English?" Figure 2 indicates that 51 percent of Cuban children who have been in the United States 5 to 8 years have a near-native pronunciation while only 15 percent of those living in the United States for 4 years or less have a near-native pronunciation. Of those children here 5 to 8 years, only 10 percent had a definite foreign accent

Child's age when
entering the
United States

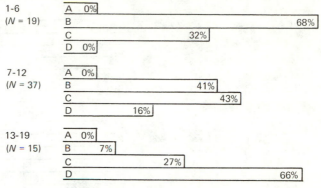

Fidelity of pronunciation

A	Native	C	Slight accent
B	Near native	D	Definite accent

FIGURE 1   English pronunciation as a function of the
Cuban child's age when entering the United States

and 39 percent had a slight accent. If the child lived in the United States 4 years
or less, 55 percent had a definite accent and 30 percent had a slight accent.

The implication is that, indeed, length of time in the United States was an
important variable. A child who lived in the United States for 5 years or more
had the highest probability of achieving a near-native pronunciation; the child
who lived here 4 years or less had the lowest probability of acquiring a near-
native pronunciation.

So far in the analysis, the age at which the Cuban child entered the United
States and the number of years he or she lived in this country were extremely
important variables in determining fidelity of pronunciation. Next we wanted to
know the interaction between these two critical variables.

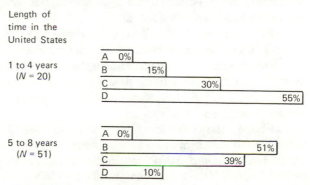

FIGURE 2   English pronunciation as a function of
years living in the United States

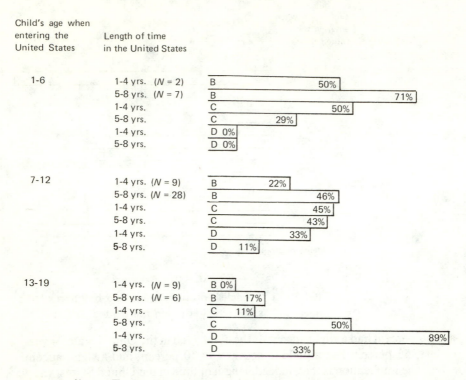

Child's age when
entering the   Length of time
United States   in the United States

1-6	1-4 yrs. (N = 2)	B	50%
	5-8 yrs. (N = 7)	B	71%
	1-4 yrs.	C	50%
	5-8 yrs.	C	29%
	1-4 yrs.	D	0%
	5-8 yrs.	D	0%

7-12	1-4 yrs. (N = 9)	B	22%
	5-8 yrs. (N = 28)	B	46%
	1-4 yrs.	C	45%
	5-8 yrs.	C	43%
	1-4 yrs.	D	33%
	5-8 yrs.	D	11%

13-19	1-4 yrs. (N = 9)	B	0%
	5-8 yrs. (N = 6)	B	17%
	1-4 yrs.	C	11%
	5-8 yrs.	C	50%
	1-4 yrs.	D	89%
	5-8 yrs.	D	33%

Note: The A category for native pronunciation was 0% in all cases.

FIGURE 3   English pronunciation as a function of entry and length of time in the United States

Figure 3 indicates that 71 percent of the Cuban children 6 years old or younger when they came to this country acquired near-native pronunciation of English if they lived in the United States between 5 and 8 years. If these children lived in the United States 4 years or less, 50 percent had a near-native sound production and 50 percent had a slight accent, but none of these children in this age group had a definite accent.

For the children in the 7 to 12 age range it can be seen in Figure 3 that 46 percent of those living in the United States between 5 and 8 years had a near-native pronunciation, 43 percent had a slight accent, and only 11 percent had a definite accent. Of those living here 4 years or less, only 22 percent had near-native pronunciation while 45 percent had a slight accent and 33 percent had a definite foreign accent.

Figure 3 shows that for children who were age 13 or older when they came to the United States, of those here between 5 and 8 years, 17 percent had near-native pronunciation, 50 percent had a slight accent, and 33 percent had a definite accent. If these children lived in the United States 4 years or less, none had a near-native pronunciation, 11 percent had a slight accent, and 89 percent had a definite foreign accent.

8

The implications from the data were that Cuban children had the greatest probability of achieving a near-native pronunciation of English if they were 6 or younger and lived in the United States more than 5 years. Children who came to America when they were 13 or older had a small chance of acquiring a near-native pronunciation even if they lived here 5 years or more. Children who were between 7 and 12 when they arrived here and then lived here 5 years or more had a 50–50 chance of achieving a near-native pronunciation.

Next, are Cuban girls better able than Cuban boys to acquire a near-native pronunciation of English? Figure 4 suggests that this may be true, since girls outnumbered the boys by 2 to 1 in near-native pronunciation. About the same proportion of boys as girls had a slight accent, but for children with a definite foreign accent, the ratio was three boys for every girl.

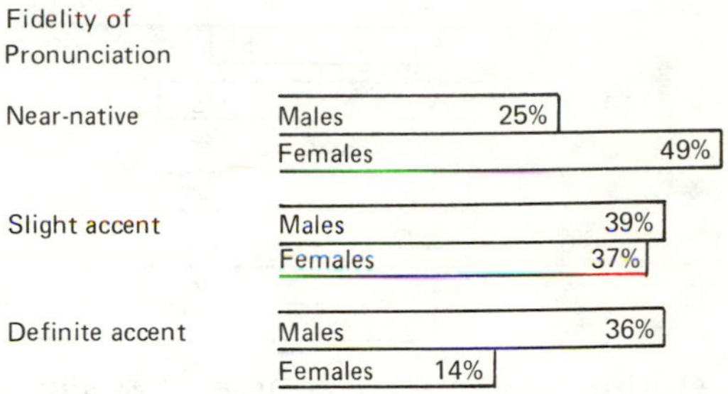

Fidelity of
Pronunciation

Near-native   Males   25%
               Females   49%

Slight accent Males   39%
               Females   37%

Definite accent Males   36%
               Females   14%

FIGURE 4   English pronunciation for males
(N = 28) versus females (N = 43)

Will girls still outperform boys in pronunciation when the age of the children upon entering the United States is considered? In Figure 5 we see that of the children who came to this country between the ages of 1 and 6, 75 percent of the girls acquired a near-native pronunciation as compared with 33 percent of the boys. This comparison should be made cautiously, since there was an extremely small sample of boys (N = 3) in this age range.

For children between 7 and 12, 50 percent of the girls had a near-native pronunciation as contrasted with 28 percent of the boys. If the children were between 13 and 19 when they entered the United States, almost as many girls (62 percent) as boys (72 percent) had a definite foreign accent.

Finally, will girls have better pronunciation than boys when the factor of time in the United States is considered? Figure 6 shows that of the children living in this country between 1 and 4 years, 80 percent of the boys had a definite foreign accent as compared with 30 percent of the girls. In this group, none of the boys had a near-native pronunciation as compared with 30 percent of the girls.

It is interesting that for those children who lived in the United States for 5 to 8 years, the differences in English pronunciation between boys and girls seemed to vanish. The girls appeared to be only slightly better in pronunciation than the boys.

Child's age when
entering the
United States

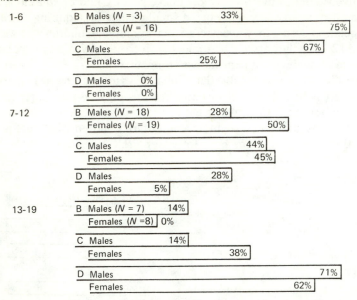

1-6	B Males (N = 3) 33%
	Females (N = 16) 75%
	C Males 67%
	Females 25%
	D Males 0%
	Females 0%
7-12	B Males (N = 18) 28%
	Females (N = 19) 50%
	C Males 44%
	Females 45%
	D Males 28%
	Females 5%
13-19	B Males (N = 7) 14%
	Females (N =8) 0%
	C Males 14%
	Females 38%
	D Males 71%
	Females 62%

FIGURE 5   English pronunciation as a function of sex and entry age

DISCUSSION

The data from the colony of Cuban children living in the San Francisco Bay area of California suggested the following:

1. No matter what the age of the child when he or she came to the United States and no matter how long the child lived here from 1 to 8 years, not one of the 71 Cuban children achieved a native English pronunciation.

2. However, many acquired a near-native English pronunciation. The highest probability of this near-native sound production occurred when the child was a boy or girl who came to the United States between 1 and 6 years of age and lived in this country between 5 and 8 years.

3. There seemed to be an inverse relationship between age when the child entered the United States and the acquisition of a near-native pronunciation. The younger the child, the higher the probability of pronunciation fidelity. This probability was further increased the longer the child lived in the United States.

For example, of the children 6 or younger who lived here between 5 and 8 years, 71 percent had a near-native pronunciation as compared with only 50 percent of those living here between 1 and 4 years. For the older children, those in the age range of 13 to 19, nobody (N = 9) who lived here between 1 and 4

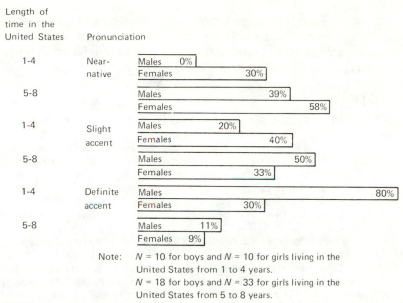

Length of time in the United States	Pronunciation			
1-4	Near-native	Males	0%	
		Females	30%	
5-8		Males	39%	
		Females	58%	
1-4	Slight accent	Males	20%	
		Females	40%	
5-8		Males	50%	
		Females	33%	
1-4	Definite accent	Males	80%	
		Females	30%	
5-8		Males	11%	
		Females	9%	

Note: $N = 10$ for boys and $N = 10$ for girls living in the United States from 1 to 4 years.
$N = 18$ for boys and $N = 33$ for girls living in the United States from 5 to 8 years.

FIGURE 6 English pronunciation as a function of sex and years lived in the United States

years had a near-native pronunciation, and only 17 percent of these children who lived in the United States between 5 and 8 years ($N = 6$) had a near-native speech.

4. More girls than boys had a near-native pronunciation. When age of entry into the United States was examined, girls still had better fidelity of pronunciation for any age group. This difference between boys and girls tended to diminish the longer the children lived in the United States. As an illustration, of the boys living here 1 to 4 years, 80 percent had a definite accent and none had a near-native pronunciation. In comparison, of girls living in the United States the same period of time, only 30 percent had a definite accent and 30 percent a near-native pronunciation. Nevertheless, in time the sex difference seemed to vanish as, for example, when the children lived here 5 to 8 years, 11 percent of the boys and 9 percent of the girls had a definite accent while 39 percent of the boys as compared with 58 percent of the girls had acquired a near-native pronunciation.

The data suggest that some variable within child development is a powerful determinant of pronunciation fidelity for second languages. This variable may indeed be biological. The curious puzzle is that although the probability of pronunciation fidelity is with the younger child, some older children—a small group to be sure—can also achieve an excellent pronunciation, which implies that biology does not completely determine the phenomenon.

When this research with Cuban children is compared with prior work having to do with listening comprehension, there is an indication that fidelity of pronunciation and listening comprehension of a second language are orthogonal dimensions or even inversely related. It may be that two different types of learning are operating. Pronunciation may be a learning based on copying, while listening comprehension may be learning rules and principles.

NOTES

1. Wilder Penfield and Lamar Roberts, *Speech and Brain-Mechanisms*, Princeton: Princeton University Press, 1959.

2. J. A. Fodor, How to learn to talk: some simple ways. In Franklyn Smith and George A. Miller (eds.), *The Genesis of Language*, Cambridge: Massachusetts Institute of Technology Press, 1966. Eric H. Lenneberg, A biological perspective of language. In Eric H. Lenneberg (ed.), *New Directions in the Study of Language*, Cambridge: Massachusetts Institute of Technology Press, 1964, pp. 65–88. D. McNeill, Developmental psycholinguistics. In Smith and Miller, op. cit.

3. Konrad Z. Lorenz, The evolution of behavior. *Scientific American*, December 1958, 199 (6), 67–78.

4. James J. Asher and Ben Price, The learning strategy of the total physical response: some age differences, *Child Development*, December 1967, 38 (4), 1219–1227.

5. Appreciation is expressed to the following linguists for their assistance in developing the test sentences: Professors Elaine Ristinen, Donald H. Alden, and Phillip Cook. We are grateful also to Professor William D. Moellering of the Department of Foreign Languages for many helpful suggestions and to Dr. Bela H. Banathy from the Defense Language Institute, West Coast.

6. The seven American children who were falsely identified as nonnative speakers of English were classified as having a "slight accent." Four of the seven were ages 7 or 8, and idiosyncratic distortions on certain words may have biased the judges' decisions.

2

MATURATIONAL CONSTRAINTS
IN THE ACQUISITION OF SECOND LANGUAGES

Herbert W. Seliger
Queens College, New York

Stephen D. Krashen
University of Southern California

Peter Ladefoged
University of California at Los Angeles

One of the fascinating aspects of the language behavior of bilinguals is the apparent difference between adult and child bilinguals. It is commonly believed that children are more complete language learners than adults and that they learn the second language more easily and in natural environments. Asher and Garcia (1969) claim that children are able to learn a new language more easily because it is synchronized with physical movement in real play situations, whereas the adult learns language in nonplay situations. Gleitman and Gleitman (1970, p. 56) argue that the reason children learn a new language with greater ease is that the language system of their peers is simpler than that to which adults are exposed.

It would be difficult to prove that the learning of the phonological system of a new language with nativelike pronunciation is either a function of the physical movement of play situations or the result of learning a simpler system. The pronunciation distinctions that together cause what is commonly referred to as a foreign accent are probably not a functional part of any play situation, since to a great extent these distinctions are often subphonemic and therefore are not instrumental in helping the child gain control of language. Explaining second language acquisition by children in this way is like returning to previous behaviorist explanations. This is especially difficult when we are attempting to explain nonfunctional language differences such as those between native and nonnative speakers of English.

13

The Gleitmans' explanation of the child's apparently superior ability to learn a new language may be valid with regard to other parts of the language system such as syntax, where the child's system is simpler, and lexicon, where it may be less abstract. However, if children are only imitating their peers, how do we explain the finding demonstrated below that bilingual children still learn the nativelike pronunciation of the adult system if they approach the second language at an early age?

Considering that phonological distinctions which cumulatively lead to foreign accent are nonfunctional in language use situations, we might suppose that they should be more easily learned by adults simply because the adult learner is better equipped than the child to utilize explanations and abstract verbalizations of such distinctions. However, in spite of this, and in spite of the fact that many adult second language learners consciously try to perfect their pronunciation of the second language, they are unsuccessful. The child pays no conscious attention to such problems and yet seems to learn nativelike pronunciation naturally.

One often cited but little documented claim is that this distinction is related to maturational differences between the child and the adult. Lenneberg (1967) considers this phenomenon to be a consequence of a biologically based "critical period" for language acquisition, extending from age 2 to puberty. The study reported below investigated the validity of the maturational constraint argument with two linguistically diverse groups of immigrants to two different language environments in an attempt to see whether the constraint would hold in different cultural environments. Any difference would suggest a nonbiological explanation for the child's language learning ability.

Previous work in this area has been limited to fairly small groups of immigrants to the United States with similar linguistic backgrounds. Oyama (1973) found a negative correlation between age of arrival in the United States and degree of foreign accent for a group of 59 Italian-born male immigrants living in New York, while Asher and Garcia (1969) reported similar results for 71 Cuban immigrants living in the San Francisco Bay area in California. In both studies, tape-recorded samples of subjects' speech were played for native-speaker judges (graduate students in linguistics in Oyama, and high school students in Asher and Garcia) who rated the samples on five (Oyama) and four (Asher and Garcia) scales for degree of foreign accent.

The survey reported here was carried out as a class assignment in linguistics classes at UCLA, Queens College, Bar Ilan University, and Tel Aviv University. Each student was asked to interview three adult immigrants, preferably one who had arrived in the adopted country before puberty, one who had arrived around the age of puberty, and one who had arrived after puberty. The following questions were to be asked: (1) country of birth, (2) present age, (3) age on arrival in the United States or Israel, (4) "Do you think most ordinary Americans (Israelis) could tell now that you are not a native speaker of English (Hebrew)?" (5) "If the answer to the last question is 'no,' how old were you when you became indistinguishable from a native speaker? In other words, it took you—years to lose your foreign accent?" (6) "When you arrived, could you speak any English (Hebrew) at all?" (7) "Consider five of your closest friends. How many of them have the same first language as you?" (8) "On a scale of 1 = very little and 10= to the greatest extent possible, rate yourself on your degree of Americanism." (Questions 7 and 8 were asked of American subjects only.) A total of 394 adult subjects were interviewed, representing 28 mother tongues.

RESULTS

Responses to the questionnaire were divided into three groups, those who arrived at age 9 or younger, those who arrived at age 16 or older, and those who arrived between the ages of 10 and 15. In the first two groups, there was no significant difference between Hebrew and English learners (chi^2 = .34 and .79 respectively, d.f. = 2, n.s.). For those who arrived between ages 10 and 15, there tended to be relatively more Hebrew learners who reported no accent (chi^2 = 6.75, d.f. = 2, p<.05).

Self-Report of Foreign Accents in Immigrants to the United States and Israel

Target language	Age of arrival	Accent	Don't know	No accent
English	9 and under	5	4	47
Hebrew		2	3	30
English	10 to 15	37	6	27
Hebrew		9	1	20
English	16 and over	106	4	7
Hebrew		50	1	5

As shown in the table, members of the 9-and-under group, for the most part, reported that most speakers of their target language thought they were native speakers, and most members of the 16-and-older group felt they still had a foreign accent. The total number of subjects in the 10-to-15 group who reported an accent (English and Hebrew learners combined) was nearly identical to the number who reported no accent (n = 47 and 46, respectively). When statistics for Hebrew and English learners were combined, very significant differences were observed between the 9-and-under and 10-to-15 groups (chi^2 = 33.95, d.f. = 2, p<.005), between the 10-to-15 and 16-and-older groups (chi^2 = 149.49, d.f. = 2, p<.005), and between the 9-and-under and 16-and-older groups (chi^2 = 209.74, d.f. = 2, p<.005).

To examine the possibility that mastery of a second language is dependent on the amount of exposure a person has had to the target language, the total number of years a subject had lived in the language area was taken as a measure of exposure (current age minus age of arrival) and analyzed with respect to responses to the questionnaire. In this survey only the 10-to-15 age group was analyzed, as the other two groups contained too few "exceptions" (subjects who had arrived before age 10 and had an accent, or who had arrived after age 15 and had no accent). For the 10-to-15 group, those who felt they were taken for native speakers had lived in their adopted country a mean of 15.03 years (s.d. = 11.48), while those who felt they were not taken for native speakers had lived in their adopted country a mean of 20.59 years (s.d. = 19.38). Although the difference between these means was not significant ($t = 1.38$, d.f. = 71, n.s.) the tendency was for those who reported an accent to have lived in the new country longer. These results are quite consistent with those reported by Oyama (1973) and Asher and Garcia (1969).

DISCUSSION

The data presented here do in fact show that puberty may be an important turning point in language learning ability. This result extends and generalizes previous studies (cited above), which were limited to small groups of subjects with similar linguistic and sociological backgrounds and confirms Lenneberg's (1967, p. 176) statement that "foreign accents cannot be overcome easily after puberty," Further, the consistency of our results with those of previous studies supports the hypothesis that the simple self-report method is a reasonably valid procedure. Our findings also corroborate observations by Labov (1970) that dialects acquired after puberty are less stable, and that maintenance of such late-learned rules requires constant self-monitoring.[1] It should be noted, however, that this confirmation of Lenneberg's critical period does not necessarily imply that its basis is the development of cerebral dominance, as Lenneberg proposes (see Krashen, 1973). Nor do our data necessarily indicate that improvement of pronunciation of second languages learned in adulthood is impossible. They do suggest, however, that there are limits to the degree of perfection that may in general be expected from adult second language learners.[2]

The American data included 10 cases of learners who arrived at age 15 or earlier and who reported that they became indistinguishable from a native speaker at some point in time after puberty (question 5); the Israeli data contained no such cases. It is hoped that further data will be obtained to indicate whether one must usually attain perfection before a certain age or merely begin living in the new environment before that age to be eventually taken for a native speaker of a second language.

Despite the clear distinctions between the groups, two small classes of exceptions did exist: adult learners who claimed no accent and prepuberty learners who felt they would still not be taken for native speakers. Twelve out of 156 adult learners (7.6 percent) fell into the former category, a percentage that corresponds surprisingly well to the estimated 5 percent of absolutely successful adult second language learners mentioned by Selinker (1972, p. 212), who suggests that these learners "may go through very different psycholinguistic processes than do most second language learners." The presence of such a group should be confirmed through use of more reliable measures of language proficiency; following that, an analysis of their characteristics would be of interest.

Seven of the 121 prepuberty learners reported accents. Possible explanations of this are: (1) the learner did not live in an environment where enough primary data in the target language were available, or (2) the subject learned an 'interlanguage' or a nonstandard local variety of the target language (Richards, 1972). The second reason clearly applies to one prepuberty learner whose mother tongue is Hindi and who most likely learned the Indian English of his parents and/or peer group. We have also observed what would be judged as nonnative American English spoken by adult Nisei, presumably because they were brought up in a Japanese speech environment.

The 10-to-15 age group may provide a natural laboratory for the investigation of factors underlying the successful acquisition of a second language. The possible fruitfulness of comparing successful and unsuccessful language learners (where success equals perfection) who arrived in their new country at around puberty is shown by an analysis of the responses to questions 7 and 8 asked of American immigrants. Those who reported "no accent" ($n = 14$) stated that a mean of 1.3 of their five closest friends spoke the same native language they did, while those who reported accents ($n = 27$) indicated that a mean of 3.3 of their five closest friends spoke their native language. This is a significant difference (Mann–Whitney $U = 92.5$, $z = 2.76$, $p = .003$, one-tail test). The no-accent group also tended to consider themselves "more American"; their mean response to question 8 was 7.1 as compared with 5.9 for the accent group ($U = 149.5$, $z = 1.26$, $p = .10$, one-tail test). While these results are consistent with the hypothesis that the presence of "integrative" motivation assists in successful language learning (Gardner and Lambert, 1972), further research will be necessary to determine whether the desire to assimilate is indeed a causative factor; it is possible that the no-accent group showed greater signs of integrative motivation as a result of their nativelike English.

Responses to question 6, dealing with the competence in the target language prior to arrival, were also analyzed for the 10-to-15 group: 31 out of 43 successful learners (68 percent) and 29 of 45 unsuccessful learners (65 percent) responded that they could not speak the target language at all when they arrived, indicating no difference between the groups. Inspection of the data revealed no obvious effect of mother tongue.

In earlier studies (Krashen and Seliger, 1976; Krashen, Seliger, and Hartnett, 1974; Krashen, Jones, Zelinski, and Usprich, 1978) we presented evidence that adults need formal environments in addition to exposure to primary linguistic data if they are to improve in second language learning. Despite evidence from error analysis studies showing the presence of similar strategies in first and second language learning (Dusková, 1969; Buteau, 1970; Bailey and Madden, 1973), our earlier work and the results presented here imply that there are real differences between child and adult language learning. It is hoped that more detailed investigations of linguistic competence in young and older second language learners, as well as further examinations of exceptions and of the 10-to-15 age group among immigrants, will clarify how and why puberty has the effect it does on language learning.

NOTES

1. Such self-monitoring may also occur in learning a second language. The speakers may learn more than one form of pronunciation of the target language but reserve the use of these forms for specific functions or roles. A particular case observed by one of the authors was that of a Puerto Rican teacher of English in New York City who pronounced English quite well in the ESL classroom as long as she was conscious of her pronunciation, but tended to lapse into a heavier Spanish accent in more informal situations. While the situation described here is a sociolinguistic one, the authors would predict that only adults would be capable of such conscious control of different varieties of the same language.

2. One variable that may affect the degree of approximation to the second language system is any form of prior learning of that language before immigration. Many American immigrants to Israel learned some form of Hebrew before immigration, mostly just enough to read a prayer book or say a few simple expressions. However, what they learned prior to immigration was in most cases learned from a nonnative speaker. The learner therefore interpreted Hebrew sounds in terms of English phonology. It is our observation that those English speakers who had little contact with Hebrew prior to immigration and who learned it in intensive language courses in the country tended to have better pronunciation than those with prior learning.

This suggests the possibility that adult learners may be both aided and inhibited by prior learning. If they have learned the second language first as a foreign language from teachers who were nonnative speakers, the likelihood is that prior learning will limit their ability to learn a new pronunciation system. The situation resembles that of having to unlearn one dialect pronunciation and learn a new one—a task that appears to be beyond the ability of most adult learners (see Krashen and Seliger, 1975).

REFERENCES

Asher, J., and Garcia, R.   The optimal age to learn a foreign language. *The Modern Language Journal.* 1969, 53, 334–41.

Bailey, N., and Madden, C. Is second language learning like first language learning? Paper presented at the Third Annual Conference of the City University of New York, 1973. .

Buteau, M.   Students' errors and the learning of French as a second language: A pilot study. *International Review of Applied Linguistics.* 1970, 8, 133–45.

Dusková, L.   On sources of errors in foreign language learning. *International Review of Applied Linguistics.* 1969, 8, 11–36.

Gardner, R., and Lambert, W.   *Attitudes and Motivation in Second-Language Learning.* Rowley, Mass.: Newbury House, 1972.

Gleitman, L., and Gleitman, H.   *Phrase and Paraphrase.* New York: Holt, Rinehart and Winston, 1970.

Krashen, S.   Lateralization, language learning, and the critical period: Some new evidence. *Language Learning.* 1973, 23, 63–74.

Krashen, S., Seliger, H., and Harnett, D.   Two studies in adult second language learning. *Kritikon Litterarum.* 1974, 2/3, 220–228.

Krashen, S., and Seliger, H.   Maturational constraints in the acquisition of a second language and second dialect. *Language Sciences.* 1975, 38, 28–29.

Krashen, S., and Seliger, H.   The role of formal and informal environments in adult second language learning. *International Journal of Psycholinguistics.* 1976, 3, 15–21.

Krashen, S., Jones, C., Zelinski, S., and Usprich, C.   How important is instruction? *English Language Teaching Journal*. 1978, 32, 257–261.

Labov, W.   *The Study of Nonstandard English*. Urbana, Ill.: National Council of Teachers of English, 1970.

Lenneberg, E.   *Biological Foundations of Language*. New York: Wiley & Sons, 1967.

Oyama, S.   A sensitive period for the acquisition of a second language. Ph.D. dissertation. Harvard University, 1973.

Richards, J.   Social factors, interlanguage, and language learning. *Language Learning,* 1972, 22, 159–88.

Selinker, L.   Interlanguage. *International Review of Applied Linguistics*. 1972, 10, 209–231.

3

A SENSITIVE PERIOD FOR THE ACQUISITION OF A NONNATIVE PHONOLOGICAL SYSTEM[1]

Susan Oyama

John Jay College, New York

INTRODUCTION

The notion that it is better to learn a second language early than late is neither new nor uncommon. It comes in a number of variations: that children acquire language "naturally" and without effort, that they do so faster or better than do adults. It is the idea that nativelike mastery of phonology can be acquired only by those who learn early that concerns us here. It is, of course, a part of folk wisdom that superior performance in certain fields, such as athletics or music, is the result of some combination of inborn propensity and early training. Such assumptions involve the realm of extraordinary capabilities, however; language, on the other hand, is the universal gift. Yet, as frustrated foreign language students can attest, really nativelike pronunciation in a second language seems as rare in an adult learner as the ability to run the 4-minute mile.

Is there, indeed, an age-related limitation on the learning of phonology? Explicit treatment of this question, let alone controlled research, is hardly abundant. In her review of the literature, Larew (1961) found a consensus that early learning is preferable, yet many students of language learning ignore the issue, or mention it only in passing as a kind of "given." Even Lambert, indefatigable student of bilingualism, has not, to this writer's knowledge, discussed the specific question of the relation between age at learning and quality of learning, although he is a vocal advocate of the introduction of foreign languages into the first grade (Lambert and Macnamara, 1969). Yet he does drop a revealing comment in writing about parents' worries that the second language will interfere with the first: "Children are often kept away from a second language until, inadvertently, it may be too late to learn it well" (Lambert, 1963,

p. 120). Thus we find the assumption that early learning is superior to late.

Larew's consensus notwithstanding, Jakobovits (1970) refutes the sensitive-period notion on two grounds: that children studying a foreign language in school do not always attain nativelike pronunciation, and that some adults can acquire nativelike pronunciation in 1000 hours of intensive training, which is also said to impart conversational knowledge of the language and a vocabulary of 3000 words. There are several objections that can be raised to this reasoning. For one thing, some children's failure to learn a language well under unnatural and restricted circumstances may say less about their general ability to acquire languages than it does about our difficulty in providing the proper conditions for learning. The differences between the classroom experience and that of a person immersed in a new language must not be overlooked. For Jakobovits to offer the customary equation of one semester of college language study to two semesters of high school study as proof that languages are not harder to acquire after the teens is an evasion of the sad fact that completing work on such a course, even attaining good grades, is no guarantee of acquisition. Further, the present writer has yet to see justification for the use of the term "nativelike" in cases like these.[2] Finally, although it may actually be that a small percentage of adults are able to perform like natives on all measurable aspects of a second language (a possibility that cannot be disproved conclusively), this would hardly lessen the importance of a sensitive period for most people, under most conditions. It should also be noted that this hypothetical exception would not preclude a "biological" explanation for a sensitive period, any more than a J. S. Mill negates the general schedule for intellectual development.

Even among those who believe in the advantages of early learning, there are numerous approaches and theoretical orientations; an intriguing characteristic of these disparate positions is that they tend to converge on puberty as the end point of the alleged period of receptivity to new languages, even when the explanatory mechanism invoked does not, in itself, imply that particular cutoff point.

As a part of a larger study, the existence of a sensitive period for acquisition of the phonological system of a nonnative language was investigated. The hypothesis, then, was that there is some developmental period, stretching roughly from 18 months to puberty, during which it is possible fully to master the phonology of at least one (and the upper limit is as yet undetermined; children have been known to learn three or four languages virtually concurrently) nonnative language, and after which complete acquisition is impossible or extremely unlikely.

METHOD

Subjects

Subjects were 60 Italian-born male immigrants, drawn from the greater New York metropolitan area, who learned English as a second language upon their arrival in the United States. Immigrants were clearly a better group to work with than people who acquired language in other ways. Students in school programs, for instance, usually begin in their teens, and thus present a very limited range of ages at which study is begun. In addition, they seldom reach high levels of proficiency from their school experience alone. Immigrants, on the other hand, begin at various ages and frequently attain good command of their adopted tongues, so that the question of how nearly they approach native performance becomes a reasonable and interesting one. The aims of the study influenced subject selection in a number of ways. Whereas the question "How well do Italian immigrants in general acquire a second language?" would have been answered by examining a random or stratified sample, the question at hand— "Can nativelike command of a second language phonology be acquired regardless of the age of beginning?"—makes some selectivity logical. That circumstance can prohibit or inhibit learning of a language by normally capable people is obvious; many large cities are full of households, for example, in which the mother, who has been in the United States for decades, still speaks practically no English. These are women whom custom and economics have conspired to keep monolingual. Such social and cultural factors, which, of course, can affect men as well as women, are pervasive and powerful. To eliminate them would have been impossible, but an attempt was made to minimize their effect on the study. Subjects who had had a good chance to acquire English, then, were sought. They were taken from the upper educational groups, some college experience characterizing all participants except the youngest; the latter were in college preparatory programs in high school.

The imposition of the education requirement was also an attempt to reduce the complexities introduced by dialectal variations (see Labov, 1966a, b, c; McDavid, 1966). As it turns out, the extraordinary social mobility of immigrant groups blurred these class lines considerably. Many young professionals in the sample had parents who came to the ethnic ghettoes of the New York area from lower-middle-class lives in Italy, found menial jobs, and remained virtually illiterate in English. Still, the education requirement ensured that such subjects had had ample exposure to Standard English, and put them substantially in the same position vis-à-vis the upper-middle-class norms as native-born upwardly mobile people, some of whom were included in the control group.

The choice of males was made because women were thought to be less likely than men to meet the education requirement and to have had the desired amount of contact with the English-speaking milieu, because of the cultural pressures mentioned above. That this decision was justified for the younger as well as the older groups is indicated by one college-age subject's assertion that he spoke English with his brothers and Italian with his sisters. Several of the teenage subjects confirmed that the social freedom of their female peers was often severely restricted, and that the girls' speech sometimes reflected this fact.

Subjects were distributed along two independent variables: age at arrival in the United States (6 to 20 years) and number of years in the United States (5 to 18 years).

Measures

Pronunciation was scored from two taped speech samples. The first was a reading of a short paragraph, introduced with taped instructions: "Here is a sample paragraph in English. Please read it out loud, in a natural voice, and at your own speed." The paragraph was constructed to include a number of phonological variables that Labov (1966c) had found to be sensitive indices of sociolinguistic stratification and stylistic shift, and that the experimenter had observed to be difficult for Italians speaking English. These variables were the (r) in words like *hard*, (eh) as in *band*, (oh) as in *small*, (th) as in *thought*, and (dh) as in *this* (following Labov's notation).

The second sample was a brief anecdote, evoked by a request to recount a frightening episode in the subject's life. The general frame of reference here is taken from Labov's (1966c) study of variability in New York speech; where he used four levels of carefulness of speech, the present study uses two. Basic to this approach is the notion of stylistic variation in different speech contexts, characterized by various degrees of self-monitoring. According to Labov, there are stylistic norms which are striven for and achieved to different degrees by different groups of people. The prestige norm is approached most nearly by the speech of the upper middle class, which shows relatively little difference between careful and casual speech. At the other end of the scale, lower-class people show rather small amounts of stylistic variation, perhaps because of a combination of reduced exposure to the prestige norm and negative attitudes toward its adoption. (Herein lies another reason for setting class limits on the subjects in this study: lower-class immigrants may not be under the same social and attitudinal pressures to acquire full command of Standard English as are the middle classes.) Between these two groups lies a population which shows rather marked stylistic shifts. The assumption here, then, is that when people are speaking formally or carefully they are in fact listening quite closely to themselves, keeping their speech in line, so to speak; when they are engaging in "casual" speech, the motor activity involved in speaking is less well regulated. In the latter state, the forms learned in childhood predominate, and where the prestige norm is essentially a layered-on correction of these early patterns, the careful forms fall away. The present study involves a conceptual variant of this idea, which will be discussed later. Included in casual speech are not only informal conversation but also excited and, one would expect, angry and weary speech as well.[3] One of the subjects taking part in the present study answered the question "Would you like to change anything about the way you speak English?" this way: "Yes: learn how to speak fluently when angry." Another claimed he could hardly understand himself when he was nervous.

Labov described a number of methods of recording casual speech; the one best suited to the project under consideration was the "danger-of-death" technique, in which the subject is asked to recount an experience in which he thought he was in danger of losing his life. This task was introduced as informally as possible; if necessary, the subject was prompted or encouraged to give a detailed and involved description of the event.

Master tapes were made of the paragraph readings and of the stories, with control samples mixed in at irregular intervals. Since the stories varied considerably in length, the last 45 seconds of each one was taken. It was thought that subjects were more likely to be emotionally involved toward the climax of the anecdote than at the beginning. The samples heard by the judges, then, were of equal length. Each sample was identified by a code number, and the tapes were judged for degree of accent, defined as nonnative American, by two American-born graduate students in linguistics. A typewritten sheet of instructions was given to the judges, who employed a 5-point scale ranging from *no foreign accent* to *heavy foreign accent*. Although they were instructed to restrict their attention to the phonological and prosodic aspects of the samples, the possibility remains, of course, that other features of the samples may have influenced the judgments. To control for fatigue and sequential effects, each master tape was split into halves, I and II. For both Paragraphs and Stories, a warmup sequence of six samples taken from Italians not included in the data analysis preceded the experimental samples. The two sets of samples were judged at separate sessions. One judge heard the Paragraph tapes first, in the order I–II, then the Stories, in the order II–I; the other listened first to the Stories, I–II, then to the Paragraphs, II–I. Thus both order of the split halves and order of the sessions were controlled for.

Finally, a questionnaire was filled out by each subject. This provided data on method of learning English, relative amount of use of native and second languages, certain attitudes, and other information.

Procedure

Subjects were seen individually. All sessions were introduced by this statement by the experimenter: "We are interested in getting an idea of the way the various aspects of language are organized in your personal system, since each person's system is slightly different from everyone else's. Most of the material and instructions are recorded and will come to you on these earphones. If at any time you have questions or want the volume adjusted, let me know."

The two accent measures were part of a battery of seven tests. Two orders were used; in one the accent measures came at the beginning, in the other they came near the end. In both orders, however, the paragraph reading preceded the danger-of-death story. This methodological detail will be treated later. Instructions were recorded on a Sony TC90 cassette machine and were presented through stereo earphones. Speech samples were recorded on a Uher Report 1400.

RESULTS

Analyses of variance and correlational methods were used to examine the relationships among the two main independent variables, the questionnaire variables and the accent measures. For the analyses of variance, a fixed-effects 2×3 was used. Following Ferguson (1971), a X^2 test was performed to determine whether the unequal cell frequencies differed significantly from chance; they did not ($\chi^2 = 1.2$, 5 d.f.). The unweighted means procedure, described by Winer (1962), was then employed; this is a method based on the harmonic mean of cell frequencies, 9.799 in this case.

The two judges agreed on the majority of their judgments of accent. If only the 60 experimental decisions for each measure were considered, the correlation coefficient between their judgments was 0.87 for the Paragraph readings and 0.80 for the Stories (both significant beyond the 0.001 level); when the 10 control subjects were included, the coefficients rose to 0.90 and 0.82.

It is worthy of note that the mean of cell 1 in the Paragraph ANOVA table differs from that of the control group at the 0.01 level (one-tailed), and that the Stories, which showed less extreme scores, showed a difference between controls and cell 2 significant at the 0.005 level. When a modified t test, one not involving the usual assumptions about population variances, was applied because an F test revealed significant differences between the pairs of variances, both comparisons were still significant beyond the 0.01 level.

The analyses of variance, based on mean values of the two judgments for each subject, showed an extremely strong Age at Arrival effect, more so

Table 1   Two-Way Analysis of Variance: Influence of Age at Arrival and Number of Years in the United States on Degree of Accent on Paragraph Reading

Number of years in U.S.	Cell 1	Cell 2	Cell 3
12–18	$M = 1.272$	$M = 2.272$	$M = 3.722$
	$SD = 0.327$	$SD = 0.862$	$SD = 0.415$
	$N = 11$	$N = 11$	$N = 9$
	Cell 4	Cell 5	Cell 6
5–11	$M = 1.375$	$M = 2.583$	$M = 3.500$
	$SD = 0.413$	$SD = 0.493$	$SD = 0.707$
	$N = 8$	$N = 12$	$N = 9$
Age at arrival	6–10	11–25	16–20

Controls

$M = 1.00$
$SD = 0$
$N = 10$

Source of variation	d.f.	Mean square	F
Number of years in U.S.	1	0.059	0.162
Age at arrival	2	25.649	70.271*
Interaction	2	0.338	0.926
Within groups	54	0.365	

*$p < 0.01$.

Table 2   Two-Way Analysis of Variance: Influence of Age at Arrival and Number of Years in the United States on Degree of Accent on Story

Number of years in U.S.	Cell 1	Cell 2	Cell 3
12–18	$M = 1.318$	$M = 1.954$	$M = 3.611$
	$SD = 0.49$	$SD = 0.721$	$SD = 0.567$
	$N = 11$	$N = 11$	$N = 9$
	Cell 4	Cell 5	Cell 6
5–11	$M = 1.437$	$M = 2.5$	$M = 3.166$
	$SD = 0.463$	$SD = 0.979$	$SD = 1.1$
	$N = 8$	$N = 12$	$N = 9$
Age at arrival	6–10	11–25	16–20

Controls

$M = 1.05$
$SD = 0.15$
$N = 10$

Source of variation	d.f.	Mean square	F
Number of years in U.S.	1	0.078	0.119
Age at arrival	2	19.970	30.442*
Interaction	2	1.205	1.837
Within groups	54	0.656	

*$p < 0.01$.

for the Paragraphs than for the Stories, virtually no effect from the Number of Years in the United States factor, and a very small interaction effect (Tables 1 and 2).

An interesting result to emerge from the analysis of the articulatory measures was that the casual samples (Stories) showed less accent than the Paragraph readings. This is contrary to the expectation, derived from Labov's writings, that casual speech would be farther from the norm than formal. Since casual speech was conceived by Labov to include not only emotionally involved speech but also speech under stress, however, those results are perhaps not so surprising after all. For immigrants, who are often painfully aware of their accents, the reading aloud of printed material may well be a more stressful task than the informal recounting of an anecdote. Cell means were higher (more accent) for the Paragraph in four out of six cases; exceptions were cells 1 and 4, which contained the subjects closest to native ability on all tests. This trend held for individual scores as well as for cell means. The numbers are small but suggestive; stylistic variation for earlier arrivals seems to resemble that of native speakers, while later arrivals tend to reverse the direction of the shift.

It was mentioned earlier that this study actually involves a variant of Labov's model. While casual speech and accented speech both depart from the prestige norm, in the case of native speakers the departure is assumed to be due to the use of another, more basic, style involving less self-monitoring, whereas for a nonnative, accent is less the expression of an early-acquired system than it is the result of imperfect control of any of the second language variants. For the nonnatives, then, the increased attention to pronunciation that presumably accompanied the reading of the Paragraph did not necessarily allow closer approximation of the norm. For those whose command of English phonology was shaky, increased attention seemed to have a deteriorative effect on performance. This recalls the Yerkes-Dodson law, familiar to psychologists, which states that high motivation enhances performance only on relatively simple tasks, whereas it may hinder performance on difficult ones. If one can assume that English phonology is harder for late arrivals than for early, then the results described above fall into place. That "difficulty" is an appropriate concept also for normal native stylistic shifting is affirmed by Labov's observation that a rapid succession of instances of his phonological variables (as in "*th*is *th*ing, *th*at *th*ing, and *th*e o*th*er *th*ing") presents problems for speakers for whom the fricative form does not predominate in everyday speech. Such speakers would sometimes begin the sequence with the prestige forms, but end it with the affricate (Labov, 1972, p. 105).

Before leaving this part of the analysis, two alternate explanations should be considered. First, judges may, for some reason, have allowed more latitude in listening to the Stories than the Paragraphs. Second, the fixed order of the two tests (Paragraph, then Story) may have had an effect. To produce the observed patterns, however, either of these would have to have been an interactive effect, influencing late arrivals differently from those who came young. Neither of the possibilities is very convincing when examined, and each would ultimately depend, circularly, on a difference in linguistic ability distinguishing early from late arrivals. At any rate, the present results can offer no more than some hints for further investigation of the covariation of accent with context.

Considering the width of the Number of Years in the United States intervals, the lack of effect from this variable in these analyses of variance is striking. Amount of use of a language must obviously be an important consideration under certain circumstances; one would fully expect a year's exposure to a second language to have more impact than a week's. Yet the continuing influence of length of stay appears from these results to be rather limited. There is, however, another aspect of these data that must be noted.

Sampling error produced, in general, descending values for Numbers of Years, as Age at Arrival values increased. The unfortunate confounding of the independent variables makes an additional correlational analysis advisable. Correlation coefficients were computed for the accent measures and Age at Arrival on the one hand, and for the measures and Number of Years in the United States on the other. Since the two independent variables were also correlated ($r = -0.30$), first-order partial correlation coefficients were calculated, first with effects of Number of Years removed ($r_{p,\,aa.\,\#\text{yrs}}$ and $r_{s,\,aa.\,\#\text{yrs}}$), then with the effects of Age at Arrival removed ($r_{p,\,\#\text{yrs.aa}}$ and $r_{s,\,\#\text{yrs.aa}}$) (Table 3).

Table 3 Partial Correlation
Coefficients Between Accent Scores
and Independent Variables*

$r_{p,aa \cdot \#yrs} = 0.83\dagger$	$r_{p,\#yrs \cdot aa} = 0.02$
$r_{s,aa \cdot \#yrs} = 0.69\dagger$	$r_{s,\#yrs \cdot aa} = -0.07$

*Subscripts: p, degree of accent on
Paragraph; s, degree of accent on Stories;
aa, age at arrival; #yrs, number of years
in the United States.
$\dagger p < 0.001$, df for t test $= 57$.

It can be seen from this analysis that the ANOVA results were not appreciably affected by sampling error, since the same set of relationships emerged from both sets of calculations. Correction for confounding of the age and practice variables, far from revealing a strong effect of length of stay, showed it to be virtually nonexistent.

To evaluate the background data gathered, the correlation of each questionnaire variable (QV) with the Paragraph scores was calculated. The similarity of the two sets of accent scores was strong enough ($r = 0.76$) that it seemed redundant to perform another set of analyses on the Story scores.

Simple correlation produced a number of significant associations between questionnaire variables and accent scores, but some were rather puzzling. The higher the initial motivation to learn English, for example, the worse had been a person's accent score. Given the substantial correlation of many QVs with Age at Arrival, a more detailed investigation of these relationships was clearly indicated. Partial correlations were therefore computed (Table 4). While the removal of the effects of the QVs resulted in highly significant partial correlations, none of the other coefficients reached significance. It appears, then, that accent is rather resistant to the effects of factors other than age at beginning the language, and that the apparent influence of such factors is an artifact of their relationship with age at learning. As with all information obtained by interview or questionnaire methods, uncertain reliability and validity of the reports are a problem. Further research might involve direct measures of motivation and practice. It is quite clear, however, that there is little evidence to support the various arguments about the effects of such variables on mastery of the phonological system of the second language.

The relationship between age at learning and degree of accent has been established for these subjects, then. Naturally other groups of people and other languages must be studied; further research may well show age to be the basic determinant, one which sets limits but which allows some room for the operation of factors such as method of study and conditions of use of the language. The next question is, what is the nature of the relationship that has revealed itself in this study? Inspection of the Scattergrams indicates no sharp discontinuities, seeming instead to be quite linear. The youngest arrivals perform in the range set by the controls, whereas those arriving after about age 12 do not, and substantial accents start appearing much earlier.

Table 4   Partial Correlation Coefficients of Paragraphs with Age at Arrival and Questionnaire Variables

	Questionnaire variables	A§	B¶
QA	(education), $N = 37$†	0.84*	0.01
QB	(American education), $N = 37$†	0.76*	0.01
QC	(occupation), $N = 28$‡	0.92*	−0.25
QD	(method of learning English)	0.84*	0.18
QE	(motivation while learning)	0.82*	−0.23
QF	(self-consciousness while learning)	0.81*	−0.22
QG	(amount of Italian used while learning)	0.83*	0.05
QH	(amount of Italian used, present)	0.81*	0.05
QI	(American orientation and identification)	0.82*	0.05
QJ	(present motivation to improve English)	0.84*	0.17

*$p < 0.001$.
†Based on a subsample who had either completed schooling or reached the highest category of education, "some graduate school."
‡Based on a subsample who either were employed full time or had reached the highest category of occupation, "professional or semi-professional."
§Column A: Partial correlation coefficient of Paragraphs and Age at Arrival with effects of questionnaire variable removed.
¶Column B: Partial correlation coefficient of Paragraphs and questionnaire variable with effects of Age at Arrival removed.

DISCUSSION

It was noted earlier that although many people seem to accept some notion of a sensitive period for second language learning, there is little agreement on explanations. Jones (1969, p. 13), for example, writes that a child's world is less complicated than an adolescent's, that the latter's "moods and perplexities" hamper "unconscious habit formation" and imitation, that the child's "pre-paredness to identify himself with others" gives him the advantage. He includes in his list of reasons, however, neurological and physiological factors as well. Huebener (1965, p. 99) claims that the child has plenty of time, gets constant practice, and is "intensely motivated because success in getting food and drink, in playing with his fellows, in securing relief from pain" depends on his use of language. The processes of learning are listed as imitation, association, and trial and error. One would have to conclude from remarks like these that ordinary loving fathers and mothers routinely withhold comfort, food, and drink until their children master the crucial tool of language. Since even rudimentary command generally takes about a year to develop, it is a wonder that so many babies survive that awful first 12 months. Anyone who has watched children play quite happily without the benefit of a common language would have to question Huebener's claim that social intercourse depends on speech, and anyone who has followed a child on the adventures of a single day would wonder whether his world is actually as simple as Jones claims. Children whose environments are truly simple—that is, impoverished—may suffer severely from lack of stimulation; one such case is mentioned below. To the assertion that a child spends more time learning language than an adult, which appeared as early as 1900 and frequently since then, Jespersen (1964, p. 141) wisely retorted that the child has much else to do, so his mastery of language is all the more wonderful.

Jones's reference to the child's identification with others is probably derived from Mowrer's (1960) theory of language acquisition through identification with a rewarding model. Mowrer's notion is explicitly cited by Lambert (1963), who attributes individual differences in language learning ability partly to differences in desire to identify with speakers of the new tongue. Accepting this principle, one could just as easily point to the adolescent's much-noted need to gain the respect and approval of his peers, his intense desire for conformity, and his susceptibility to slavish imitation (Horrocks, 1962; Cole, 1954), and argue that a foreign-born teenager would inevitably perfect his pronunciation as a consequence of the strong motivation generated by his identification with his peers, not to mention his exacting imitation of them.

Common in the literature is the insistence that children are more adept than adults at imitation. This, coupled with the assumption that imitation is the basis for language acquisition, leads to the conclusion that children therefore make superior language learners. Caution must be exercised in accepting this syllogism, though, for both premises are questionable. First, imitation of any given string requires a memory span sufficient to the task. Children's spans are notoriously short. As Lenneberg (1964b) points out, blind reproduction of even a 10-word sentence would be impossible for an adult because of the tremendous amount of information involved. A certain amount of structure must be known. "The *sine qua non* for reproduction is, therefore, the ability to recognize the patterns—which is tantamount to saying the reproduction presupposes prior learning of grammar" (p. 123). The mimicry of young children, furthermore, is often considerably more primitive than the speech of their models, and erroneous renderings can be extremely resistant to correction by well-meaning elders.

To compound the confusion, one discovers that some writers in the field confound the first-second language opposition with that of early-late second language acquisition. The two distinctions are, of course, conceptually independent. A notion which, ostensibly at least, has specifically to do with the relationship of first to second language is that of "stamping in" or overlearning. It has its roots in the behaviorist vocabulary of habit, stimulus-response, and interference, and is presumably based on the paradigm of proactive interference, defined by Shiffrin (1970) as a decrement in performance for an item caused by prior presentation of the other items. Such interference can be of two types: item specific, in which one stimulus is linked with two or more responses, and nonspecific, in which the effects proceed from similarity among nonidentical stimuli. Drawn from paired associate and word list learning experiments, the concept of proactive interference involves clearly identifiable stimulus-response ties. Language is seen by some theorists as a series of habits, stamped in by repetition and reinforcement, and the assumption is that old well-practiced "responses," by continuing to occur in the context of a new language in the form of errors, make full mastery of the new tongue difficult. Mackey (1965) and Politzer (1970), then, explain that learning a foreign language while young is easy because the native language habits are still relatively new and thus easily replaced by other habits. By adolescence, these habits are too deeply ingrained, and create enough interference that mastery of another language becomes difficult, if not impossible. What is interesting is that both these writers, along with others, take adolescence as the point at which old habits become disruptive. Such a timetable does not in any way follow from their assumptions about the mechanics of learning. When one considers that learning experiments generally deal with time lapses of minutes, hours, and days, the postulation of a 12-year-long stamping-in process seems rather puzzling. Ultimately, these people seem to be talking about age limitations, after all, and trying to explain the phenomenon with the vocabulary of learning theory.

Much can be said about this view of language, and, indeed, much has been said (e.g., see Bever et al., 1968; Chomsky, 1959, 1970; Ervin-Tripp, 1969; Jenkins and Palermo, 1964; Skinner, 1957). A complete review of the arguments for and against the associationist approach cannot be made here, but a few things can be noted. There is every indication that patterns and interrelationships are more important in language acquisition than practice per se. The question of what constitutes a response or a habit of phonology, furthermore, is not easily answered. It will be recalled, at any rate, that amount of use of English had little long-range effect on skill in employing the new sound system.

It should be pointed out that the store of possible explanations for the phenomenon observed in this study is not exhausted by the pedagogical literature cited. It is possible that there are simply age-related limits on the ability to acquire a second phonological system (and all the prosodic trimmings that go with it). By this is meant not the incidental relation to chronological age implied by the overlearning hypothesis, but a biologically determined reduction in acquisitional capacity.

Penfield and Roberts (1959), in their lengthy discussions of language and the brain, urge early teaching of second languages on the basis of the plasticity of the young brain. "Plasticity," of course, implies malleability. The learning of a language certainly must involve changes in the brain, whatever the elusive engram may ultimately show itself to be. So must the learning of solid geometry or sociology by a college student and the learning of a new income tax regulation by an 80-year-old, and few advocate teaching these things to 5-year-olds. If there is a physiological "stiffening" of the brain as it reaches maturity, it cannot affect all faculties equally, then, and we are left with a specifically linguistic phenomenon, or at least one less general than the ability to learn. Apparently, either something happens to those parts of the brain that are instrumental in acquiring language or there is something about language that makes it different from geometry or sociology and therefore not appropriately delayed until the student's intellectual development is equal to the extreme intricacy of the subject.[4] There is, in fact, reason to believe both are true. That there are parts of the cortex closely involved in language is not be be disputed (e.g., Goldstein, 1948; Ajuriaguerra, 1966; Lenneberg, 1960, 1964b, 1966, 1967).

In addition to presenting a fine summary of much of these data on the evolutionary aspects of language and other related subjects, Eric Lenneberg argues persuasively for the existence of an inherent propensity for the learning of language. If this is true, and the position taken in this article is that it is, then language is indeed different from intellectual disciplines ordinarily approached after childhood is passed, and is more akin to a biologically programmed activity like walking, a parallel drawn convincingly by Lenneberg (1967).

Ironically enough, neither of the most cited sources in this area takes second language learning as its primary subject. Lenneberg (1966, 1967) takes a few lines to observe that foreign accents are hard to lose after puberty and that after that age a person seems to lack the ability to acquire a language without conscious effort and study. Penfield and Roberts (1959), although they devote some space to an eloquent plea for early teaching of languages, make their recommendations by rather loose extension of their work on the brain. Although neither Lenneberg nor Penfield and Roberts mention actual research on second language learning, their findings on the neurological evidence for age limits on the acquisition of the native language are of considerable import. Briefly, these authors note that when the brain reaches maturity around adolescence (probably the origin of the previously mentioned authors' perplexing choice of puberty as the point at which the various alleged inhibiting factors come into play) much of the impressive flexibility of the young brain seems to be lost.

In the literature of aphasia, for example, one finds that disruptions of linguistic functioning can be caused by lesions, especially on the left side, in the area of the Rolandic and Sylvian fissures, and in some parts of the temporal and parietal lobes. If the injury occurs early, the chances for complete recovery are excellent. It seems, then, that until a certain point, the right hemisphere, not normally differentiated for language, has the capacity fully to develop the linguistic potential generally left unrealized. With increased age, the prognosis becomes progressively less optimistic. Whether lateralization is a decade-long process completed around puberty[5] (Lenneberg, 1960, 1966, 1967; Penfield and Roberts, 1959) or a rapid one ending by age 5 (Krashen, 1973) is a matter of debate. Although it has been widely assumed that the accomplishment of lateralization and a decrease in language learning ability are causally related, and although Lenneberg (1967, p. 153) at one point linked the two by implication, it is not necessarily true that lateralization per se prohibits subsequent language acquisition in either hemisphere. While the pattern of *occurrence* of aphasia gives evidence of lateralization, the pattern of *recovery* from aphasia can give information on language learning capacity (although not all recovery is due to literal relearning). Thus, while the question of when dominance is definitively established is an interesting one, evidence for limitations on language learning must be directly derived from the linguistic phenomena themselves.

Further evidence for limitations on primary language acquisition ability, this time in the left, or normally dominant, hemisphere, is presented by Lenneberg (1967), who reports that among severely retarded children (and retardation must be severe before a correlation between intelligence and language is seen) the various developmental landmarks of motor and speech functions tend to occur in their proper sequence and in the normal relationship to each other, but that the sequences are stretched out in time, progressing slowly until puberty, then ceasing.

Writing about deaf children, Hirsh (1966) states that if a deaf child has not acquired language by age 10, or has acquired only sign language, it is very hard to teach him. Below that age, he claims, the younger the child, the more easily he learns. On the other hand, reports on the linguistic development of Genie, a child who suffered extreme social and sensory deprivation for over a decade, indicate that she has gained some command of language since she was discovered at the age of 13 (Fromkin et al., 1974). It is impossible, unfortunately, to evaluate the impact of the exposure to language that Genie had prior to her sequestration at nearly 2 years of age, and since she is still improving it is not yet known how proficient she will become. Another limitation on the relevance of Genie's case to the issue at hand is that the relationship between various kinds of deprivation and sensitive periods is complex. In some cases, sensory deprivation prior to exposure to crucial patterns of stimuli seems to extend the sensitive period beyond its normal boundary; such effects do not challenge the validity of the sensory period as a phenomenon that occurs under a wide range of normal conditions. If Genie fails to develop full linguistic proficiency, of course, one will not know whether to attribute the failure to maturational factors or to the devastating effects of her long isolation.

Clearly, this is an exceedingly complex area, and the significance of these data and concepts for second language acquisition is still uncertain. It may well be the case that phonology has a different natural history from syntax; certainly vocabulary can always be expanded in both native and nonnative tongues (appropriate use is another thing). Along with the massive literature on imprinting and sensitive periods in many species of animals, however, these writings on the relation between age and language provide a rich and varied theoretical basis for the postulation of a sensitive period of the type suggested here.

This sensitive period is obviously not an all-or-nothing phenomenon; adults can and do learn to speak new languages, and often very well. Whether the efficiency of the acquisition process simply decreases as a person grows older or whether the process actually ceases to function, so that one must use other abilities whose efficiency is not so closely tied to maturation, learning to "speak like a native" seems to be quite difficult for all but the very young. Another possibility is suggested by Thorpe (1961, p. 17), who points out that the development of advanced skills and more complex perceptions may make the person less willing (unable?) to function in the more primitive mode of the infant. In its extreme form, however, this argument would reduce to one of those given above. Recall that retardation does not usually affect acquisition; although the process may be slowed, it too ceases at the same time its normal counterpart does: at puberty. It may be that the "higher" intellectual and emotional faculties which enable a normal adult to overcome at least partially the handicap imposed by loss of the primary ability are just those faculties that are lacking in the severely retarded. Furthermore, it is probably precisely this lack which leads to the classification of retardates as such on the standard intelligence scale.

It cannot be assumed, however, that "general intelligence" is the best predictor of second language learning ability. Several studies have shown that there are not only many factors involved but a large unknown factor as well. Even in the specialized situation of the foreign language class in school, which frequently emphasizes a heavily intellectualized approach to language, IQ explains only about 18 to 20 percent of the variance in student success in courses. Jakobovits (1970) summarizes five studies that result in correlations of this order.

While the term "biological" is implied in the notion of the sensitive period, it should be clear what, in turn, is and is not implied by biology. If it should turn out, for example, that the diminution in language acquisition ability is always mediated by emotional factors, the invariant appearance of such factors would need to be explained, and that explanation could certainly be couched in maturational terms (some researchers, interestingly enough, point to the appearance of fear to explain the termination of the imprinting period in birds). Similarly, a formulation involving the development of general cognitive or linguistic processes could qualify as a biological explanation. What is excluded from this perspective is the kind of treatment cited earlier, in which elementary learning mechanisms are invoked, from which a truly developmental view is absent, and in which a relation between quality of learning and age is coincidental, not fundamental.

At this point, it can be said that the sensitive period for the acquisition of phonology seems to be an empirical reality, not just an illusion resulting from selective informal observation. The relation seems to be a roughly linear one, with no sharp discontinuities. The rectangle that describes some imprinting could hardly have been expected to apply to something as complex as human language. Although there was considerable individual variation, the high correlation between the two accent measures suggests consistency for subjects across speech situations.

Since anyone can probably learn *some* aspects of an unfamiliar tongue at any age, and since there is reason to believe that a person's native linguistic system continues to evolve subtly well into the adult years, the question that raises itself is, what kinds of phonology learning are subject to age restraints and what kinds are not? How are they related to more general cognitive processes? What is the role of motor coordination? Where do the phonological variations involved in regional dialects fit in, since adults sometimes pick up features of an adopted region? (Labov, 1966c, has some interesting things to say about this question and about acquisition of the various stylistic variants in a single region.) Many issues must be clarified before we can claim to understand what actually happens in acquisition.

What are the practical implications of this study? There seems to be little excuse remaining for not designing and implementing programs which take full advantage of this interval of receptivity, especially since this same research project produced evidence that the sensitive period is not confined to phonology, but may involve perception and syntax as well. Those involved in the socially, psychologically, politically, and educationally very complex problem of bilingual instruction in the schools would do well to add yet another consideration to their deliberations, at least in those cases in which the school provides contact with English that would otherwise be lacking, so that the issue becomes one of postponing introduction to the second language.

Although elimination of accents is obviously not necessary for effective use of a language, and although it is doubtful that perfection of pronunciation should be made the major goal of training, there are several reasons for serious attention to this question. The social penalty, first of all, that may be paid by accented speakers is sometimes serious. A related problem is that imperfect pronunciation may act as an inhibitor on speakers themselves, affecting their social interaction and their aspirations, perhaps even leading them to avoid certain situations. One would hope that such considerations might diminish in importance as we become more enlightened in our linguistic attitudes, but as long as they remain a social reality we ignore them at our students' peril.

Certain implications, on the other hand, do *not* follow from the findings reported here. Adult courses would not necessarily be contraindicated, although they would have to be considered a second choice to early teaching. For one thing, all subjects in this study had been in the United States at least 5 years; even if language courses had no long-term effects (which is suggested by the data), they might well have short-term advantages that could be extremely important in certain cases. For nonimmigrants, of course, courses may be the only possible method of learning, anyhow. There is a defensive tone to the writing of some educators, as though talk of the advantages of early learning negated the usefulness, even the possibility, of adult language education. Clearly this is not so. Just as clearly their work, too, would be facilitated by more basic knowledge of the nature of these processes.

Perhaps, then, the similes suggested at the beginning of this article were not unfair. A young learner of a second language, given sufficient environmental support, is like any infant learning to sit up: the feat is stupendous, and an individual victory, but is rendered unremarkable by its predictability; the mature learner who succeeds in mastering a new phonological system, fully and perfectly, may belong in the rarefied company of the concert violinist and the 4-minute miler.

Final note: Two studies on accent and age of learning have come to my attention.[6] The first, conducted by Krashen (personal communication), was an informal survey of self-reported accent and age of beginning the second language. While its method was admittedly limited, the study had the virtue of a large N (around 400 people in two countries), and the added virtue of confirming the present results, even when the student experimenters' judgments were used instead of the subjects' own. If learning began before age 11 or so, accents were rare, between 11 and 15 they were not uncommon, and after 15 they were virtually universal.

The second study actually predated the present project (Asher and Garcia, 1969), was in some respects similar, and produced results that merit attention. Subjects this time were Cuban immigrant students, aged 7 to 19, whose taped readings of four sentences were judged by native junior high students for accent. None of the 71 Cuban children was judged to speak like a native, although the earlier arrivals had much less accent than the later ones. Longer stays in the United States were also associated with better pronunciation.

Although differences in subject population, method, and statistical treatment make detailed comparisons difficult, these results seem to be at variance with those reported here. One could, of course, hypothesize that it is harder for Cubans to learn English than for Italians, or that junior high school students are more astute at detecting accents than students of linguistics, but a more plausible suggestion arises from the fact that nearly a quarter of the 30 American controls were judged to have accents by Asher and Garcia's student helpers. The authors speculate that peculiarities of speech in some American students account for these false positives. Whatever the reason, these errors cast some doubt on the "100 percent correct identification" of the Cubans; some of them like the wrongly classified controls, may have been erroneously labeled as accented speakers. The length of stay finding does not directly contradict the present findings, either, since the values used by Asher and Garcia are quite low (1 to 8 years), while the Italian subjects had all been in the United States over 5 years, with the range extending up to 15 years. It is entirely possible that length of stay has an effect precisely in the lower range, whereas the long-range effect (with a less homogeneous sample) may well be as weak as is indicated by the results reported in this article. Many other speculations could obviously be made about these findings, and it is to be hoped that research will soon be done to clarify the issues, but it is probably fair to say that no strong argument against the sensitive period for phonology has materialized.

NOTES

1. This article was adapted from a doctoral dissertation for the Department of Psychology and Social Relations, Harvard University, 1973 (unpublished), which was supported by NSF Grant No. GS-36263 and the Radcliffe Institute.

2. In an effort to determine whether such claims are made by the best-known programs of intensive study, that of the U.S. Armed Forces and that of the Berlitz Schools, the experimenter made inquiries at several branches of each. All the persons contacted denied that "nativelike" pronunciation, in the sense of "indistinguishable from native," could be attained by their methods or by any other methods they knew of. It seems, then, that it would be wise to interpret this term more modestly, perhaps as "resembling native speech in some ways," when reading Jakobovits' account. The former meaning, however, is intended when the present writer uses "nativelike."

3. This represents a collapsing of two categories, casual and spontaneous speech, that Labov found to be similar in many respects.

4. Oddly enough, Roberts claims elsewhere that "Language must be, and is, simple . . . every normal person can learn to speak" (1966, p. 20). Yet no linguist has yet succeeded in making a complete description of all the vagaries and details of any natural language. Roberts' comment reflects one of two general ways of explaining children's learning their native tongue at an age at which they are decidedly intellectually immature. If one can contend that language itself is simple or that acquisition proceeds by elementary learning mechanisms, the incongruity of early childhood acquisition may seem to be lessened. One can, on the other hand, acknowledge the monumental complexity of the task and attempt to explain acquisition in the light of that complexity.

5. There is, of course, no reason to assume a *direct* relationship between maturation of linguistic capabilities and the endocrine changes involved in puberty. The entire period, though, is characterized by general physical and intellectual maturation as well.

6. I thank S. Krashen for informing me of both.

REFERENCES

Ajuriaguerra, J. Comment on Roberts, Central brain mechanisms in speech. In E. C. Carterette (ed.), *Brain Function, Vol. III: Speech, Language and Communication.* Berkeley: University of California Press, 1966, 117–140.

Asher, J. J., and Garcia, R. The optimal age to learn a foreign language. *Modern Language Journal.* 1969, 53, 334–342.

Bever, T. G., Fodor, J. A., and Garrett, M. A formal limit on associationism. In T. R. Dixon and D. L. Horton (eds.), *Verbal Behavior and General Behavior Theory.* Englewood Cliffs, N.J.: Prentice-Hall, 1968, 582–585.

Chomsky, N. A review of B. F. Skinner, *Verbal Behavior. Language.* 1959, 1, 26–58.

Chomsky, N. Linguistic theory. In M. Lester (ed.), *Readings in Applied Transformational Grammar,* New York: Holt, Rinehart and Winston, 1970.

Cole, L. *Psychology of Adolescence,* New York: Rinehart, 1954.

Ervin-Tripp, S. Commentary to session on "How and when do persons become bilingual?" In L. G. Kelly (ed.), *Description and Measurement of Bilingualism.* Toronto: University of Toronto Press, 1969, 26–35.

Ferguson, G. A. *Statistical Analysis in Psychology and Education,* 3d ed., New York: McGraw-Hill, 1971.

Fromkin, V., Krashen, S., Curtiss, S., Rigler, D., and Rigler, M. The development of language in Genie: A case of language acquisition beyond the "critical period." *Brain and Language,* 1974, 1, 81–107.

Goldstein, K. *Language and Language Disturbance.* New York: Grune and Stratton, 1948.

Hirsh, I. J. Comment on Lenneberg's "Speech development." In E. C. Carterette (ed.), *Brain Function, Vol. III: Speech, Language and Communication.* Berkeley: University of California Press, 1966.

Horrocks, J. E. *The Psychology of Adolescents.* Boston: Houghton Mifflin, 1962.

Huebener, T. *How to Teach Foreign Languages Effectively.* New York: New York University Press, 1965.

Jakobovits, L. A. *Foreign Language Learning: A Psycholinguistic Analysis of the Issues,* Rowley, Mass.: Newbury House, 1970.

Jenkins, J. J., and Palermo, D. S. Mediation processes and the acquisition of linguistic structure. In U. Bellugi and R. Brown (eds.), *The Acquisition of Language*, Monographs of the Society for Research in Child Development, 1964, 29 (1), 141–168.

Jespersen, O. *Language, Its Nature, Development and Origin*. New York: Norton, 1964 (orig. ed. 1922).

Jones, R. M. Theme, session on "How and when do persons become bilingual?" In L. G. Kelley (ed.), *Description and Measurement of Bilingualism*. Toronto: University of Toronto Press, 1969, 12–25.

Krashen, S. Lateralization, language learning, and the critical period: Some new evidence. *Language Learning*. 1973, 23, 63–74.

Labov, W. Hypercorrection by the lower middle class as a factor in linguistic change. In W. Bright (ed.), *Sociolinguistics*. The Hague: Mouton, 1966a, 84–113.

Labov, W. The effect of social mobility on linguistic behavior. *Sociology Inquiry*. 1966b, 36, 186–203.

Labov, W. *The Social Stratification of English in New York*. Washington, D.C.: Center for Applied Linguistics, 1966c.

Labov, W. *Sociolinguistic Patterns*, Philadelphia: University of Pennsylvania Press, 1972.

Lambert, W. E. On second language learning and bilingualism. *Modern Language Journal*. 1963, 47, 114–121.

Lambert, W. E., and Macnamara, J. Some cognitive consequences of following a first-grade curriculum in a second language. *Journal of Educational Psychology*. 1969, 60, 86–96.

Larew, L. The optimum age for beginning a foreign language. *Modern Language Journal*. 1961, 45, 203–206.

Lenneberg, E. Review of Penfield and Roberts, Speech and brain mechanisms. *Language*, 1960, 36, 97–112.

Lenneberg, E. The capacity for language acquisition. In J. A. Fodor and J. J. Katz (eds.), *The Structure of Language: Readings in the Philosophy of Language*. Englewood Cliffs, N.J.: Prentice-Hall, 1964a, 579–603.

Lenneberg, E. Speech as a motor skill with special reference to nonaphasic disorders. In U. Bellugi and R. Brown (eds.), *The Acquisition of Language*, Monographs of the Society for Research in Child Development, 1964b, 29 (1), 115–126.

Lenneberg, E. Speech development: Its anatomical and physiological concomitants. In E. C. Carterette (ed.), *Brain Function, Vol. III: Speech, Language and Communication*, Berkeley: University of California Press, 1966, 37–66.

Lenneberg, E. *Biological Foundations of Language*. New York: Wiley, 1967.

Mackey, W. F. *Language Teaching Analysis*. Bloomington: Indiana University Press, 1965.

McDavid, R. I., Jr. Dialect differences and social differences in an urban society. In W. Bright (ed.), *Sociolinguistics*. The Hague: Mouton, 1966, 72–83.

Mowrer, O. H. *Learning Theory and the Symbolic Processes*. New York: Wiley, 1960.

Penfield, W., and Roberts, L. *Speech and Brain Mechanisms*. Princeton: Princeton University Press, 1959.

Politzer, R. L. *Foreign Language Learning*. Englewood Cliffs, N.J.: Prentice-Hall, 1970.

Roberts, L. Central brain mechanisms in speech. In E. C. Carterette (ed.), *Brain Function. Vol. III: Speech, Language and Communication*. Berkeley: University of California Press, 1966, 17–36.

Shiffrin, R. M. Memory search. In D. A. Norman (ed.), *Models of Human Memory*. New York: Academic Press, 1970, 375–447.

Skinner, B. F. *Verbal Behavior*. New York: Appleton-Century, 1957.

Thorpe, W. H. Sensitive periods in the learning of animals and men. In W. H. Thorpe and O. L. Zangwill (eds.), *Current Problems in Animal Behavior*, Cambridge: Cambridge University Press, 1961.

Winer, B. J. *Statistical Principles in Experimental Design*. New York: McGraw-Hill, 1962.

4

THE SENSITIVE PERIOD
AND COMPREHENSION OF SPEECH

Susan Oyama
John Jay College, New York

When it has not been taken for granted, the ability of the young child to acquire its native language, with a minimum of observable effort and, of course, "perfect" results, has excited both wonder and puzzlement. That this childhood facility extends to second and even third languages (though more reliably when those languages are learned by exposure than when they are taught in the classroom) is especially noteworthy when it is compared with the limited success of older learners.

Among teachers of languages and applied linguists there has long been a degree of consensus that the outcome of adult second language learning is at least in some ways inferior to that of children (Larew, 1961; Jones, 1969). Until relatively recently, however, explanations tended to reflect both the behaviorist view of learning that dominated the field for many years and the structuralist view of language that was associated with it; if a childhood advantage in language acquisition was conceded (and sometimes it was not; see Ausubel, 1964; Jakobovits, 1970; and Macnamara, 1973), it was often attributed to more frequent reinforcement, more practice, more intense motivation to master language in order to have basic needs met, while adults were seen as the habit-ridden victims of linguistic interference, self-consciousness, weak motivation, and inadequate rewards (Huebener, 1965; Mackey, 1965; Politzer, 1970).

In the late 1960s, largely as a result of work by Penfield and Roberts (1959) and by Lenneberg (1967) on the biological aspects of language, one began to see occasional references to a biologically based decline in language acquisition ability toward puberty (Jones, 1969; Lakoff, 1969; Scovel, 1969); such references existed side by side with the view of adult difficulties as a matter of recalcitrant stimulus-response bonds. Lenneberg (1960, 1967, 1969), with whom the notion of an age limitation on language acquisition is most often associated, analyzed material from developmental neurology, studies of traumatic aphasia, deafness, and severe retardation, as well as from other sources. From these data he constructed a multifaceted argument that there exists a period, lasting roughly from the second to the tenth or twelfth year, during which the child is able fully to exploit its extraordinary capacity to acquire its native language, and after which primary linguistic development is severely constrained. He also suggested in passing (1967) that children are not only biologically prime learners of their native tongues, but that their special state of receptivity extends to nonnative languages as well, and further, that the drop-off in acquisitional efficiency around age 10 affects the ability to learn *any* natural language completely.

The notion of the critical period, then, which as Kagan points out, "was born in experimental embryology and nurtured in comparative psychology. . ." (1971, p. 239), has come to be applied to the rather lengthy interval during which linguistic systems are effectively and "automatically" processed by the developing child, and after which full mastery seems to be unlikely. Though "critical period" seems to have been the term that has moved into the language acquisition literature, "sensitive period" will be used in this paper. Hinde (1970) advocates using the latter because it reflects more accurately the gradual nature of such phenomena, as well as their responsiveness to variation in experience. Hess (1970) and Erlenmeyer-Kimling (1975) contrast the relatively short and well-defined critical period with the longer, more gradual sensitive period. Lenneberg himself, who in 1968 wrote that the "notion of the critical period has come of age and may be accepted as a legitimate concept in the study of behavior. . . ." (p. 169) recommended 3 years later (personal communication) that "sensitive period" be used to refer to language acquisition because the connotations of the original term had become so absolute, implying sudden, all-or nothing events, often on the imprinting model presented by Lorenz (1970, for example). It should be pointed out that not all ethologists agree with Lorenz's view of development, however; see Moltz (1963) for comments.

In recent years the "biological" conception of acquisition, though not by any means universally accepted, has been frequently discussed (Andersson, 1973; Hill, 1970; Fromkin, Krashen, Curtiss, Rigler, and Rigler, 1974; Krashen, 1973; Macnamara, 1973; Neufeld, 1977; Rosansky, 1975; Schumann, 1975) and several empirical studies of second language phonology acquisition by immigrants have appeared. Oyama's 1976 report on productive mastery of English phonology by a group of immigrants showed a strong relationship between degree of accent and age of learning English; length of stay in the United States, however, did not predict degree of accent, and neither did a variety of other variables investigated. Oyama also discussed several other studies of accent among immigrants, and concluded that the findings were similar enough to be consistent with the existence of a sensitive period for second language acquisition.

The case for a sensitive period would be strengthened, though, by the discovery of comparable age effects for linguistic abilities other than productive phonology. Because comprehension of speech can exist in the absence of articulatory ability (see Lenneberg, 1962, for a description of language in a child with congenital anarthria), and especially because people often say their ability to understand a second language exceeds their ability to speak it, it makes sense to examine this aspect of language use. It could even be argued, after all, that Oyama's findings are more relevant to "motor coordination" than to language per se; this would imply that old dogs may be able to learn new tricks; they just have trouble doing them. It goes without saying that a conception of motor coordination that is divorced from the underlying regulating structure is unrealistic; still, there is certainly ample precedent for distinguishing encoding from decoding processes (see Fodor, Bever, and Garrett, 1974, and Kinsbourne, 1975, for some sophisticated discussion).

An attempt was made, therefore, to assess the ability of Italian immigrants to understand spoken English which had been masked with white noise to reduce redundancy; this reduced redundancy made comprehension more difficult without necessitating complex syntax or esoteric vocabulary which would have complicated interpretation. It was hypothesized that the most powerful predictor of comprehension would be the age at which the individual had begun using English, and that the amount of practice he had had with his second language and other attitudinal and usage variables would show, at best, only indirect relationships with comprehensional skill.[1]

METHOD

Subjects. Subjects were 60 Italian-born male immigrants to the United States who had begun learning English upon their arrival. To ensure ample exposure to Standard English all subjects, who ranged in age from 14 to 37 years, had had some college education (except the youngest, who were recruited from college preparatory high schools), and some had attended graduate school as well. Roughly a third of them had arrived in the United States between the ages of 6 and 10, another third between 11 and 15, and the rest between 16 and 20. The first of these groups, of course, consists of subjects who began their second language during the alleged sensitive period, the second group began toward the end of the period, and the third represents post-sensitive-period learners. About half of these same 60 people had spent 5 to 11 years in the United States, and the others had spent 12 to 20 years. People who had used English for shorter periods were not included, because it was ultimate command of the language that was of interest, not the acquisition process itself.

Baseline data were supplied by 10 native speakers of American English, also male, selected to provide a rough match for the Italians in age, education, and social characteristics.

Procedure. Twelve short sentences, five to seven words long, were tape-recorded by a native American female on a Uher 1400 Report. Each sentence was then rerecorded four times in succession on an identical machine, each time with masking white noise at a different signal-to-noise ratio. The first time the sentence was heard by the subject at a signal-to-noise ratio shown by pretesting with natives to render it virtually unintelligible; the ratio was increased on each of the following three trials until the sentence was clear enough to be easily and completely perceptible to natives. Subjects were instructed, by a taped voice, to listen to each sentence and to repeat whatever they had understood. Stimuli and instructions were presented through earphones. The masking white noise was produced by a Grason Stadler noise generator, model 901B; signal-to-noise ratios ranged from approximately 5 to 16½ decibels.

Adapted for this study from a technique developed by Spolsky and his colleagues (1968, 1969), the masked speech test was meant to tap an ability to integrate various kinds of linguistic knowledge, not only of phonology, but of syntax, intonation, and redundancy patterns as well. In contrast to discrete point tasks, which check for specific bits of knowledge, this comprehension test requires the subject to use virtually all available information to reconstruct the sentence from an incomplete acoustic signal, rather like a cloze procedure raised to the third power.

A word was scored a point each time it was correctly heard, and each sentence was played four times; so this method had a built-in weighting mechanism. A word heard on the first playing added four points to the sentence score, whereas it added only one if heard on the last repetition.[2] A subject's score, then, was cumulative over four repetitions of each of 12 sentences.

In addition, information was gathered by interview and questionnaire on each subject's language background, pattern of language use, education, motivation, and attitudes.

Results. A general impression of the results can be gained from Table 1. Although sampling error produced a significant confounding between age of arrival and length of stay in the United States ($r = -.30, p<.05$), subjects have been grouped by both variables and mean scores are shown for six subgroups. In this way various informal comparisons can be made. As predicted, those subjects who began learning English before age 11 showed comprehension scores similar to those of native speakers, whereas later arrivals did less well; those who arrived after the age of 16 showed markedly lower comprehension scores than the natives. No overall practice (length of stay) effect, on the other hand, is evident from these figures.

The main analyses were correlational. When Comprehension scores were correlated with Age of Arrival, holding constant the effects of Length of Stay, the resulting partial correlation coefficient was $-.57$, significant well beyond

Table 1 Mean Comprehension Scores of Nonnative and
Native Speakers of English

Natives	165.8 ($n = 10$)			
Nonnatives				

Length of stay	Age of arrival			
	6–10	11–15	16–20	Combined
12–18	163.4 ($n = 11$)	119.1 ($n = 11$)	110.1 ($n = 9$)	132.2 ($n = 31$)
5–11	141 ($n = 8$)	131.6 ($n = 12$)	123.7 ($n = 9$)	131.7 ($n = 29$)
Combined	153.9 ($n = 19$)	125.6 ($n = 23$)	116.9 ($n = 18$)	

the .001 level. To a large extent, then, the impression conveyed by Table 1, that younger arrivals were best able to compensate for the effects of masking noise, was confirmed by more precise analysis.

The reverse partial correlation coefficient was a puzzling $-.39$, also statistically significant ($p<.01$). What is odd about this result is that it indicates a negative relationship; when Age of Arrival was partialed out, the longer subjects had been in the United States the worse they were at comprehending masked speech. The first explanation that presents itself is that auditory acuity, which begins to decline rather early in life, is actually the operative factor, showing up in the guise of length of stay simply because older subjects tended to have been in the United States longer. To test this possibility a series of second-order partial correlation coefficients was computed, allowing the examination of the relationship between two variables, with the effects of two others held constant. When the effects of both Age and Age of Arrival were removed, the association between Comprehension and Length of Stay dropped to an insignificant $-.17$. The correlation between Comprehension and Age with Age of Arrival and Length of Stay held constant was even smaller, $-.07$, rather effectively eliminating the possibility that comprehension decreased as subjects grew older. When, on the other hand, the originally highly significant association between Comprehension and Age of Arrival was reexamined, this time with both Age and Length of Stay partialed out, it was a substantial $-.40$.

It seems, then, that Age of Arrival is indeed the prime variable ordering these data, and that the apparently negative correlation between Comprehension and Length of Stay does not offer any insight into possible explanations for sensitive period phenomena, though it may point to some hitherto unidentified cohort effect.

When simple correlation coefficients were computed on the background data on linguistic and social factors, some unsurprising associations were

Table 2 Partial Correlation Coefficients of Comprehension
Scores with Age of Arrival and Questionnaire Variables

Column A: Partial correlation coefficient for Comprehension
and Age of Arrival with effects of Questionnaire
Variables removed.

Column B: Partial correlation coefficient for Comprehension
and Questionnaire Variables with effects of Age of
Arrival removed.

Questionnaire variable	A	B
Education level ($n = 37$)*	−.64§	−.16
Amount of American education ($n = 37$)*	−.51‡	.04
Amount of exposure to English upon arrival	−.58§	−.12
Motivation while learning	−.56§	.12
Self-consciousness while learning	−.42§	−.18
Amount of Italian used while learning	−.56§	−.25
Amount of Italian used, present	−.60§	.21
American orientation and identification	−.53§	.10
Present motivation to improve English	−.60§	.29†

*Based on a subsample who had completed schooling or had
reached the highest educational category, "some graduate
school."

†$p < .05$

‡$p < .01$

§$p < .001$

revealed: the lower a subject's reported self-consciousness while learning, for example, or the more oriented to American culture, the higher the Comprehension score. When the partial correlation coefficients were done, however, a rather instructive pattern emerged. With one modest exception, the simple correlations between Questionnaire Variables and Comprehension were seen to have been artifacts of a confounding of those variables with Age of Arrival (Table 2). While it was true, that is, that higher comprehension scores were associated with low self-consciousness while learning English or greater American orientation and identification, these correlations were a function of the tendency for *early learners* of English to be unselfconscious while learning, to be oriented toward American culture, and so forth. When the effects of Age of Arrival were controlled for, all but one of these relationships disappeared; the sole survivor of this procedure was a variable called "Present motivation to improve English," which showed a coefficient of .29 (column B). When the reverse set of partial correlations was computed, that is, between Age of Arrival and Comprehension with the various Questionnaire Variables held constant, an extremely strong confirmation of the importance of age was found (column A). The association between performance on the comprehension task and age of beginning the second language, then, is robust and clear.

DISCUSSION

There is evidence, then, that there is a strong age effect, not only on the ability to speak a second language with a convincing accent, but also on the ability to understand it effectively. Though "accent" is the aspect of second language functioning most often believed to be rather closely age-related, late learners' difficulties with their adopted language are not exclusively a matter of getting the articulatory apparatus to do the right things.

These results do not, of course, imply that late learners have comprehension problems under normal circumstances. Everyday use of language generally offers multiple redundancies, situational and gestural as well as linguistic. What is at issue here is not whether adults can learn language, or even whether they can learn language very well. Communicational skill and even eloquence are often compatible with less-than-perfect deployment of the various aspects of a second language. What is of interest is the nature of the long-term outcome of acquisition; to what extent does it resemble native (fully elaborated and integrated) linguistic performance? Since the process of language comprehension is not at all well understood, and since the testing technique used here gives a good index of overall comprehension ability but does not permit refined analysis of specific psycholinguistic mechanisms, it is not yet possible to say precisely what underlies the deficit observed in this sample. Further research should reveal the extent to which individual phonemic confusions, for example, are responsible for the differences observed in this study; if such confusions are involved, are they "interference" errors (do they seem to reflect the phonemic structure of the native language) or do they seem to be the result of more general processes? What part is played by intonation, by syntax, by the ability to produce a rapid sequence of hypothetical readings of a given acoustic signal? Such aspects of language are interrelated in notoriously complex and subtle ways; so any answer to these questions will presumably be correspondingly complex and subtle. Lacking an integrated theory of language use, we must for the time being content ourselves with relatively broad quantitative statements.

These subjects, on the whole, performed in a way that was consistent with the predictions made. Those who began learning English by the age of 10 tended to resemble native speakers in their ability to deal with masked speech, those who began in early adolescence diverged from native levels, and those who began after midadolescence showed markedly lower average comprehension scores. When scores were plotted against age of arrival, the relation appeared to be a linear one, though data are clearly needed on people beginning new languages in their twenties, thirties, and beyond.

There seems to be less and less reason to reject the idea that human beings are better able to analyze, integrate, and fully utilize a new language if they approach it early in life than if they do so after the early teens. Late learners, however effectively they may use their adopted tongue in their everyday lives, not only announce themselves when they speak but can be shown in the laboratory to process masked speech less well than early learners.

The sensitive period hypothesis has been associated with what Hill calls "innatist explanations" of language acquisition (1970, p. 237), as well as with "nativism" and with "biology" when biology is used as a cover term for naive nativism. The proper way to construe it, however, is not as a banner signaling allegiance to one side of a false dichotomy but as a descriptive term for a certain type of developmental phenomenon. In relating the concept of the psychological stage to that of the critical period, Kagan says, "Biology has prepared the child for a change in cognitive structure, motivation, affect or behavior, with experience playing the role of inducer. Exquisite, time-locked mechanisms alter the individual's psychic competence so that he is able to react to events in a new way." (1971, p. 239) As Hinde remarks, "In general it is a useful working assumption that no particular case of learning would occur with equal facility at all stages of the life cycle. . . . The problem of sensitive periods for learning is the problem of ontogeny of behavior itself." (1970, p. 556.)

An empirically demonstrated sensitive period, then, shows that there is a tendency for receptivity to certain aspects of the environment to be tied to maturational state in some way. It is a developmental phenomenon not in that it is "determined by the genes" in some rigid or direct way, but rather insofar as it reflects an intricate sequence of interactions between the developing phenotype and the environment, which is sufficiently typical of the species that it appears despite individual differences and widely varying experiences.

Demonstrating a sensitive period, however, is certainly not the same as explaining it. Various attempts have been made to identify the bases for age limits on acquisitional capacity; though they will not be reviewed here, a few comments will be made about two themes that occur frequently in the acquisition literature: the importance of motivation and the role of input.

A common argument, for instance, is that the child is highly motivated to acquire a new language because it is necessary for social interaction and for the satisfaction of basic needs (Ausubel, 1964; Huebener, 1965; Jones, 1969; Macnamara, 1973). The fact is that prospective playmates do not make their friendship contingent on flawless syntax and perfect articulation. Studies of bilingual children are full of charming examples of cheerful and vigorous interaction among children who have very little common linguistic ground. Wagner-Gough (1975) has observed how forgiving adults are of children's errors; one has the impression that other children are equally tolerant. If this is so, then the young learner probably has less reason to perfect a second language than the mature student. It is important to distinguish, incidentally, between modest proficiency, which will get a person through most situations, and perfect nativelike performance. It is not clear that children would be more highly motivated than adults to attain either level. Interaction among adults is rarely possible without a common language, and adults are more likely than children to be concerned about minor imperfections in lexical choice, syntax, or articulation either in themselves or in others. Yet children perfect their second language, and adults, often professing concern over their linguistic shortcomings, do not. It should be noted that it is not being argued that children lack motivation to acquire new languages; children's superior abilities, however, cannot easily be explained by invoking greater motivation. Self-consciousness, furthermore, which has often been seen as a hindrance to effective language mastery, should be recognized in this context as a frequent companion to motivation, and it will be recalled that both seem to arise largely as a *result* of late learners' frustrating failure to progress in a new language as they would like to.

The other theme running through the literature is that of input variables. Far from explaining either the first or the second language in any simple way, investigation of input can give useful information on what constitutes some of the raw material for any given individual's construction of the language, thus perhaps illuminating the types of learning strategies used. Whether the differences betwen what the child hears and what the adult hears can account for the differential success of these two groups of second language learners, though, is another question.

It has often been noted, for example, that speech addressed to children is highly redundant, syntactically simple, repetitious, related to objects or events in the immediate environment, and parceled out in short utterances (Brown and Bellugi, 1964; Landes, 1975; Wagner-Gough and Hatch, 1975). Though these qualities have often been assumed to facilitate analysis and acquisition of a language, use of the same characteristics in the classical foreign language courses has not reliably produced native proficiency levels. Certainly such structuring does not appear to be sufficient for full acquisition. Nor have truly native levels been reached with more recent techniques, though this is not to say that they are without value or that there are no criteria for choosing among them.

The fact is, of course, that input is not only an independent variable but a dependent one as well; conversation, even with a 4-year-old, is an interactive process involving continual mutual adjustment and influence. Speakers tend to gauge the hearer's abilities (not necessarily accurately) and to tailor their vocabulary, syntax, speaking rate, and clarity accordingly (not necessarily effectively). Landes (1975, p. 376) points out, "It is clear that adults are not only sensitive to and affected by the need to communicate with their children, but that interaction patterns between parents and offspring change with the increasing language skills of the child." What is also soberingly clear is that we do not know what input characteristics facilitate or hinder acquisition. Wagner-Gough and Hatch describe speech directed at a 5-year-old learning English as consisting of "a limited body of graded language data where simple patterns and formulas complemented the activity he was engaged in. Moreover, they were constantly recycled in the input to him." (1975, p. 306.) A 13-year-old also learning English as a second language is described by the same authors as receiving complex sentences and idioms in no obvious sequence, difficult concepts and linguistic patterns. Though there seems to be an implication that these differences make the acquisitional task more difficult for the older child, the authors concede that it is hard to interpret the effects of such input characteristics.

Taking a different tack, Hakuta (1975) mentions the peculiar distortions of native speech when it is addressed to a foreigner, commenting that such pidginized speech, more often directed at the adult than at the child, may make acquisition more difficult for the mature learner. Apart from the reservations one must have about this intriguing hypothesis until it is empirically supported, it would seem that even if pidginized input proves to be detrimental to acquisition, it could not explain the enduring language deficit of the adult who has spoken a second language for many years, has attained a high degree of communicative skill, is no longer addressed in anything but normal speech, and who still does not reach perfect command of the adopted tongue. There are also striking similarities among pidginized speech, baby talk, and the simplified discourse normally directed to children. Further, we have yet to find out what part is played by speech that is overheard (and therefore presumably not simplified for the listener's benefit), and by input from speakers who themselves have imperfect command of the language; these would include other children, other second language learners, and so on. Finally, one must keep in mind that bilingual children are often the most linguistically adept members of their households, possessing second language skills far in advance of their elders.

In the same way that people seem to be arguing both that late learners of a second language are too highly motivated (too self-conscious, too concerned with performance) and that they are not motivated enough, it is held on the one hand that input to adults is too complex to be helpful, and on the other hand, that it is too simple and fragmentary. Certainly any child acquiring a language, first or second, is also frequently faced with input that is alternately too advanced and too infantile, well formed and ill formed. Just as surely, it is part of the genius of young learners that they are able to sift, process, and utilize this disparate material to construct a linguistic system that is ultimately indistinguishable from that of the community.

Our understanding of language acquisition is still primitive, in spite of the concerted efforts of investigators in many fields. If we are to approach linguistic phenomena with any hope of explaining them, we must be armed with a set of concepts that are appropriately complex and that reflect the interactive nature of development (Oyama, 1979). Certainly coherent input is necessary for acquisition at any age, but what constitutes coherence at any given time is partly a function of developmental state. Similarly, the idea of "motivation," if it is to be useful in dealing with language, must not be oversimplified, either by being cast in an exclusively instrumental or operant mold or by being seen only as cause, never as effect. Surely the sensitive period for language acquisition is actually a finely graded sequence of periods, involving different types of motivation which are intimately tied to, and responsive to, the cognitive and emotional level of the learner. Each period presumably involves both a special sensitivity to certain aspects of input, perhaps highly abstract, and a special propensity to process these data in a certain way. The existence of a sensitive period, then, is not at all inconsistent with the importance of motivational and input factors; what is to be avoided is simplistic conceptions of these factors, as well as the premature assigning of explanatory primacy to any one of them. The essence of ontogenesis is not "factors," after all, but synthesis. Explanation of the sensitive period, then, must await elucidation of the developmental processes underlying the continuous incorporation of various kinds of data into the ever-changing structures that constitute the emerging linguistic system.

APPENDIX

Instructions. You will now hear 12 sentences. You will hear each one several times, each time with some accompanying noise. The first time you hear a sentence you probably will not be able to understand it, since the noise will be quite loud. Each successive time you hear it, there will be less noise and you will begin to hear more and more. After each reading, please repeat as much as you heard, in the order in which you heard it. Are there any questions?

The sentences:

1. Shepherds seldom lose their sheep.
2. Sixteen great leaders were lost.
3. Robert put the dishes down.
4. She sounded sad on the phone.
5. The bird lost all its feathers.
6. People always want more time.
7. She went away after lunch.
8. The oak tree shook in the wind.
9. Children went over the high wall.
10. The sun hasn't gone down yet.
11. Young people like red apples.
12. This fish is in its own bowl.

NOTES

1. In the absence of any evidence to the contrary, that is, it seemed simplest to begin with the assumption that comprehension skills would show the same pattern of responsiveness to these factors as accent does.

2. Very rarely a subject heard a word correctly early in the sequence of replays, and then changed or omitted it later. In such cases, the "built-in weighting" did not hold, since a point was scored only if the word was actually repeated correctly.

REFERENCES

Andersson, T. Children's learning of a second language: another view. *Modern Language Journal.* 1973, 47, 254–259.
Ausubel, D. Adults versus children in second-language learning: psychological considerations. *Modern Language Journal.* 1964, 48, 42–424.

Brown, R., and Bellugi, U. Three processes in the child's acquisition of syntax. *Harvard Educational Review.* 1964, 34, 133–151.

Erlenmeyer-Kimling, L. Commentary I on paper by N. D. Henderson. In K. W. Schaie, V. E. Anderson, G. E. McClearn and J. Money (eds.), *Developmental Human Behavior Genetics.* Lexington, Mass.: D.C. Heath and Co., 1975, 25–31.

Fodor, J. A., Bever, T. G., and Garrett, M. F. *The Psychology of Language: An Introduction to Psycholinguistics and Generative Grammar.* New York: McGraw-Hill Book Co., 1974.

Fromkin, V., Krashen, S., Curtiss, S., Rigler, D., and Rigler, M. The development of language in Genie: a case of language acquisition beyond the "critical period." *Brain and Language.* 1974, 1, 81–107.

Hakuta, K. Becoming Bilingual at Age 5: The Story of Uguisu. Unpublished senior honors thesis, Department of Psychology and Social Relations, Harvard University, 1975.

Hess, E. H. The ethological approach to socialization. In R. A. Hoppe, G. A. Milton, and E. C. Simmel (eds.), *Early Experience and the Processes of Socialization.* New York: Academic Press, 1970. Reprinted in J. Sants and H. J. Butcher (eds.), *Developmental Psychology: Selected Readings,* Harmondsworth, Middlesex, England: Penguin Books, Ltd., 1975, 57–74.

Hill, J. H. Foreign accents, language acquisition, and cerebral dominance revisited. *Language Learning.* 1970, 20, 237–248.

Hinde, R. A. *Animal Behavior,* 2d ed. New York: McGraw-Hill Book Co., 1970.

Huebener, T. *How to Teach Foreign Languages Effectively.* New York: New York University Press, 1965.

Jakobovits, L. A. *Foreign Language Learning: A Psycholinguistic Analysis of the Issues.* Rowley, Mass.: Newbury House, 1970.

Jones, R. M. Theme, session on "How and when do persons become bilingual?" In L. G. Kelly (ed.), *Description and Measurement of Bilingualism.* Canada: University of Toronto Press, 1969, 12–25.

Kagan, J. A conception of early adolescence. Originally under title, "Twelve to Sixteen: Early Adolescence." *Daedalus* Fall 1971. Reprinted in Annual Editions: *Readings in Human Development '73–'74.* 1971, 239–243.

Kinsbourne, M. Minor hemisphere language and cerebral maturation. In E. H. Lennebrg and E. Lenneberg (eds.), *Foundations of Language Development.* New York: Academic Press, 1975, 2, 107–116.

Krashen, S. D. Lateralization, language learning and the critical period: some new evidence. Language Learning. 1973, 23, 63–74.

Lakoff, R. Transformational grammar and language teaching. *Language Learning.* 1969, 19, 117–140.

Landes, J. E. Speech addressed to children: issues and characteristics of parental input. *Language Learning.* 1975, 25, 355–379.

Larew, L. The optimum age for beginning a foreign language. *Modern Language Journal.* 1961, 45, 203–206.

Lenneberg, E. J. Review of Penfield and Roberts' Speech and Brain Mechanisms. *Language.* 1960, 36, 97–112.

Lenneberg, E. H. Understanding language without ability to speak: a case report. *Journal of Abnormal Psychology.* 1962, 65, 419–425.

Lenneberg, E. H. *Biological Foundations of Language.* New York: Wiley, 1967.

Lenneberg, E. H. The effect of age on the outcome of central nervous system disease in children. In R. Isaacson (ed.), *The Neuropsychology of Development.* New York: Wiley, 1968, 147–170.

Lenneberg, E. H. On explaining language. *Science.* 1969, 164, 635–643.

Lorenz, K. *Studies in Animal and Human Behavior.* Trans. R. Martin. Cambridge, Mass.: Harvard University Press, 1970.

Mackey, W. F. *Language Teaching Analysis.* Bloomington: Indiana University Press, 1965.

Macnamara, J. Nurseries, streets and classrooms: some comparisons and deductions. *Modern Language Journal.* 1973, 57, 250–254.

Moltz, H. Imprinting: an epigenetic approach. *Psychological Review.* 1963, 70, 123–138.

Neufeld, G. Language learning ability in adults: a study on the acquisition of prosodic and articulatory features. *Working Papers on Bilingualism.* 1977, 12, 45–60.

Oyama, S. A sensitive period for the acquisition of a non-native phonological system. *Journal of Psycholinguistic Research.* 1976, 5, 261–285.

Oyama, S. The concept of the sensitive period in developmental studies. *Merrill-Palmer Quarterly.* 1979, Vol. 25, No. 2.

Penfield, W., and Roberts, L. *Speech and Brain Mechanisms.* Princeton, N.J.: Princeton University Press, 1959.

Politzer, R. L. *Foreign Language Learning.* Englewood Cliffs, N.J.: Prentice-Hall, 1970.

Rosansky, E. J. The critical period for the acquisition of language: some cognitive developmental considerations. *Working Papers on Bilingualism.* 1975, 6, 93–100.

Schumann, J. H. Affective factors and the problem of age in second language acquisition. *Language Learning.* 1975, 25, 209–235.

Scott, J. P. *Early Experience and the Organization of Behavior.* Belmont, California: Brooks/Cole Publishing Co., 1968.

Scovel, T. Foreign accents, language acquisition, and cerebral dominance. *Language Learning.* 1969, 19, 245–254.

Spolsky, B. Reduced redundancy as a language testing tool. Paper read at Language Testing Session of Second International Congress of Applied Linguistics, Cambridge, England, September 1969.

Spolsky, B., Bengt, S. Sato, M., Walker, E., and Arterburn, C. Preliminary studies in the development of techniques for testing overall second language proficiency. *Language Learning, Special Issue,* 1968, 3, 79–101.

Wagner-Gough, J. Comparative Studies in Second Language Learning. Unpublished MA thesis, UCLA, 1975.

Wagner-Gough, J., and Hatch, E. The importance of input data in second language acquisition studies. *Language Learning.* 1975, 25, 297–308.

5

THE SENSITIVE PERIOD
FOR THE ACQUISITION OF SYNTAX
IN A SECOND LANGUAGE[1]

Mark S. Patkowski
English Language Program, Hofstra University

The notion of a sensitive period for the acquisition of a second language has been debated in the field of second language acquisition for some time. This notion derives from Lenneberg's (1967) hypothesis concerning the existence of a critical period for the acquisition of a first language extending from about 2 years of age to the close of puberty. The term "critical period" refers to the notion that the age limitation is absolute. In theory, first language acquisition is not possible past the critical point. The term "sensitive period," on the other hand, refers to the fact that the age limitation is not absolute. It is indeed possible to acquire a foreign language at an adult age, but it is not possible to do so to the extent of being able to "pass for native."

Lenneberg, in advancing the critical period hypothesis, pointed out that "many animals traverse periods of peculiar sensitivities, response-propensities, or learning potentials. Insofar as we have made such a claim for language acquisition, we have postulated nothing that would be extraordinary in the realm of animal behavior." (p. 175.)

Lenneberg presented two important arguments implicating puberty as the close of the critical period: The first is based on studies in neurology and aphasia which seem to show that the chances for recovery of lost language functions are very different for children and adults. The second argument concerns language development in Down's syndrome children. Lenneberg observed that the linguistic development of these children follows a normal but slowed-down course and that this development is "frozen" at puberty.

Lenneberg's critical period hypothesis concerns specifically first language acquisition. However, he did address himself to the issue of second language acquisition, as shown in the following passage:

Our ability to learn foreign languages tends to confuse the picture. Most individuals of average intelligence are able to learn a second language after the beginning of their second decade, although the incidence of "language learning blocks" rapidly increases after puberty. Moreover, a person can learn to communicate in a foreign language at the age of forty. This does not trouble our basic hypothesis on age limitations because we may assume that the cerebral organization for language learning as such has taken place during childhood, and since natural languages tend to resemble one another in many fundamental aspects, the matrix for language skills is present. (p. 176.)

Studies on accent by Oyama (1976) and Seliger et al. (1975) which investigated the relation of age of acquisition with the attainment of nativelike pronunciation have adduced supporting evidence for the notion of a sensitive period for the acquisition of a second phonological system. The results, in both cases, showed that age of acquisition is a strong predictor of accent, while various motivational and practice factors (including length of stay in the United States) have little effect.

The study reported here investigated the existence of a sensitive period for the acquisition of syntax in a second language. The hypothesis tested was that full, nativelike acquisition of syntax in a nonnative language can be achieved only if learning begins before the age of 15 years. It should be noted that native proficiency (meaning the ability to produce and comprehend speech in a manner which is indistinguishable from that of a native speaker) is not the necessary product of any second language acquisition experience prior to puberty, but rather is a possible outcome under optimal sociolinguistic conditions. Adult second language acquisition, on the other hand, would be expected never to result in total native fluency.

METHOD

Sixty-seven immigrants who had come to the United States and started learning English at various ages and who had lived in this country for various periods of time were tested for syntactic proficiency in English and were administered a questionnaire to gather information concerning linguistic, educational, and professional variables. All participants had resided in this country for a minimum of 5 years. This was to ensure that participants had had ample time to acquire their second language. Most subjects either held professional positions or were continuing their education. Such selectivity was necessary in order to best answer the question at hand, namely, "Can nativelike command of syntax in a second language be acquired regardless of age?" This goal was met by drawing upon highly educated, upwardly mobile subjects who could be assumed to have been exposed to near optimal sociolinguistic conditions. Additionally, this selectivity reduced the complexities introduced by dialectical variations in the language, since the subjects had been exposed to the educated, middle-class, "standard" version of the language upon which the language measures were based.

Control subjects were 15 native-born Americans of similar background. Insofar as little variance was to be expected among the controls, their main purpose was to provide evidence concerning the reliability and validity of the linguistic measures.

As part of a larger study, a number of measures of syntactic proficiency were employed. The most interesting measure turned out to be the syntactic ratings which were assigned by two trained judges to written transcripts of tape-recorded oral interviews. These interviews were patterned after the Foreign Service Institute's language proficiency interview test. The rating system was adapted to meet the needs of a situation involving the assessment of written rather than oral materials (see Appendix). The interviews themselves lasted from 15 to 35 minutes. Five-minute samples (or three pages of single-spaced typewritten transcript, whichever came first) were selected from toward the end of the conversations. Only minimal punctuation was provided, mispronunciations of correct structures were not indicated, and references which might have given away the national background of subjects were deleted.

Evaluation was performed on a 0- to 5-point scale (with a possible + value for any level except the 5 level, for a total of 11 possible ratings). The judges were two ESL teachers with master's degrees in TESOL and at least 5 years' experience. They were trained over a 2-week period. They were then given all the transcripts to take home and rate over the following 3 weeks.

The independent variables employed in this research were the following: (1) Age at the Beginning of Second Language Acquisition, which was simply the age of the participants upon arrival in the United States; (2) Years in the United States, which represented a practice variable; (3) Informal Exposure to English, a more refined practice variable, which was calculated by weighting the number of years spent in the United States with the subjects' self-reported patterns of language use; (4) Formal Instruction in English, which was calculated in hours of instruction in English as a second or foreign language received by participants. Information concerning these variables was gathered by means of a questionnaire. All subjects were seen individually.

RESULTS

Interrater reliability on the syntactic ratings proved adequately high. The Pearson product-moment correlation coefficient between the judgments of the two raters for the 82 transcripts (67 nonnatives and 15 controls) was .78 ($p<.001$). Only 12 of the 82 pairs of ratings differed by more than one step. This left 70 pairs (85.4 percent) either in "perfect agreement" (identical ratings by both judges) or in "tolerable disagreement" (ratings differing by just one step).

In assigning final ratings to the subjects where the two judges differed, one-step differences were resolved in favor of the higher level (e.g., 4+ and 5= 5). Two-step differences were resolved in favor of the middle level (e.g., 4 and 5= 4+) and three-step differences, which occurred only twice, in favor of the first level down from the higher rating (e.g., 3+ and 2= 3). Under this system, all 15 native controls received 5 ratings (one rater had assigned all 15 natives 5 ratings and the other assigned nine 5 ratings and six 4+ ratings).

The sample consisted of highly educated individuals who were either still pursuing their studies at the time of testing or were engaged in careers in the professions, government, and business. Fifty-one of the total sample of 83 had earned at least a master's degree. The sample consisted of 36 males and 46 females. The number of years spent in the United States (for the nonnative group) ranged from 6 to 61 years (mean = 19.5, SD = 10.7). The age at which second language acquisition began ranged from 5 to 50 years (mean = 18, SD = 11.1). The Formal Instruction Score, calculated in terms of hours of English language instruction, ranged from 0 to 9000 hours (mean = 780, SD = 1565). The subjects' native languages included Spanish (24 cases), Polish (17 cases), Chinese (9 cases), as well as French, Haitian Creole, Czech, Arabic, Turkish, Rumanian, Hebrew, Bengali, Russian, Italian, and Serbo-Croatian (each with three cases or less).

There were 33 subjects who had come to the United States before the age of 15 years (prepuberty group) and 34 subjects who had arrived after (postpuberty group). The mean age upon arrival was 8.6 years for the first group (SD = 2.7) and 27.1 years for the second group (SD = 8.2). The postpuberty group had received considerably more formal instruction (apparently to little avail, as seen below). The mean number of hours of instruction for the postpuberty group was 1201 hours compared with 345 hours for the prepuberty group ($t = 2.31$, $p = 0.025$). Both groups had lived in the United States for comparable periods of time; the mean number of years was 20.4 for the prepuberty group and 18.7 years for the postpuberty group ($t = 0.65$, $p<.500$). However, the prepuberty group scored higher on the informal exposure variable; the mean number of hours of informal exposure was 84,452 for the prepuberty group and 58,479 for the postpuberty group. This finding is discussed below in light of subsequent results.

The population distribution curve for the dependent variable (syntactic rating) exhibited a bimodal aspect for the entire nonnative sample. However, when the population curves for subjects having arrived before and after the age of 15 years were examined separately, the following results emerged. The curve for the prepuberty group was strongly skewed to the right (mean = 4.8, mode = 5) and showed very little scatter (32 of 33 cases scored at the 4+ or 5 levels). The curve for the postpuberty group, on the other hand, exhibited a strikingly "normal" distribution centered about the 3+ level (mean = 3.6, SD = .6).

This difference, which is illustrated in Figure 1, is quite revealing. The population curve for the postpuberty group, with its normal characteristics, suggests the usual scatter of abilities which is often found in psychological and social research. The population curve for the prepuberty group, however, strongly suggests that some special factor is at work and is the cause of such a skewed population distribution. Thus, even at a purely descriptive level, the distributional characteristics of the two nonnative groups are clearly consonant with the notion of a sensitive period for the acquisition of syntax in a second language.

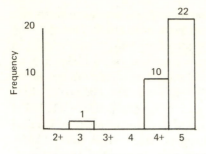

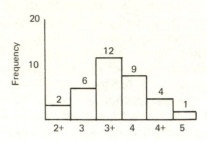

Bar chart for prepuberty learners (n = 33)   Bar chart for postpuberty learners (n = 34)

FIGURE 1 Bar charts showing population frequencies for pre- and post-puberty learners on syntactic rating

Table 1 Two-Way Analysis of Variance: Influence of Age at
Arrival and of Years in the United States on Syntactic Rating

Age at arrival		
Under 15 years	$M = 4.8$	$M = 4.7$
(prepuberty)	$SD = 0.2$	$SD = 0.5$
	$N = 16$	$N = 17$
Over 15 years	$M = 3.7$	$M = 3.6$
(postpuberty)	$SD = 0.5$	$SD = 0.6$
	$N = 18$	$N = 16$
	Under 18 years	Over 18 years

Number of years in the United States

Source of variation	d.f.	Mean square	F
Age at arrival	1	21.99	88.76*
Years in the United States	1	0.30	1.18
Interaction	1	0.01	0.04
Within groups	63	0.25	

*$p < .001$

In order to test the hypothesis of a sensitive period for second language syntax, analyses of variance (2×2 factorial designs, unweighted means method) and correlational analyses were used. All calculations were carried out on an IBM 360 using the DATATEXT and SPSS statistical programs.

In dichotomizing continuous variables for the purposes of the ANOVAs, the median of each variable was selected as the cutoff point between "high" and "low" categories. The two-way analyses of variance, involving Age at L2 (age at the beginning of second language acquisition) as the first factor and taking each one of the remaining three independent variables (Years in the United States, Informal Exposure, and Formal Instruction) in turn as the second factor

Table 2   Two-Way Analysis of Variance: Influence of Independent Variables on Syntactic Rating

Source of variation	d.f.	Mean square	F
Age at arrival	1	15.82	61.69*
Formal instruction	1	0.02	0.08
Interaction	1	0.10	0.41
Within groups	63	0.26	
Source of variation	**d.f.**	**Mean square**	**F**
Age at arrival	1	21.37	83.41*
Informal exposure	1	0.02	0.07
Interaction	1	0.12	0.48
Within groups	63	0.26	

$*p < .001$

Table 3   Correlation Coefficients between Syntactic Rating and Independent Variables

	Age at arrival	Years in the U.S.	Informal exposure	Formal instruction
Syntactic rating	−0.74*	−0.01	0.22†	−0.19

$*p < .001$
$†p < .05$

showed strong main effects for Age at L2 and no main effects for the other independent variables. Furthermore, there were no significant interaction effects (see Tables 1 and 2).

Pearson product-moment correlation coefficients were also computed. The results, presented in Table 3, show a strong negative relationship between Age at L2 and Syntactic Rating ($r = -.74$, $p<.001$) and little relationship between the dependent variable and the practice and instructional variables. The correlation between Informal Exposure and Syntactic Rating did reach significance at the .05 level ($r = .22$, $p = .03$), but such a low correlation "explains" less than 5 percent of the variance. Moreover, this relationship disappeared when the effect of Age at L2 was removed (first order partial $r = .06$, $p = .31$).

Second-order partials, which are presented in Table 4, showed no significant change in the strong negative relationship between Age at L2 and Syntactic Rating when all possible three-way combinations of independent variables were tested. They also showed little or no relationship between the dependent measure and the practice and instructional variables.

Table 4 Second-Order Partial Correlation Coefficients between Syntactic Rating and
Independent Variables

Column A:	Second-order partial correlation coefficient of syntactic rating and Age at Arrival with effects of Informal Exposure and Formal Instruction removed		
Column B:	Second-order partial correlation coefficient of syntactic rating and Informal Exposure with effects of Age at Arrival and Formal Instruction removed		
Column C:	Second-order partial correlation coefficient of syntactic rating and Formal Instruction with effects of Age at Arrival and Informal Exposure removed		
	A	B	C
Syntactic rating	$-0.72*$	0.04	-0.15

$*p < .001$

Thus, all the results discussed above seem to be strongly consistent with the notion of an age limitation on the acquisition of syntax in a second language. Descriptive statistics reveal strikingly dissimilar population distribution characteristics for the pre- and postpuberty groups on syntactic proficiency; analyses of variance show strong main effects on syntactic proficiency for age at which learning begins and no significant effects for instructional and practice variables. Correlational analyses further reinforce this picture.

In the light of these results, the difference noted earlier between the pre- and postpuberty groups on the variable of informal exposure (with the former group spending a considerably greater proportion of time exposed to English despite a similar mean number of years of residence in the United States) can be interpreted as follows. Since the prepuberty group spoke better English, its members tended to immerse themselves in English language environments more often. At the same time, the fact that the postpuberty learners had received almost four times as much formal instruction might indicate that they recognized their linguistic shortcomings and sought to correct them.

For the purpose of replicating Oyama's (1976) study on the sensitive period for the acquisition of a nonnative phonological system, the two judges involved in this research had also been asked to rate on a 0- to 5-point scale 30-second taped passages from all 82 interviews after they had finished rating the written transcripts. The results strongly upheld Oyama's. Interrater reliability was high ($r = .84, p < .001$). F tests revealed strong main effects for age upon arrival ($F = 118.5, p<.001$) and no significant main or interaction effects involving the other independent variables. The Pearson product-moment correlation between accent rating and age upon arrival showed a strong negative relationship ($r = -.76, p<.001$), and this relationship did not weaken with second-order partials controlling for all possible three-way combinations of independent variables.

DISCUSSION

The sample investigated in this study was composed of people who were in an optimal position to acquire the new language. All had resided in this country for at least 6 years (and some for as many as 35 or more years). All were highly educated and were either continuing their studies or employed in professional positions. Under these circumstances, all could be surmised to have been highly motivated to acquire English, and yet the only factor which was highly associated with the level of syntactic proficiency attained by learners was the age at which acquisition of English began. Practice and instructional variables showed little or no association with the dependent variable. The results, then, appeared to strongly support the hypothesis of an age-related limitation on the ability to acquire full command of a second language.

As Krashen et al. (1979) point out, there have been surprisingly few studies investigating child-adult differences in eventual attainment in a second language. However, such studies (e.g., Oyama, 1976; Seliger et al., 1975) consistently show age at the beginning of second language acquisition to be the most highly associated independent variable with eventual attainment.

Some studies have shown child-adult differences favoring adults. Snow et al. (1978) tested (and rejected) the prediction that second language acquisition would be relatively quick and successful if it occurs before puberty by following during a period of 1 year a group of English speakers who were learning Dutch in a natural setting. The results, on a battery of tests, showed that the general order from proficient to poor on most tasks was (1) 12- to 15-year-olds, (2) either adults or 8- to 10-year-olds, (3) 6- to 7-year-olds, (4) 3- to 5-year-olds. The authors then noted that "the adults, despite their initial rapid acquisition, fell increasingly behind because their subsequent improvement was very slow. The teenagers had almost achieved native performance very rapidly." (p. 1122.) Krashen et al. (1979) note that this study involved a very short exposure time (1 year) and thus concerned learning rates and not eventual achievement. This writer would like to suggest that the above results are quite compatible with the hypothesis of an age limitation. The optimal age for acquiring a second language, at least with respect to ease and rapidity, would logically be the age at which the learner has attained a high level of cognitive development while he or she still retains use of the genetically based language acquisition system. This optimal age, then, would have to be somewhere prior to the critical threshold of puberty, in the low teens (say 12 to 15 years). Studies comparing acquisition rates between children (e.g., Fathman, 1975; Ervin-Tripp, 1974) have indeed generally shown other children outperforming their younger counterparts.

Other studies (e.g., Burstall, 1975; Stern, 1976) have shown essentially no differences in second language attainment between younger and older children. As Krashen et al. (1979) remark, such studies compared children in formal language learning situations in school settings. According to Lamendella (1977), such settings are conducive to an essentially rational, intellectual, and conscious learning process where little use is made of the language acquisition system. Thus, it is only under conditions of prolonged exposure to the target language in a "natural" setting that the intrinsically greater potential for rapid and effective second language acquisition of children can be detected. Studies of formal language learning situations therefore do not bear directly upon the hypothesis of an age limitation.

Appeal to innate mechanisms is widely regarded with great suspicion; yet the results of studies on the sensitive period run counter to competing theories of language acquisition. A strict behavioral approach (e.g., Skinner, 1957) would lead to the prediction that, all other things being equal, a longer period of exposure (i.e., a longer conditioning process) would result in superior linguistic performance. This clearly does not appear to occur. The high strength of the age factor also seems to mitigate against a "social learning" approach (e.g., Gardner et al., 1976) which holds that the cultural and sociolinguistic milieu in which individuals find themselves affects the attitudinal and motivational factors which determine success or failure, irrespective of age factors. Lastly, those who posit that cognitive structures provide the sole basis for language acquisition (e.g., Sinclair, 1975) are left with the task of explaining why, upon the onset of formal operations (the highest level of cognitive development) at about puberty, the capacity to master a second language appears to greatly subside. Indeed, it seems that a "rationalist position" (Chomsky, 1979) holding that the mind possesses a genetically determined language acquisition system which functions during a critical period (Lenneberg, 1967) is the most compatible with the evidence uncovered in this and similar research.

APPENDIX

Language Proficiency Levels[2]

	0.	Unable to function in the language.
Elementary proficiency	1.	Can use stock expressions; almost no control of syntax; speaks largely by juxtaposition of words; vocabulary is adequate only for survival, basic courtesy needs; except for memorized expressions, speech is so fragmentary that little meaning is conveyed.
Limited working proficiency	2.	Has fair control of basic patterns; uses simple "kernel" sentences; very frequent errors of all types; vocabulary is adequate for simple social conversation and routine job needs; relatively simple meanings are accurately conveyed, but linguistic abilities are clearly strained in doing so.
Minimum professional proficiency	3.	Has good control of most basic syntactic patterns; reasonably complex sentences used; errors quite frequent; vocabulary is adequate for participation in all general conversation and for professional discussion in a special field; despite errors and possible circumlocutions, always accurately conveys meanings of relative complexity.
Full professional proficiency	4.	Has excellent control of the grammar; few errors are made and these reveal no overall pattern of deficiency; vocabulary is broad, precise, and literate; occasional unidiomatic use of words or expressions; can convey complex messages in fluent and literate fashion.

Native	5.	Has native control of grammar; occasional slips do not have a "foreign" quality
proficiency		to them; vocabulary is equal to that of an educated native; speech is as fluent as a
		native's.

Numerical Rating Procedure

Instructions: For all of the three areas (grammar, vocabulary, communicative ability), choose the proficiency descriptions—from 1 to 6—which best represent the interviewee's competence. Then, in the weighting table, find the number corresponding to each of the three descriptions and add all three numbers. Then, determine from the conversion table the rating level within which the total score falls. *This numerical procedure is intended only to supplement the verbal descriptions and should not be used by itself to determine a rating.*

Note that the numbers 1 through 6 are simply used to designate the different proficiency descriptions for each language area and do not have any direct relationship to the rating levels 1 through 5.

After some practice, you may in some cases want to give a score that is in between two of the descriptions. For example, if you feel the interviewee's competence in grammar is about midway between description 3 ("Frequent errors showing . . .") and description 4 ("Occasional errors showing . . ."), you might give a weighted score of 21 for grammar, rather than 18 or 24.

Proficiency Descriptions

Grammar

1. Grammar almost entirely inaccurate except in stock phrases.
2. Constant errors showing control of very few major patterns and frequently preventing communication.
3. Frequent errors showing some major patterns uncontrolled and causing occasional irritation and misunderstanding.
4. Occasional errors showing imperfect control of some patterns but no weakness that causes misunderstanding.
5. Few errors, with no pattern of failure.
6. No more than two nonnativelike errors during the interview.

Vocabulary

1. Vocabulary inadequate for even the simplest conversation.
2. Vocabulary limited to basic personal and survival areas (time, food, family, etc.).
3. Choice of words sometimes inaccurate; limitations of vocabulary prevent discussion of some common professional and social topics.
4. Professional vocabulary adequate to discuss special interests; general vocabulary permits discussion of any nontechnical subject with some circumlocution.
5. Professional vocabulary broad and precise; general vocabulary adequate to cope with complex practical problems and varied social situations.
6. Vocabulary apparently as accurate and extensive as that of an educated native speaker.

Communicative Ability

1. Speech is so fragmentary that little meaning is conveyed; appears to understand little or nothing.
2. Except for routine sentences, speech is very fragmentary; needs constant repetition for minimal comprehension.
3. Speech is hestitant, sentences are often left uncompleted; requires careful, somewhat simplified speech with much repetition and rephrasing.
4. Speech is occasionally hestitant; sentences may go uncompleted quite often; gropes for words; understands normal speech but may require rephrasing or repetition.
5. Speech is smooth and fluent but occasional unidiomatic utterances are perceptibly nonnative; understands everything in normal educated conversation.
6. Speech and understanding appear nativelike in all respects.

Weighting Table

Proficiency description →	1	2	3	4	5	6	
Grammar	6	12	18	24	30	36	_____
Vocabulary	4	8	12	16	20	24	_____
Communicative abilitiy	6	12	18	23	29	35	_____
						Total	_____

Conversion Table

Total score	Level	Total score	Level	Total score	Level
12–21	0+	39–48	2	69–78	3+
22–28	1	49–58	2+	79–88	4
29–38	1+	59–68	3	89–95	4+

NOTES

1. This article was based on a doctoral dissertation for the Department of Bilingual Education, New York University, 1980 (unpublished), which was supported in part by an E.S.E.A. Title VII Graduate Fellowship from the United States Department of Health, Education and Welfare (Grants #G 007603258, G 007700569, G 007700509).

2. The Language Proficiency descriptions and the Numerical Rating Procedure are adapted from materials provided by the Foreign Service Institute's Testing and Publications Office. Special thanks are owed to Mrs. Marianne Adams. Assistance was also obtained from Mr. John Clark of the Educational Testing Service, to whom gratitude is also expressed.

REFERENCES

Burstall, C. Primary French in the balance. *Educational Research.* 1975, 17, 193–198.

Chomsky, N. *Language and Responsibility.* New York: Pantheon, 1979.

Ervin-Tripp, S. Is second language learning like the first? *TESOL Quarterly.* 1974, 8, 111–127.

Fathman, A. The relationship between age and second language learning ability. *Language Learning.* 1975, 25, 245–253.

Gardner, R., Smythe, P., Clement, R., and Gliksman, L. Second language learning: a social psychological perspective. *The Canadian Modern Language Review.* 1976, 32, 198–213.

Krashen, S., Long, M., and Scarcella, R. Age, rate and attainment in second language acquisition. *TESOL Quarterly.* 1979, 13, 573–582.

Lamendella, J. General principles of neuro-functional organization and their manifestation in primary and non-primary language acquisition. *Language Learning.* 1977, 27, 155–196.

Lenneberg, E. *Biological Foundations of Language.* New York: Wiley, 1967.

Oyama, S. A sensitive period for the acquisition of a nonnative phonological system. *Journal of Psycholinguistic Research.* 1976, 5, 261–283.

Seliger, H., Krashen, S., and Ladefoged, P. Maturational constraints in the acquisition of second language accent. *Language Sciences.* 1975, 36, 20–22.

Sinclair, H. The role of cognitive structures in language acquisition. In E. H. Lenneberg and E. Lenneberg (eds.), *Foundations of Language Development: A Multidisciplinary Approach.* New York: Academic Press, 1975, 223–229.

Skinner, B. *Verbal Behavior.* Englewood Cliffs, New Jersey: Prentice-Hall, 1957.

Snow, C., and Hoefnagel-Höhle, M. The critical period for language acquisition: evidence from second language learning. *Child Development.* 1978, 49, 1114–1128.

Stern, H. Optimal age: myth or reality? *The Canadian Modern Language Review.* 1976, 32, 283–294.

II

SHORT-TERM STUDIES
OF CHILDREN AND ADULTS

As in Section I, this section also presents studies that compare second language performers who begin second language acquisition or instruction during childhood with those who begin later in life. There is one important difference between these groups of studies, however. While studies in Section I were of long duration, all studies here are "short-term," ranging from an exposure time of 25 minutes in Asher and Price to approximately 1 year (Snow and Hoefnagel-Höhle). Because of this difference, we suggest (Krashen, Long, and Scarcella, reprinted in Section IV) that the different results reported in studies in this section reflect differences in *rate* of acquisition; all studies presented here are consistent with the hypothesis that adults are generally faster than children in early stages of second language acquisition.

As in Section I, the studies vary in certain ways. First, the "treatments" differ. In Asher and Price, subjects were given language instruction using Asher's "total physical response" teaching system. Olson and Samuels used traditional phoneme drills in pronunciation lessons. Snow and Hoefnagel-Höhle used imitation testing and also compared child and adult progress in second language acquisition in the natural environment.

Different linguistic skills were examined. Phonology was probed in several studies (Snow and Hoefnagel-Höhle, Olson and Samuels), and syntactic acquisition was examined in others (Asher and Price), with Snow and Hoefnagel-Höhle examining a variety of syntactic and morphological abilities in their 1978 paper. Also, a variety of target languages were used: Russian (Asher and Price), German (Olson and Samuels), Dutch (Snow and Hoefnagel-Höhle). In all cases, however, the first language was English.

The studies contained in this section also indicate that older children are superior to younger children in rate of acquisition. Section III presents additional studies comparing older and younger children.

6

THE RELATIONSHIP
BETWEEN AGE AND ACCURACY
OF FOREIGN LANGUAGE PRONUNCIATION

Linda L. Olson and S. Jay Samuels
University of Minnesota

The assumption that younger children can master the phonological system of a second language more easily than those who are older was tested under laboratory conditions. This assumption is based on observations of immigrant children in natural settings and findings related to the ability of various age groups to recover full use of speech function following trauma to the dominant cerebral hemisphere. In the study, each of three groups of 20 elementary, 20 junior high, and 20 college students received 10 sessions, each 15 to 25 minutes in length, of pretaped German phoneme pronunciation instruction. A total of 33 phonemes were taught in 2 weeks using various mimicry drills. The students were pretested and posttested and given the Raven Progressive Matrices Test. Analysis of variance and covariance on the pretest indicated no difference in pronunciation. Contrary to common belief, on the posttest the junior high and college groups were significantly ($p < .01$) better at pronunciation than the elementary group.

It has been assumed for many years that foreign language training in the elementary school was advantageous to comprehensive foreign language skill development. Specifically, many people, such as Carroll (1963), believe that younger children can acquire a more native-like accent in a second language than older students. Others have carried this assumption further to say that a child will be superior in other foreign language skills such as syntax and vocabulary acquisition. In addition, the child's enthusiasm and open-mindedness to the study of foreign language and culture and the need for a long study sequence have led many to press for foreign language education in the elementary school (FLES). However, there is a lack of firm evidence to back these assumptions.

The literature regarding age and foreign language study, focusing on foreign language pronunciation, can be divided into three classifications: theory, common (anecdotal) observations, and experimental research.

The theoretical support for notions regarding the relationship between age and foreign language acquisition comes from inferences drawn from psychological and physiological investigations. One example is the brain plasticity theory (Asher and Garcia, 1969). According to this theory, the younger child has a "cerebral receptivity" to language acquisition—in other words, because of differences in brain functioning, younger children find it easier to acquire language. The receptivity may be a function of the organizational plasticity of the brain or lack of cortical specialization. As the child matures, the organization of the cerebral cortex becomes more specialized until speech is completely lateralized in the left cerebral hemisphere. As the organization of the brain becomes more specialized, the individual's capacity to learn a language tends to decrease.

Clinical evidence for such a theory comes from physiological studies. Penfield and Roberts (1959) found that children—but not adults—can regain speech functions following injury to the speech area in the left or dominant cerebral hemisphere. For those children who learned to speak again, the speech area shifted from the left to the right cerebral hemisphere. This shift was demonstraed by injecting sodium amytal into the carotid artery, which produced interference with the function of the right cerebral hemisphere, resulting in hemiplagia and a temporary loss of speech (aphasia) until the drug wore off. This shift of the speech area of the cerebral cortex which occurs in children but not adults, strongly suggests cerebral plasticity in children but not adults. From this and other evidence, Penfield concluded that the critical period in the change of plasticity was near age 10. Therefore, Penfield suggested that foreign language instruction begin before age 10 to take advantage of this critical period in developing good foreign language skills in the child.

Lenneberg (1967), summarizing case histories of brain damage with acquired aphasia, also infers a physiological age limitation for normal first language acquisition, which corresponds with cerebral lateralization of the speech function and change in organizational plasticity. Two lines of evidence support the physiological age limitation viewpoint. Evidence for the first is shown by the difference in probability of recovery from acquired aphasia between children and adults, which is a function of the age at which the brain damage occurred. Below the age of 10, children can relearn language without permanent aphasic symptoms. However, between 10 and puberty traces of aphasia remain permanently in the patient's speech. The amount of permanent aphasic symptoms increases during the middle teens. In adulthood (after the age of 18), those with well-established aphasia fail to overcome their language difficulties despite training. Therefore, Lenneberg infers that language learning can take place, at least in the right hemisphere, only between the ages of 2 and about 13. Thus we can see that as far as ease of primary language learning and relearning following injury are concerned, Lenneberg and Penfield are in agreement regarding physiological age limitations.

Although Lenneberg (1969, 176) believes there is a fundamental difference between first and second language acquisition, he believes that age seems to influence most the retention of foreign accent and the ability to learn a foreign language just from exposure in the natural setting without formal training. It must be emphasized that the conclusion that children have a foreign language capacity which adults do not, as inferred above, is not based on direct experimental data.

The ability of children to achieve a more nativelike pronunciation of a foreign language than older students is the most common reason given for beginning foreign languages in the elementary school. This is based on the frequent observation that immigrant children acquire nativelike speech much more rapidly than their parents. But there are many factors which obscure the foreign language learning process in the natural setting and thereby limit the relevance of observations such as the above until they are verified by empirical research.

EXPERIMENTAL RESEARCH

Asher and Garcia (1969) proposed that the child's observed language facility in the natural setting may be due to learning the foreign language in a physically active, play situation, whereas, adults do so in a non-physically active, nonplay situation. As a test of this concept, Asher and Price (1967) investigated the relationship between age and Russian listening comprehension. When both college age adults and children (ages 8, 10, and 14) were taught Russian comprehension in situations in which the Russian utterances were synchronized with physical movement, the adults did much better than the children, and in turn the older children surpassed the younger children in Russian listening comprehension. This experiment, however, does not address itself specifically to problems of age and foreign language pronunciation.

In the area of age and foreign language pronunciation, the existing experimental research provides conflicting evidence supporting the superiority of both children and adults. There is informal evidence from a number of FLES program evaluations which supports the superiority of younger children. One such program was conducted by Dunkel and Pillet (1957). Following 2 years of French instruction, given 15 to 20 minutes each day, beginning in grades 3 and 4, the third and fourth graders were judged by the staff and by outside graduate students to have better pronunciation and intonation than the older students. According to the opinion of the experimenters "the pronunciation of the children, as a group, was superior to that generally achieved by adults in classes during an equal or even much longer span of time." Kirch (1956) came to a similar conclusion after teaching German to normal first, third, and sixth graders, that the younger the student the better the pronunciation. In comparison with his university students, he felt all three groups had excellent pronunciation. The findings of both these studies were based on uncontrolled classroom situations, comparisons of disimilar programs, and the personal judgment of the teachers of experimenters, and therefore need to be viewed with caution.

Opposite results were reported by Grinder, Otomo, and Toyota (1961), who found that pronunciation accuracy of Japanese increased with the child's age in second, third, and fourth grade. Bland and Keislar (1966) found in a French audiolingual pilot program with four kindergarten students and six fifth-graders "no evidence that younger children had better pronunciation." The sample here was too small to be broadly generalized, but it does provide suggestive data.

Lambert and MacNamara (1969), in evaluating a year-long experimental program to develop second language (French) skill by using it as the sole means of instruction with native-English speaking first graders, found that the children's ability to produce French phonemes was average with reference to native speakers as judged by a French linguist. But they were still poorer than the native French-speaking controls, who were taught the same material in a comparable French environment. While the observation on pronunciation is experimentally sound, it does not give any comparison with older children in a comparable program.

Asher and Garcia (1969) attempted to determine the factors related to the achievement of native pronunciation of English as a second language. Cuban immigrants, ranging in age from 7 to 19, who had learned English in a natural setting while living and going to school in the United States were judged by American high school students. The evaluation indicated that no Cuban child achieved a native pronunciation of English. But a near-native pronunciation was most apt to occur if the child was 6 or younger when coming to the United States and had lived in this country between 5 and 8 years.

Further information applicable to foreign language pronunciation learning is found in controlled experimental studies of dialect training (the teaching of standard white speech), which resembles second language learning. Torrey (1971) found, after an hour of individual training on a single grammatical point with both black and white Connecticut second graders, a change in written comprehension but no change in spontaneous oral production. Rystrom (1970) found no difference in the ability to pronounce standard white phonemes between Georgia Negro first graders with dialect training and those with none. Kennedy and Rentel (1971) also found no phonological differences after 6 weeks of dialect training of rural Appalachian first graders. Kennedy and Rentel concluded that grammar comprehension is much easier to modify than phonology in the "classroom learning situation where systematic attention is not directed toward linguistic features." This emphasizes the difficulty of teaching native foreign language pronunciation in the classroom situation during a limited period of time, and suggests that to attain the goal of good phonology, a longer sequence of instruction is required.

None of the previous experiments or FLES program evaluations have shown whether elementary children can achieve more nativelike pronunciation of the foreign language than older teenage or college students under properly controlled conditions in a setting which is applicable to the normal foreign language classroom. The purpose of this study was to test the commonly held assumption that younger children are superior to those who are older in learning to speak a second language with a good accent. In the test of the assumption, the critical age periods for brain lateralization were incorporated into the design.

METHOD

Each of three groups of 20 elementary (ages 9.5 to 10.5), 20 junior high (ages 14 to 15), and 20 college students (ages 18 to 26) were randomly selected. All Ss had no previous formal foreign language instruction and came from homes in which no foreign language was used. A fairly even division between girls and boys existed in the two younger groups but was not possible in the oldest group (elementary: 11 girls, 9 boys; junior high: 9 girls, 11 boys; college: 2 girls, 18 boys). A 2×3 (sex by age group) factorial design was used.

Instructional materials consisted of 10 prerecorded tapes, each 15 to 25 minutes in length containing German phoneme drills based on *The Sounds of English and German* (Moulton, 1962). The 33 phonemes selected for the drills were those which differ from English phonemes and which therefore present the most difficulty for English speakers learning German. A native German speaker read the German part of the script and the English-speaking experimenter the English. The experienced foreign language teachers who developed the materials and procedures judged them to be suitable for each of the groups in the study.

The format for the drills was: German utterance, pause for unison repetition by the experimental group, repetition of the German utterance for reinforcement, pause for unison repetition by the group. For key drills this format was enlarged upon by breaking the large group into four smaller groups and having each of the smaller groups repeat the same utterance as the entire group had just done. After the fourth small group had responded, the entire group repeated the utterance as at first. The drills used successive approximation, syllable variation, contrasting words, and short sentences. Previously taught phonemes were reviewed regularly. A standard classroom tape recorder was used for instruction.

PROCEDURE

Each group participated in 13 sessions over a period of 3 weeks. Ten sessions consisted of pretaped German phoneme instruction, each group being given the same 10 tapes. Three additional sessions for each student were devoted to administering the Standard Progressive Matrices (Raven, 1960) test and taping individual pre- and posttests.

The students were taught to pronounce the words by modeling their pronunciation after the German voice on the tape as accurately as they could. The experimenter led the Ss during the sessions by quietly uttering or mouthing the words on tape and by using hand signals and facial gestures to reinforce procedures and directions on the tape.

Testing and Evaluation. Students were given the Standard Progressive Matrices (Raven, 1960) test to measure intellectual ability. Derived z scores from the Ss' raw scores on the test were used as a covariate in the data analyses.

Equivalent taped pre- and posttests, each containing 25 target phonemes in short words and sentences to be repeated onto a blank tape, were given to each S individually using two tape recorders, head sets, and patch cord links.

In order to prevent bias in scoring phoneme production, before the tapes were evaluated, the experimenter randomly spliced together the Ss' responses for all three age groups. This was done for a pretest and posttest tape. These tapes were evaluated by a native German speaking graduate student and an American graduate student majoring in German. The judges did not know the nature of the experiment and were told only that they were to evaluate different people in pronouncing German phonemes. They made separate evaluations and scored each phonemic test item for each S on a scale of 0 to 4. Four was nativelike pronunciation; 3, good; 2, average; 1, poor but an attempt; and 0 was no attempt. Only the target phoneme in each test item was evaluated.

To check on intrajudge reliability, the judges unknowingly scored 18 Ss' responses twice on both the pretest and posttest. Interjudge reliability was checked by comparing the evaluations of judge 1 against judge 2.

RESULTS

Table 1 presents the data on intrajudge and interjudge reliability. Table 2 shows the German phoneme pronunciation scores for each of the groups. The mean score represents tests 1 to 25 where a maximum score of 100 was possible on either the pretest or posttest.

The covariates used in data analysis are derived Raven 2 scores to which 1 was added to get rid of negative numbers. Therefore, a score of 1 indicates a mean Raven's score for the group using the Raven norms.

The pretest results, using analysis of variance and analysis of covariance, showed no significant difference in pronunciation for sex, for age groups, or for their interaction.

Table 1   Intra- and Interjudge Reliability

Intrajudge reliability	Judge 1			Judge 2		
	0	−1	0+−1	0	−1	0+−1
Average pretest, %	58	32	90	49	42	91
Posttest, %	47	46	93	48	44	92
Total, %	52	39	91	48	43	91

Interjudge reliability	Pretest			Posttest		
	0	−1	0+−1	0	−1	0+−1
Average elementary, %	84	16	100	83	14	97
Junior high, %	80	18	98	82	17	99
College, %	71	24	95	88	8	97
Total, %	78	19	97	84	13	97

0 indicates perfect correspondence.
−1 indicates a difference of 1 out of a range from 0 to 4.
0+−1 is the sum of the two.

On the posttest, the analysis of variance indicated the following: no significant sex effect ($F = < 1$; 1/54 d.f.) and no significant interaction between age groups and sex ($F = < 1$; 2/54 d.f.). However, there was a significant age group effect on accuracy of pronunciation ($F = 5.29$; 2/54 d.f.; $p < .008$).

The analysis of covariance produced highly similar results: no significant sex effect ($F < 1$; 1/53 d.f.) and no significant interaction ($F < 1$; 2/53 d.f.). Again, there was a significant age group effect on pronunciation accuracy ($F = 5.17$; 2/53 d.f.; $p < .009$).

Table 2   German Pronunciation Scores for Boys and Girls for Elementary, Junior High, and College Groups

	Pretest*		Posttest*		Raven scores†	
	$\bar{X}$	SD	$\bar{X}$	SD	$\bar{X}$	SD
Elementary						
Boys—$N = 9$	52.39	8.57	60.44	11.05	1.30	0.87
Girls—$N = 11$	56.68	11.61	67.55	11.04	2.11	0.36
Junior high						
Boys—$N = 11$	57.50	12.71	73.91	9.27	1.69	0.87
Girls—$N = 9$	56.00	7.30	71.78	7.60	1.70	0.54
College						
Boys—$N = 18$	59.97	11.54	74.19	9.56	2.01	0.37
Girls—$N = 2$	53.25	0.35	78.25	4.60	1.60	0.28

*Means and standard deviations for pretest and posttest scores are based on the sum of the scores for variables (test items) 1 to 25.
†Raven score is based on z scores $+1$.

Newman-Keuls tests were computed to determine among which age groups there were significant differences in accuracy of pronunciation on the posttests. Contrary to common assumptions, both the junior high and college groups were superior to the elementary age group ($p < .01$). There was no significant difference between the two older groups in pronunciation accuracy.

DISCUSSION

The general assumption is that younger children learn to produce foreign words with a more nativelike accent than older people. Not only is this assumption not supported by the test results but the trend is in a reverse direction favoring older students.

There is good evidence, however, that the age-language acquisition relationships favoring younger students hold for first languages only. Therefore, we must distinguish between first and second language learning as Lenneberg did, in stating that the biological conditions which are important in primary language learning are not so important in second language learning.

Our evidence suggests that adults are superior to children in foreign language pronunciation. Therefore, the question needs to be answered as to why there is a difference between common observations that children are superior and the findings of this study. One possible answer lies in the fact that in the present study important factors in foreign language pronunciation learning, such as amount of time spent on training and quality of the language model, were controlled for all groups.

The common observation that children acquire better second language pronunciation than adults may have an environmental-sociological explanation. Studies have shown that people model their foreign language pronunciation after their peers. Immigrant adults tend to associate more with peers who speak their native language than children. For instance, husbands would continue to use the native language when speaking with their wives or with other members of their families. Often immigrant families have tended to settle in areas where there are other families of similar origin. These adult peers reinforce poor second language pronunciation habits. Similarly, the contacts which these adults would have with good pronunciation models are limited. Children, on the other hand, would be more apt to come in contact with teachers and native-speaking classmates, who have a good accent to model. Thus, it is more probable that children would have a closer approximation to nativelike pronunciation because they are surrounded by good models more of the time than are their adult counterparts.

The dialect training studies show the difficulty in modifying phonological behavior in a relatively short period of time. If further experiments confirm the results of this study, the old reason for starting foreign languages in the elementary school should be abandoned, namely, that children have a natural advantage in learning to produce the sound system of a new language. This statement does not imply that foreign language training should not start in the elementary school, since a long period of time is required for mastery of a foreign language.

REFERENCES

Asher, J. J., and Garcia, R. The optimal age to learn a foreign language. *Modern Language Journal.* 1969, 8, 334–341.

Asher, J. J., and Price, B. The learning strategy of the total physical response: some age differences. *Child Development.* 1967, 38, 1219–1227.

Bland, M., and Keislar, E. R. A self-controlled audio-lingual program for children. *French Review.* 1966, 40, 266–276.

Carroll, J. B. Research on teaching foreign languages. In N. L. Gage (ed.), *Handbook of Research on Teaching.* Chicago: Rand McNally, 1963, 1060–1100.

Dunkel, H. B., and Pillet, R. A. A second year of French in elementary school. *Elementary School Journal.* 1957, 53, 143–151.

Grinder, R. E., Otomo, A., and Toyota, W. Comparison between second, third, and fourth grade children in the audio-lingual learning of Japanese as a second language. Department of Psychology, University of Hawaii, Honolulu, 1961.

Kennedy, J. J., and Rentel, V. M. Effects of pattern drill on the phonology, syntax, and reading achievement of Appalachian dialect youth. Paper submitted to the AERA Convention, 1971.

Kirch, M. S. At what age elementary school language teaching? *Modern Language Journal.* 1956, 40, 399–400.

Lambert, W. E., and MacNamara, J. Some cognitive consequences of following a first grade curriculum in a second language. *Journal of Educational Psychology.* 1969, 40 (2), 86–90.

Lenneberg, E. H. *Biological Foundations of Language.* New York: John Wiley, 1967.

Moulton, W. G. *The Sounds of English and German.* Chicago: University of Chicago Press, 1962.

Penfield, W., and Roberts, L. *Speech and Brain Mechanisms.* Princeton: Princeton University Press, 1959.

Raven, J. C. *The Standard Progressive Matrices Tests,* Sets A, B, C, D, and E. London, England: H.K. Lewis and Co., Ltd., 1960.

Rystrom, R. Dialect training and reading: a further look. *Reading Research Quarterly.* 1970, 5, 581–599.

Torrey, J. W. Teaching standard English grammatical morphemes to speakers of another dialect. Paper submitted for the APA Convention, 1971.

7

THE LEARNING STRATEGY
OF THE TOTAL PHYSICAL RESPONSE:
SOME AGE DIFFERENCES[1]

James J. Asher and Ben S. Price
San Jose State University

There is a common belief that children are better able than adults to learn a foreign language. This belief may be an illusion if children living in a foreign country learn the new language through play activity while their parents try to learn independently of physical behavior.

Using Russian, this study compared the listening comprehension of 8-, 10-, and 14-year-old children, and college adults when each S was in physical action during retention tests. The results showed that (1) the adults were superior to the children of any age group at $p < .0005$; (2) the youngest children, the 8-year-olds, had the poorest retention; and (3) the 10- and 14-year-old children were intermediate between the adults and the 8-year-olds.

There is an almost irrefutable belief that children are better able than adults to learn a foreign language. This belief may be the result of a common observation that when children live in a foreign country they acquire speaking fluency of a new language while their parents are retarded in understanding and vocalizing.

It may be that children outperform adults in foreign language comprehension because the new language is learned through play activity in which the child makes action responses. For the child, the second language tends to be synchronized with physical responses ("Come on, Sam. Let's ride our bikes!"). The adult, by contrast, tries to manipulate the foreign language quite independently of physical behavior. Adults tend to be physically static when they receive or transmit the new language ("It's a beautiful day today, isn't it?").

If the child in a foreign country uses an action response but the adult does not, this may partially explain why children become more fluent than adults. An intriguing question then is, how do adults compare with children when both apply action responses in controlled situations?

In previous research (Asher, 1964, 1965, 1966; Kunihira and Asher, 1965) with a technique called the "learning strategy of the total physical response," it has been demonstrated that when adults learn listening comprehension of either Russian or Japanese there is a highly significant difference in retention ($p<.0005$) if the adults are in action rather than passively writing English translations. For short-term experiments, it was found that dramatic differences in understanding complex utterances in a foreign language are associated with action of Ss *during retention tests,* but not necessarily during training. For example, there were no significant differences when, in training, adult Ss listened to Russian commands and acted along with a model or merely sat and observed a model act. However, listening comprehension scores were vastly superior at $p<.0005$ when each S individually listened to Russian commands and physically acted during retention tests, rather than sitting down, listening to Russian commands and writing English translations.

In the study to be described next, the listening comprehension for various complexities of Russian utterances were compared for children whose average ages were 8 years-1 month, 9 years-9 months, and 13 years-8 months. Also included in the comparison were college adults between the ages of 18 and 21. The children and adults had identical training, and action responses were required of each S during retention tests.

METHOD

Subjects

The children ($N = 96$) were drawn from the second, fourth, and eighth grades of a public school[2] in San Jose, California. The adults ($N = 37$) were college students recruited from undergraduate general psychology courses at San Jose State College. None of the children or adults had prior training or exposure to Russian. The Ss from the 8-year-olds to adults were divided into two groups at each age level. The two groups, called an "act-act group" and an "observe-act group," will be described next. The average IQ for the children in each group as measured by the California Test of Mental Maturity was 115 for the 8-year-olds, 113 for the 10-year-olds, and 114 for the 14-year-old children.

Procedure

The act-act group: In Unit I of the training, two Ss sat on each side of E and were instructed that a voice on tape would utter a command in Russian. When the Ss heard the Russian utterance, they were to do exactly what the instructor did. In the 3 minutes of training, Ss and the adult model physically responded to the following Russian commands: stand, sit, walk, stop, turn, squat, and run. Each utterance was presented ten times in a sequence which was varied so the Ss did not simply memorize a fixed pattern of behavior.

Then a retention test was individually administered, followed by Unit II of training for 9 minutes in which the Russian was increased to this complexity: Walk to the door; walk to the window; walk to the chair; walk to the table; run to the door; rund to the window; run to the chair; run to the table.

The session ended with a retention test, and 24 hours later Ss returned for another retention test and Unit III of training. For 6 minutes, Ss and the model acted in response to Russian commands, such as: Pick up the pencil; put down the pencil; pick up the book; put down the book; pick up the paper; put down the paper; pick up the paper and pencil; put down the pencil, book, and paper.

In the retention test, S physically responded to Russian utterances which they had heard in training, but they also heard novel Russian commands. Novelty was defined as the recombination of elements into sentences never experienced in training, as for example: Run to the table, and pick up the paper; pick up the pencil, and walk to the window; run to the chair, and put down the book.

Forty-eight hours later, Ss returned for another retention test and then $7\frac{1}{2}$ minutes of Unit IV training, which consisted of the recombination and expansion of learned patterns, such as: Pick up the paper and pencil, and put them on the chair; run to the table, put down the paper, and sit on the chair; walk to the door, pick up the pencil, put it on the table, and sit on the chair.

At the end of this training there was another retention test, and 2 weeks later Ss returned for a final retention test. The total amount of time in small-group training was $25\frac{1}{2}$ minutes as compared with almost an equal amount of time in individual retention tests of 19 minutes.

Observe-act group: The conditions were exactly the same as those for the act-act group, except that these Ss were instructed to sit silently in their chairs, listen to the Russian commands, and imagine that they were acting along with the model. Only the model performed while the Ss observed his behavior.

However, during the retention tests each S listened individually to commands in Russian and showed understanding by *acting* (e.g., if the command in Russian was, "Walk to the chair and sit down," S indicated comprehension by physically walking to a chair and sitting down).

RESULTS

We expected to find that the children and adults in the act-act situation would perform similarly to the Ss in the observe-act situation. The reason is that prior research has shown that physical action *during retention tests* facilitated learning. Since Ss in the act-act group and observe-act group all were in physical action during the recall tests, we expected no difference between treatments. The observe-act condition may then be viewed as a replication, in a sense, of the act-act; and, therefore, if the performance pattern is similar, this is an indication of reliability.

Indeed, Figures 1 to 5 show that children and adults in the act-act treatment perform quite like the children and adults in the observe-act treatment.

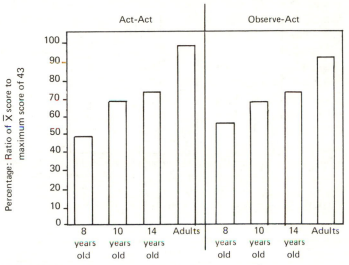

FIGURE 1   Retention of single Russian words

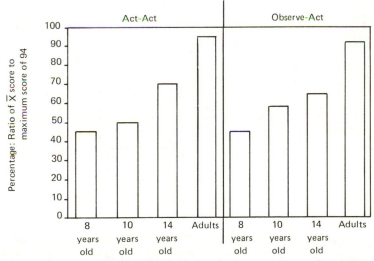

FIGURE 2   Retention of short Russian words

The difference in retention of the Russian was between age groups. Adults performed near the maximum possible score in comprehension of Russian while the 8-year-old children were the lowest of all groups tested. Intermediate

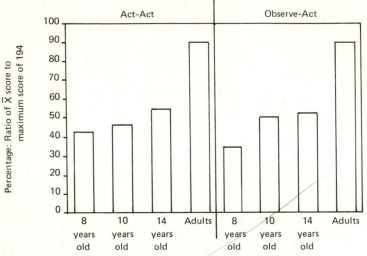

FIGURE 3   Retention of long Russian words

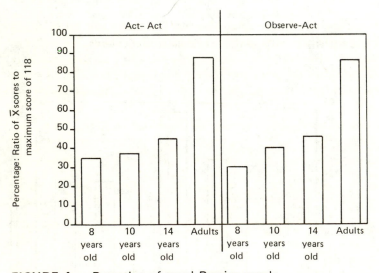

FIGURE 4   Retention of novel Russian words

between adults and the 8-year-olds were the 10- and 14-year-old children. This generalization held for single, short, long, or novel Russian utterances.

A statistical analysis was obtained by applying two-tail t tests. The results, presented in Tables 1 and 2, show that the adults, on the average and for any level of language complexity, dramatically excelled the children of any age group tested. Every t between the adults and any group of children was highly

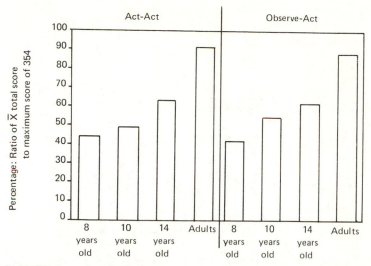

FIGURE 5 Retention as measured by the total score from all retention tests

significant beyond the .0005 level of confidence. Generally, the 14-year-old students were not significantly different in retention when compared with the 10-year-old students. However, the older children, the 14-year-olds, tended to be significantly better than the youngest children, the 8-year-olds. The 10-year-old children excelled the 8-year-old children only in the act-act condition.

Table 1 Means and Standard Deviations for Each Age Group

Retention tests	2d grade (N = 16)		4th grade (N = 16)		8th grade (N = 16)		Adults (N = 18)	
	$\overline{X}$	SD	$\overline{X}$	SD	$\overline{X}$	SD	$\overline{X}$	SD
Act-Act Group								
Single	22.56	7.58	28.93	9.09	32.68	7.54	44.72	2.10
Short	41.43	17.86	54.25	16.68	59.25	21.89	87.22	5.47
Long	66.68	33.86	95.31	27.76	98.43	37.13	173.33	21.00
Novel	34.87	17.61	49.93	16.17	51.68	23.47	103.11	15.81
Total	146.31	57.73	191.50	51.56	208.00	67.34	323.61	27.07
Observe-Act Group								
Single	21.81	7.16	29.81	10.05	32.50	9.66	43.05	3.29
Short	40.81	16.29	46.31	21.35	64.81	21.74	86.42	3.24
Long	79.12	28.86	85.25	35.67	106.31	46.05	172.26	19.36
Novel	41.50	14.46	41.93	19.31	56.68	29.44	101.68	14.56
Total	154.93	49.48	173.75	64.57	220.87	74.34	318.26	23.14

Table 2 t Tests between Age Groups

Retention tests	2d vs. 4th		2d vs. 8th		2d vs. Adult		4th vs. 8th		4th vs. Adult		8th vs. Adult	
	t	p	t	p	t	p	t	p	t	p	t	p
					Act-Act							
Single	2.08	.05	3.66	.001	11.54	.0005	1.23	NS	6.94	.0005	6.30	.0005
Short	2.03	NS	2.44	.05	10.04	.0005	.70	NS	7.68	.0005	5.08	.0005
Long	2.53	.02	2.45	.02	10.83	.0005	.26	NS	9.02	.0005	7.12	.0005
Novel	2.44	.05	2.22	.05	11.55	.0005	.24	NS	9.40	.0005	7.34	.0005
Total	2.26	.05	2.69	.02	11.32	.0005	.75	NS	9.21	.0005	6.50	.0005
					Observe-Act							
Single	2.51	.02	3.44	.01	11.23	.0005	.75	NS	5.25	.0005	4.33	.0005
Short	.79	NS	3.42	.01	11.58	.0005	2.35	.05	7.84	.0005	4.15	.0005
Long	.52	NS	1.94	NS	11.03	.0005	1.40	NS	8.89	.0005	5.51	.0005
Novel	.07	NS	1.79	NS	11.86	.0005	1.62	NS	10.12	.0005	5.70	.0005
Total	.90	NS	2.86	.01	12.45	.0005	1.85	NS	8.82	.0005	5.25	.0005

DISCUSSION

The study suggests that when adults learn a second language under the same conditions as children, the adults are superior. This generalization should be limited, at this time, to listening fluency. Future studies may show that children have an advantage in fidelity of sound production.

The comparison of college adults to children may be blurred somewhat because of a selectivity factor for the adults. The college students at San Jose State College are selected from among the top one-third of high school graduates in California. Therefore, we would expect above-average mental ability for the adults. However, it has been shown by Pimsleur (1966) and others that general mental ability is a lightweight variable in second language learning, accounting for less than 20 percent of the variance.

The second finding was that among children, the older child, the 10- or 14-year-old, tended to be significantly better than the 8-year-old in understanding of spoken Russian. Short attention span has been suggested as an explanation for the poor performance of the 8-year-old in understanding the Russian commands. When the Russian utterance was long and involved ("Pick up the pencil, walk to the chair, put down the pencil, and run to the window"), one might expect the 8-year-old child to have difficulty even if the utterance were spoken in English. Short attention span seems plausible for complex Russian commands, but this explanation does not account for the relatively low scores by the 8-year-old for single Russian words such as "run," "walk," and "sit."

NOTES

1. This study was supported by a research contract from the Personnel and Training Branch of the Office of Naval Research (NONR-4817[00], NR-154-257/12-8-64). Reproduction in whole or part is permitted for any purpose of the U.S. government. Appreciation is expressed to Drs. Rose Ginsberg and Gene R. Medinnus for their valuable suggestions in reviewing this paper. Author Asher's address: Psychology Department, Child Research Center, San Jose State College, San Jose, California.

2. Appreciation is expressed to Mr. William M. Phelps and the school personnel of the Blackford School in San Jose, California.

REFERENCES

Asher, J. J. Toward a neo-field theory of behavior. *Journal of Humanistic Psychology.* 1964, 4, 85–94.

Asher, J. J. The strategy of the total physical response: an application to learning Russian. *International Review of Applied Linguistics.* 1965, 3, 291–300.

Asher, J. J. The learning strategy of the total physical response: a review. *Modern Language Journal.* 1966, 50, 79–84.

Kunihira, S., and Asher, J. J. The strategy of the total physical response: an application to learning Japanese. *International Review of Applied Linguistics.* 1965, 3, 277–289.

Pimsleur, P. In Albert Valdman (ed.), *Trends in Language Teaching.* New York: McGraw-Hill, 1966, 175–214.

8

AGE DIFFERENCES IN THE PRONUNCIATION OF FOREIGN SOUNDS[1]

Catherine E. Snow
Harvard University

Marian Hoefnagel-Höhle
University of Amsterdam

The hypothesis that the years up to the age of puberty constitute a critical period for language acquisition was tested. Two kinds of data are presented which suggest that younger children are not better than older children and adults in learning a foreign language. In a laboratory study, it was found that the ability to imitate foreign words under controlled input conditions increased linearly with age. In a study of naturalistic second language acquisition, it was found that the older subjects had an initial advantage in pronunciation, and that age differences in pronunciation ability disappeared by 4 to 5 months after starting to learn the second language. By 10 to 11 months after starting to speak the second language, the younger children excelled in pronouncing some sounds, though there was still no overall age difference. These results are impossible to reconcile with the predictions of the critical period hypothesis for language acquisition.

It is commonly held that it is impossible to learn a language perfectly in adulthood. Whereas children are said to pick up a second language quickly and easily, adults are thought to have to work hard at learning a second language and to be less successful at achieving nativelike skill. The relative ease of second language acquisition in childhood has been used as evidence in support of the hypothesis that there is a critical period for language acquisition, a period of optimal brain plasticity which ends at about the time of puberty (Lenneberg, 1967). Language acquisition which occurs after the critical period is thought to be characterized by different learning processes and to be less complete, thus explaining why adults are less successful at second language acquisition than children.

The critical-period hypothesis is held to be especially relevant for the acquisition of second language pronunciation. Even those who reject its implications generally concede that some special facility for phonological acquisition may disappear at puberty (Braine, 1971). The belief that correct articulation of the sounds of a language is the aspect of second language skill most difficult to acquire after the critical period is supported by the many cases of adults who learn to speak a second language fluently but still maintain a strong foreign accent. It has been claimed that this foreign accent can be eliminated in adults only by special phonetic training (Christophersen, 1973), whereas children lose it automatically. A stringent test of the critical period hypothesis would thus involve comparing the speed of acquisition of correct second language pronunciation in different age groups.

Two kinds of data relevant to the question of age differences in learning to pronounce a foreign language are presented: data from a laboratory study in which exposure to the foreign language could be strictly controlled, and data from a study of naturalistic second language acquisition. In the laboratory study, the ability of English speakers who had no knowledge of Dutch to imitate Dutch words was tested. In the naturalistic study, the pronunciation ability of English speakers who were learning Dutch as a second language while living in Holland was assessed. Subjects in both the laboratory and the naturalistic studies represented a wide age range, so that performance of children well within the critical period could be compared with that of teenagers and adults. In addition, groups of children in the age range of 8 to 12 years were included so as to be able to decide whether any decline of acquisition ability occurred gradually during the several years around the age of puberty, or whether puberty marked a sharp drop-off in second language learning ability.

LABORATORY STUDY

One hundred thirty-six speakers of British English ranging in age from 5 to 31 years took part in the study. The subjects were divided into eleven age groups: ten 5-year-olds, ten 6-year-olds, eight 7-year-olds, fifteen 9-year-olds, thirteen 10-year-olds, fifteen 11-year-olds, twenty-four 12-year-olds, eleven 13-year-olds, fourteen 15-year-olds, eight 17-year-olds, and seven adults (21 to 31 years old). Eighty males and 56 females were tested.

The subjects were tested individually. Each subject listened through earphones to the stimulus tape, which contained five different Dutch words, and was asked to repeat each word immediately after hearing it. The subjects were told the purpose of the experiment, were warned that the words would be quite difficult, and were asked to listen carefully and repeat them as well as possible. Each word was presented ten times in a row (block 1), and then the entire sequence of five words was repeated (block 2), so that each subject imitated each word 20 times. The stimulus tape was made by a native Dutch speaker, who pronounced the test words slowly and carefully. Each word was pronounced 20 different times by the native speaker, so that normal variation in their pronunciation was available to the subjects.

The subjects' imitations were tape-recorded for later scoring by one of three judges. Scoring was done on the basis of a five-point scale, in which the points had the following definitions:

1   uninterpretable as target sound
2   correct target sound, very strong accent
3   correct target sound, noticeable accent
4   correct target sound, slight accent
5   indistinguishable from a native speaker's pronunciation

The three judges, who met regularly to discuss problems and check their criteria by scoring some subjects together, achieved about 85 percent agreement, with disagreements never involving more than one point. The judges were unaware of the subjects' ages.

The five test words were scored separately on a total of nine different sounds:

reiger /rɛix̄əɾ/ was scored for /ɛi/ and for final /ɾ/.
ui /ʌy/ was scored as a whole.
gelukkig /xəlœkəx/ was scored for initial /x/ and for /k/.
rollen /rɔlən/ was scored for initial /r/ and for /l/.
scheur /sxøɾ/ was scored for /x/ and for /ø/.

These sounds were selected as being likely to cause difficulty to English speakers. A subject's total score was the mean of the nine individual scores.

Results

Since it was impossible to test any girls in the 9-year-old and 10-year-old groups, sex differences were tested with separate Mann-Whitney U tests on the total scores for the 5- to 7-year-olds, for the 11- to 13-year-olds, for the 15-to 17-year-olds, and for the adults. None of these differences was significant, nor was the overall sex difference significant; so the results for males and females were pooled for further comparisons.

A Kruskal-Wallis one-way analysis of variance was performed on the total scores (mean of all the individual sound ratings per subject) to test for effect of age. The difference among the groups was significant ($H = 31.96$, $X^2 = 19.68$, $p < 0.05$), with the scores showing a general increase with age (see Figure 1).

Although the pattern of increase with age was not extremely regular, it is clear that the two youngest groups tested showed the lowest scores and the two oldest groups the highest, a result impossible to reconcile with the critical-period hypothesis. A test for linearity of increase, performed with the subjects pooled into five groups (5- to 7-year-olds, 8- to 10-year-olds, 11- to 13-year-olds, 15-

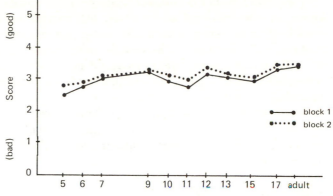

FIGURE 1   Means of the 11 age groups in the laboratory study

year-olds, and 17-31-year-olds) indicates that the increase with age was linear ($T = 2.37$, $p<0.05$).

The overall better performance of the older subjects can be explained in either of two ways: their initial pronunciations were closer to the target, or they showed faster improvement. It can be seen from Figure 1 that the differences among the age groups were the same for block 1 and block 2, and that all groups showed approximately equal improvement between the two blocks. Thus, the older groups showed better performance than the younger groups from the very beginning. If one looks at the cases of differences between block 1 and block 2 on scores for individual sounds over all the subjects, the percentage of improvement showed no relation to age.

The differences in difficulty among the nine sounds tested were so clear as not to require statistical testing. The most difficult sounds were initial /r/, final /ɾ/, /x/ in a cluster, and /ʌy/ (see Table 1). Interestingly, it is precisely these four difficult sounds which showed no significant improvement between block 1 and block 2, as tested with the Wilcoxon signed-ranks test. The five easier sounds did show significant improvement between the first and the second 10 trials.

Table 1   Mean Ratings for the Nine Sounds Tested in the Laboratory Study

	Sounds showing no improvement				Sounds showing significant improvement				
	Final /ɾ/	/x/ in a cluster	/ʌy/	Initial /r/	/k/	Initial /x/	/ø/	/l/	/ɛi/
Block 1	1.78	2.15	2.71	2.91	3.31	3.35	3.78	4.23	4.36
Block 1	1.82	2.18	2.85	2.84	3.71	3.68	4.14	4.37	4.55

The most common mistakes made with the sounds were the following. Initial /r/ was rendered as /h/ or /ł/, presumably under influence of the medial /l/ in the word /rɔlən/ , or was pronounced with a preceding velar fricative or /h/. Final /ɾ/ was deleted or was pronounded as a partly devoiced /d/. The /x/ in /sxøɾ/ was pronounced as /l/ , /j/ , /k/ , or deleted, or was influenced by the final /ɾ/ so that the word was pronounced /sɾøɾ/. The diphthong /ʌy/ was pronounced as /au/ , /o/ , or /ø/. The easier sounds showed fewer mistakes, with initial /x/ being pronounced most often as /h/ , /k/ as /x/ , /ø/ as /y/ , /u/, or /ɑ/, and /ɛi/ without diphthongization as /e/ or /ai/ . The /l/ was pronounced like the English /l/ rather than the clearer Dutch /l/ .

NATURALISTIC STUDY

Forty-seven English speakers ranging in age from 3 to 60 who were learning Dutch while living in Holland, by attending Dutch schools or working in Dutch-language environments, were followed during their first year of second language acquisition. The subjects, who spoke several different varieties of Australian, British, and North American English, fell into five age groups: ten 3- to 5-year-olds, eight 6- to 7-year-olds, ten 8- to 10-year-olds, eight 12- to15-year-olds, and eleven adults. There was some attrition in group size in the course of the year (33 subjects remained at the last test session). A pronunciation test was given to the subjects as part of a more extensive test battery, which was administered three times: within 6 weeks of the subjects' starting to speak Dutch and then again at 4- to 5-month intervals (see Snow and Hoefnagel-Höhle, 1977, for reports on the other tests). The pronunciation test consisted of 80 words. Each word in the test was pronounced twice, once immediately following a native speaker's pronunciation of the word (Imitation condition), and once without an immediate auditory model, in response to a picture (Spontaneous Production condition). All the words used were simple, familiar, and likely to be acquired as early vocabulary items even by the youngest subjects. The situation was in this respect entirely different from the laboratory study, in which the words used were meaningless to the subjects and contained difficult combinations of sounds. The 80 words were selected so as to require production of all Dutch vowels and diphthongs in various consonantal contexts, as well as initial /r/ and various initial and final clusters (see Table 2). The subjects' pronunciation of the difficult sound in each word was scored on a five-point scale by a native speaker. The five points were defined as in the laboratory study. The judge scored all the subjects twice, and achieved 89 percent agreement between the two scorings, with only 14 percent of the deviations greater than one point. A subject's total score was the mean of all the individual sound ratings.

Results

The medians per age group at each of the three test sessions are presented in Figure 2 for the Imitation and Spontaneous Production conditions separately.

Table 2 Correlations between Age and the Ability to Pronounce the Sounds Tested in the Naturalistic Study

Sound	Time 1		Time 3		Time 2	
	Imit.	Sp. Prod.	Imit.	Sp. Prod.	Imit.	Sp. Prod.
Vowels						
/a/	−0.18	0.29	−0.27	0.30	−0.08	−0.45*
/ɑ/	−0.24	0.26	−0.23	−0.24	−0.68*	−0.68*
/e/	0.09	0.48*	−0.14	0.20	−0.21	−0.04
/ɛ/	−0.11	0.33*	−0.15	0.17	−0.63*	−0.05
/eu/	0.02	0.53*	−0.27	0.08	−0.28	−0.27
/i/	−0.26	0.09	−0.24	−0.10	−0.38*	−0.33
/ɪ/	−0.03	0.32*	−0.26	−0.12	−0.11	−0.20
/o/	−0.17	0.20	−0.46*	−0.09	−0.41*	−0.29
/ɔ/	−0.21	0.35*	−0.13	−0.38*	−0.65*	−0.79*
/y/	0.05	0.45*	−0.15	0.04	−0.48*	−0.15
/œ/	0.04	0.24	−0.18	−0.21	−0.69*	−0.50*
/ɛi/	−0.12	0.29	−0.45*	−0.28	−0.72*	−0.65*
/ʌy/	−0.07	−0.03	−0.35*	−0.36*	−0.59*	−0.46*
/u/	−0.16	−0.14	−0.23	−0.26	−0.74*	−0.72*
/ø/	−0.12	0.31	−0.11	−0.21	−0.74*	−0.39
/au/	0.16	0.61*	−0.12	0.22	−0.34	0.18
Initial r	0.30	0.19	0.27	0.31	0.06	−0.09
clusters						
cons *R*	0.51*	0.42*	0.30	0.29	0.20	0.42*
R cons	−0.01	0.38*	0.20	0.06	0.19	−0.32
cons cons *R*	0.25	0.58*	0.37*	0.44*	0.28	−0.14
cons *l*	−0.02	0.35*	0.01	0.08	−0.22	0.24
l cons	0.21	0.51*	−0.06	0.37*	0.11	0.01
/sx/	0.34*	0.45*	0.15	0.25	0.09	−0.20
/sxr/	0.18	0.54*	0.11	0.50*	0.17	0.06
Total	0.18	0.41*	0.03	0.10	−0.18	−0.15

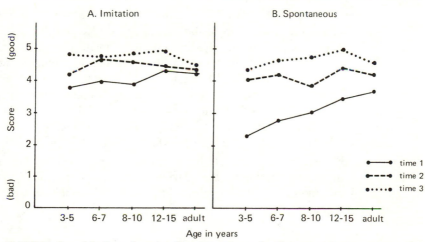

FIGURE 2 Medians for the five age groups in the naturalistic study on Imitation and Spontaneous Production

Kruskal-Wallis one-way analyses of variance performed on the total scores per subject for each time and condition revealed a significant age effect only for the Spontaneous Production condition at time 1; this significant effect reflects a linear increase with age (see Figure 2). In the other cases, the different age groups were all equally good at pronunciation. Thus, the naturalistic study supports the conclusion of the experimental study, that the critical-period hypothesis for pronunciation must be rejected.

As would be expected on the basis of the significant age differences for total scores, there were a number of positive correlations between age and individual sounds in the Spontaneous Production condition at time 1 (see Table 2). Fifteen of the 24 sounds tested showed significant positive correlations with age, including all the clusters and eight of the 16 vowels. In the Imitation condition at time 1, only two clusters showed significant correlations with age. At time 2, there were a small number of significant positive correlations with age, all for clusters, and a small number of significant negative correlations, all for vowels, in both Imitation and Spontaneous Production. By Time 3 all but one of the positive correlations had disappeared, and the number of negative correlations had increased to 11 in the Imitation condition and seven in the Spontaneous Production condition, all for vowel sounds. Thus, despite the general initial advantage of the older subjects, both for total scores and for many individual sounds, the younger subjects had become better at pronouncing some of the sounds after a period of 10- to 11 months' learning.

None of the subjects in the naturalistic study achieved perfect pronunciation of Dutch within 10 to 11 months of starting to speak the language. In fact, 11 of the subjects could be tested a fourth time, about 18 months after their first contact with the language, and even then all but one teenager still had English accents. This inability to achieve nativelike pronunciation was as true of the younger subjects as of the adults, though the adults showed somewhat lower scores than the children at time 4.

Differences in the difficulty of the various sounds tested were much less clear in the naturalistic study than in the laboratory study, and the order of difficulty varied considerably in the different conditions and test sessions. In the naturalistic study, unlike the laboratory study, the more difficult sounds showed greater improvement. The sounds with mean scores below the overall mean at time 1 showed improvement above the level of mean improvement between time 1 and time 2 ($\chi^3 = 13.59$, $p<0.001$ for Imitation; $\chi^2 = 20.65$, $p<0.001$ for Spontaneous Production); the same tendency was present for improvement between time 2 and time 3 ($\chi^2 = 1.52$, $p<0.05$ for Imitation; $\chi^3 = 4.20$, $p<0.05$ for Spontaneous Production). Thus, although the easier sounds showed greater improvement in the very short term (the 20 trials of the laboratory study), in the long term (4 to 5 months) it was the more difficult sounds which showed the greatest improvement.

DISCUSSION

The primary conclusion to be drawn from these two studies is that youth confers no immediate advantage in learning to pronounce foreign sounds. In the short term, older subjects were considerably better than younger subjects at pronunciation, and only after a period of about a year did the younger subjects begin to excel. The finding that the ages 3 to 15 constitute an optimal period for ultimately achieving near-perfect foreign pronunciation is very difficult to relate to any known facts concerning brain maturation or brain plasticity. According to Lenneberg (1967), all the parameters of brain growth have achieved adult values by about age 12, and interhemispheric transfer of function is possible only up to the age of puberty. Krashen (1973; Krashen and Harshman, 1972) has argued that cerebral dominance is fully established by age 5, and that complete recovery from aphasia is not possible beyond this age. The fact that the age range 3 to 15 was found to be optimal for achieving near-perfect foreign pronunciation cannot be explained in terms of any neurologically determined critical period.

The question arises why the belief is so generally held that young children can learn second language pronunciation easily. A clue to the answer might be available from the pattern of correlations with age found in the naturalistic study. Younger subjects, who were initially worse, seemed to continue their period of active acquisition longer, so that they eventually surpassed the older subjects, who leveled off at a lower point. The longer period of acquisition for the younger subjects may have resulted from their greater motivation to achieve nativelike skill, or from their greater need to pronounce correctly in order to achieve communication. The older subjects were much better at other aspects of second language skill—vocabulary, syntax, morphology—than the younger ones (see Snow and Hoefnagel-Höhle, 1977), and were thus perhaps less reliant on correct pronunciation to communicate effectively. Alternatively, such factors as wishing to fit in and to be indistinguishable from native speakers, the so-called integrative motive (Lambert et al., 1968), may have motivated the younger subjects to continue to a higher level of achievement. Adults are presumably less subject to peer pressure to conform than young children, and are thus less motivated to fail in achieving perfect mastery of a second language, because of fear of losing their cultural-personal identities (Christophersen, 1972). These various motivational factors might provide an explanation for the long-term superiority of younger second language learners. The short-term superiority of older speakers, both in a laboratory and in a naturalistic learning situation, is strong evidence that a critical period for language acquisition cannot provide the explanation.

NOTE

1. This research was supported by the Netherlands Foundation for the Advancement of Pure Research (Z.W.O.). We are grateful to the following schools for allowing us to test: The Friends' School, in Saffron Walden, Kings' College School, St. Johns' College School, St. Faith's School, The Perse School for Girls, and the Perse School for Boys in Cambridge. We are also grateful to Leo van Herpt, Jan Blom, and Heleen Deighton of the Institute for Phonetics, University of Amsterdam, for their help.

REFERENCES

Braine, M. D. S. The acquisition of language in infant and child. In C. E. Reed (ed.), *The Learning of Language*. New York, 1971, 7–95.

Christophersen, P. *Second-Language Learning: Myth and Reality*. Harmondsworth, Middlesex, 1973.

Krashen, S. Lateralization, language learning, and the critical period: some new evidence. *Language Learning*. 1973, 23, 63–74.

Krashen, S., and Harshman, R. Lateralization and the critical period. *UCLA Working Papers in Phonetics*. 1972, 23, 13–21.

Lambert, W. E., Gardner, R. C., Olton, R., and Tunstall, K. A study of the roles of attitudes and motivation in second-language learning. In J. A. Fishman (ed.), *Readings in the Sociology of Language*. The Hague, 1968.

Lenneberg, E. *Biological Foundations of Language*. New York, 1967.

Snow, C. E., and Hoefnagel-Höhle, M. The critical period for language acquisition: evidence from second-language learning. Unpublished paper, Institute for General Linguistics, University of Amsterdam, 1977.

9

THE CRITICAL PERIOD FOR LANGUAGE ACQUISITION: EVIDENCE FROM SECOND LANGUAGE LEARNING[1]

Catherine E. Snow
Harvard University

Marian Hoefnagel-Höhle
University of Amsterdam

The critical period hypothesis holds that first language acquisition must occur before cerebral lateralization is complete, at about the age of puberty. One prediction of this hypothesis is that second language acquisition will be relatively fast, successful, and qualitatively similar to first language only if it occurs before the age of puberty. This prediction was tested by studying longitudinally the naturalistic acquisition of Dutch by English speakers of different ages. The subjects were tested three times during their first year in Holland, with an extensive test battery designed to assess several aspects of their first year in Holland. It was found that the subjects in the age groups 12 to 15 and adult made the fastest progress during the first few months of learning Dutch and that at the end of the first year the 8- to 10-, and 12- to 15-year-olds had achieved the best control of Dutch. The 3- to 5-year-olds scored lowest on all the tests employed. These data do not support the critical period hypothesis for language acquisition.

The critical period hypothesis (CPH) as proposed by Lenneberg (1967) holds that primary language acquisition must occur during a critical period which ends at about the age of puberty with the establishment of cerebral lateralization of function. A strong implication of this hypothesis is that the processes involved in any language acquisition which takes place after the age of puberty will be qualitatively different from those involved in first language acquisition. A commonly drawn, though not absolutely necessary, corollary of the CPH is that any language learning which occurs after the age of puberty will be slower and less successful than normal first language learning (Krashen, 1975; Lenneberg, 1967, 1969; Scovel, 1969).

There are few reported cases of successful first language acquisition after the age of puberty. Buddenhagen (1971) reported successful establishment of verbal language in a previously mute mental retardate at age 18. Recent reports on Genie, a girl isolated from social interaction until age 13, suggest that although her language acquisition is very slow, it is in many respects following the same course as that of young first language learners (Fromkin, Krashen, Curtiss, Rigler, and Rigler, 1974), and her language skills are continuing to improve several years after puberty (Curtiss, Fromkin, Rigler, Rigler, and Krashen, 1975). The very small number of cases of postpubertal subjects without any language and the abnormal circumstances which are associated with those cases make it extremely difficult to draw any general conclusion, but the findings of Buddenhagen and those concerning Genie suggest that some degree of postpubertal first language acquisition is possible.

Another area for collecting data relevant to the CPH is second language acquisition. Two research designs can be expected to produce data relevant to the evaluation of the CPH: (1) comparing second language acquisition with first language acquisition; (2) comparing second language acquisition across a wide age range, such that the youngest subjects tested are still well within the critical period age range. Several recent studies using the first approach have shown that the course of second language acquisition is similar to that of first language acquisition, in terms of the order in which rules and structures are acquired (Dulay and Burt, 1974; Fathman, 1975), of the learning strategies employed (Cook, 1973; Ervin-Tripp, 1974), and of the errors made (Taylor, 1975). In addition, a few studies using the second approach have shown that older children are faster than younger children in acquiring second language morphology and syntax (Ervin-Tripp, 1974; Fathman, 1975, Ekstrand[2]) and listening comprehension (Asher & Price, 1969). Studies of age differences in the acquisition of second language pronunciation have produced conflicting results. Ekstrand[2] and Snow and Hoefnagel-Höhle (1977) found better pronunciation in older subjects, whereas Fathman (1975) found a negative effect of age. However, Seliger et al. did report on a few postpubertal second language learners who had achieved accentless pronunciation in their second language, as well as some cases of prepubertal learners who maintained foreign accents.

Although these studies do not generally support the prediction of the CPH, it would be premature to reject the CPH on their basis, for several reasons:

1. The studies cited have looked at only a restricted age range: 6 to 15 in Fathman's study, 8 to 16 in Ekstrand's, 8 to adult in Asher and Price's, and 4 to

9 in Ervin-Tripp's. No single study has included subjects in the entire age range of interest, from 3 to several years postpuberty, and none except Asher and Price has compared adult with child second language learners. The fact that children younger than 5 have rarely been studied is especially unfortunate in view of (1) the evidence that some degree of cerebral asymmetry is present at birth (reviewed in Buffery, 1978; Kinsbourne, 1975) and (2) the suggestion, based on dichotic listening techniques, that lateralization of receptive language function is fully established by age 5 (Krashen and Harshman, 1972).

2. Age differences have been assessed cross sectionally rather than longitudinally. Since age differences found at any given point after the commencement of second language acquisition might reflect recent spurts of acquisition for a particular group, rather than constant differences in rate of acquisition, only a longitudinal study can provide the basis for conclusions concerning overall age differences in rate of acquisition and in ultimate achievement.

3. A relatively restricted range of second language abilities has been tested in most studies. A complete test of the CPH requires that different language abilities be tested separately, since the acquisition of different language abilities may depend to differing degrees on brain plasticity. Testing different language abilities in the same set of subjects may enable one to explain the contradictory findings, cited above, for morphology, syntax, and listening comprehension on the one hand and pronunciation on the other.

In this paper the acquisition of several components of second language ability by subjects of different ages is described, and the implications of these observations for the CPH are considered. The acquisition of Dutch as a second language by 51 English speaking subjects in five age groups was followed for a period of 1 year. All the subjects were learning Dutch by "picking it up" at school or at work, with little or no formal instruction. The context of acquisition was thus very similar to the normal context of first language acquisition— communicative interactions with native speakers. The subjects' accomplishments at three points during their first year in the Netherlands were compared both quantitatively and qualitatively with the accomplishments of two additional groups: advanced speakers of Dutch as a second language, and native speakers.

The subjects were tested on as many components of skill in speaking a language as possible, and some open-ended tests which would reveal qualitative differences in language ability were also included. An extensive test of pronunciation was included, since nativelike pronunciation is often specifically mentioned as requiring prepubertal exposure to the language (e.g., Lenneberg, 1967, p. 176). In addition, tests for knowledge of morphology, syntax, and vocabulary; for the ability to give syntactic judgments; and for the comprehension and production of fluent speech were included.

PROCEDURE

Subjects

Two groups of English-speaking subjects were included in the study: monolingual English speakers who were just starting to learn Dutch (Beginners), and English speakers who had been living in Holland and speaking Dutch for at least 18 months (Advanced). The Beginners were tested three times at 4- to 5 month intervals. The first session was held within 6 months of their arrival in Holland and within 6 weeks of their starting at school or work in a Dutch language environment. The Advanced subjects were tested only once. The Beginners were distributed in the following way over the age groups: ten 3- to 5-year-olds, eight 6- to 7-year-olds, thirteen 8- to 10-year-olds, nine 12- to 15-year-olds, and eleven adults. The Advanced group had the following distribution: six 6- to 7-year-olds, six 8- to 10-year-olds, eight 12- to 15-year-olds, and ten adults. There was some attrition in the course of the year, and a few subjects did not complete all the tests, leading to slight variability in the numbers actually reported on for the various tests.

Although it would have been ideal to match the age groups on factors like social class, IQ, exposure to Dutch, and motivation to learn Dutch, the small size of the potential subject pool made such matching impossible. The majority of the subjects in all age groups were members of middle-class families which had moved to Holland for job-related reasons. The English version of the Peabody Picture Vocabulary Test (PPVT) was administered to all the subjects as a check on verbal intelligence. A comparison of the IQs of the four younger age groups (no IQ norms for adults are available for the PPVT) using a Kruskal-Wallis one-way analysis of variance revealed no significant differences either for the Beginners or for the Advanced subjects. Thus, age differences in speed of second language learning cannot be attributed to differences in verbal intelligence. The age groups differed unavoidably in degree of exposure to Dutch: the 3- to 5-year-olds were all attending Dutch schools and were therefore exposed to a Dutch language environment a minimum of 30 hours a week. Regular play with Dutch peers may have increased this by several hours for some children. The five adult men were all working in Dutch language environments; however, since most Dutch adults speak English well and readily, none of the men used Dutch regularly as a working language. The six adult women were all housewives, who heard Dutch only in the context of shopping, social encounters, and contacts with their children's schools, government offices, etc. Most of the adults also took courses in Dutch, but these did not exceed 26 hours of total class time in any case. Thus, if exposure to Dutch is considered a crucial variable in determining speed of acquisition, one would expect the adults to learn more slowly than any of the younger groups.

Since entire families of English speakers were tested whenever possible, 10 families accounted for 28 of the 51 subjects in the Beginners group. A separate statistical analysis of the results within families will be presented, since several extraneous variables which cannot be controlled for the group as a whole are matched for subjects of different ages within any family.

In addition to the English speakers, two groups of monolingual Dutch speakers were tested in order to establish age norms for the tests employed. There were eight 6- to 7-year-old and eight 12- to 15-year-old native speakers. They were drawn from a school in the middle-class area where most of the English speakers lived and were selected by their classroom teachers as being of average intelligence and verbal ability.

Testing

The subjects were tested individually at school or at home, in a relaxed session lasting about 1½ hours. The test session was tape-recorded for later scoring or checking, except for the Auditory Discrimination, Sentence Judgment, and Peabody Picture Vocabulary tests, which were scored during the test session.

Pronunciation. In order to assess productive control of Dutch phonology, the subjects were asked to pronounce 80 words under each of two conditions: immediately after hearing a native speaker say the word (Imitation) and a few minutes later, with no immediate auditory model (Spontaneous). The words were elicited by means of pictures, and were selected to present initial /r/, initial and final consonant clusters, and all Dutch vowels and diphthongs in various consonantal contexts. The results were scored per word on a six-point scale (0 = English word; 1 = uninterpretable as target word; 2 = target word pronounced with a strong accent; 3 = target word pronounced with noticeable accent; 4 = target word pronounced with a slight accent; 5 = indistinguishable from a native speaker) by a native speaker of Dutch. Rescoring of the subjects several months later produced 89 percent agreement with the original scores.

Auditory discrimination. Receptive control of Dutch phonemic distinctions not made in English was tested by asking subjects to point to the correct picture after auditory presentation of a word. Both words of a minimal pair were presented, all words selected to be familiar and picturable, (e.g., *man* /mɑn/ "man" and *maan* /man/ "moon"; *kuiken* /kʌykən/ "chicken" and *keuken* /kȫkən/ "kitchen"). The order of presentation was random. Fifty-six items were presented testing 14 oppositions. As the results were affected by knowledge of the vocabulary items, the subjects' scores were computed by taking the ratio of auditory confusions to correct responses plus auditory confusions, thus ignoring mistakes which did not result from auditory confusion (e.g., moon for kitchen).

Morphology. Berko's (1958) "wug-test" technique was used to test for control of the Dutch morphological rules for formation of plural, diminutive rules for formation of plural, diminutive, agentive, past tense, and past participle, as well as for final devoicing when producing the singular form of a word presented in the plural. These rules are quite complicated and do not resemble their English counterparts except in that affixes are used in both cases. The subjects were given real words and asked to produce the appropriate form (e.g., If you have one *boy*, then you have two . . .?). Pictures were used for the younger children. After the task was explained with real words, nonsense words were introduced as the test items. The subject's score was the number of correct responses (maximum = 82).

Sentence repetition. Thirty-seven Dutch sentences of increasing length and grammatical complexity were read to the subjects, who were asked to repeat them. The sentences ranged from 2 to 10 words in length. Vocabulary was kept simple in all the sentences, so that the results could be interpreted as primarily relevant to control of syntax. A subject's score was the number of words correctly produced (maximum = 238).

Sentence translation. Sixty sentences of increasing length and grammatical complexity were given in English, and the subjects were asked to translate them. Any necessary help was given with lexical items, as the test was designed to reflect control of syntax. Subjects' responses were scored by giving a point for each grammatical structure correctly produced (e.g., verb, auxiliary verb, adverb, prepositional phrase, indirect object) and for correct word order in each clause (maximum = 325).

Sentence judgment. Fourteen pairs of sentences were read to the subjects. In each case, one was a correct and one an incorrect rendering of the same content. The subjects were asked to say which sentence was better. Subjects' scores are given as the number of incorrect answers.

Peabody Picture Vocabulary Test. A version of the PPVT standardized for Dutch up to age 8 was administered (Manschot and Bonnema, 1974). This is a passive vocabulary test, in which the subject points to the correct one of four pictures after the experimenter reads a word. The 3- to 7-year-olds were tested to 50 words and the older subjects to 100 words, since the later vocabulary items were not appropriate for the youngest subjects. Accordingly, age differences on the PPVT were assessed by comparing the 3- to 5-year-olds with the 6- to 7-year-olds and by comparing the 8 to 10, 12 to 15, and adult groups in a separate analysis.

Story comprehension. A simple tape-recorded story in Dutch was played to the subjects, who were then asked to retell the story in English (or Dutch if they preferred). Comprehension was scored on the basis of mentioning 30 key points in the story.

Storytelling. Subjects were asked to tell a story on the basis of a set of pictures provided, both in Dutch and in English. A fluency score was calculated by taking the ratio of number of words to seconds talking.

RESULTS

The results for all the groups on the various tests are presented in Figures 1 through 9. Age differences between three or more groups were tested with the Kruskal-Wallis one-way analysis of variance. Differences between two groups were tested with the Mann-Whitney U.

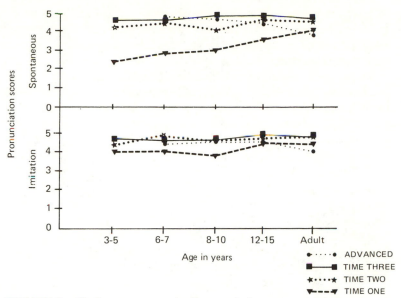

FIGURE 1   Median scores on the Pronunciation test

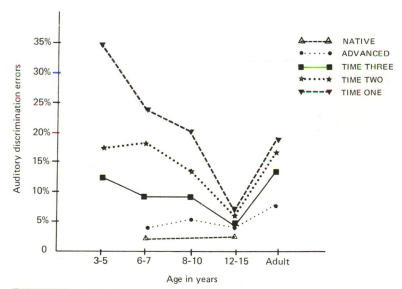

FIGURE 2   Median percentages of relevant responses which were errors on the Auditory Discrimination test

Significant improvement occurred between time 1 and time 2 for the Beginners on all the tests (tested with the Wilcoxon signed-ranks test) and between time 2 and time 3 for all tests except Auditory Discrimination (see Figures 1 to 9). Significant differences between the levels of achievement of the

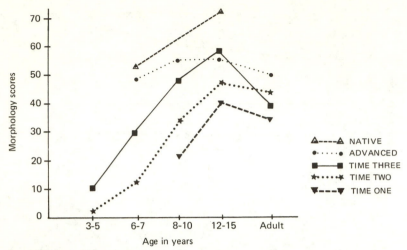

FIGURE 3   Median scores on the Morphology test

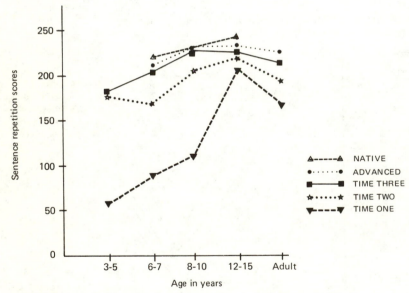

FIGURE 4   Median number of words correctly repeated in the
Sentence Repetition test

Beginners at time 3 and the Advanced groups existed, for the adult group only, on Auditory Discrimination, Sentence Repetition, and Sentence Translation. These differences suggest that further significant improvement could be expected for the adults in these areas after 1 year's exposure to the second language but that the acquisition of Dutch by the 6- to 15-year-olds was essentially completed within 1 year.

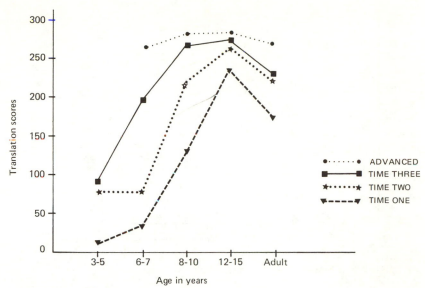

FIGURE 5   Median number of grammatical structures correctly translated in the Translation test

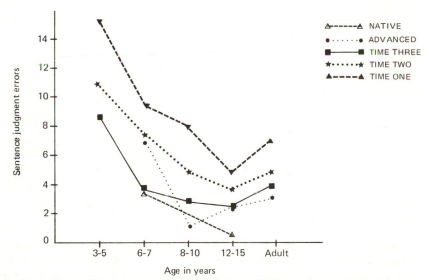

FIGURE 6   Median numbers of errors on the Sentence Judgment test

Significant age differences were observed for all the tests at time 1, except for the Imitation condition of the Pronunciation test. In all cases, the age differences favored the older subjects over the younger ones (see Figures 1 to 9). For all tests except Pronunciation, the order of the groups, from proficient to

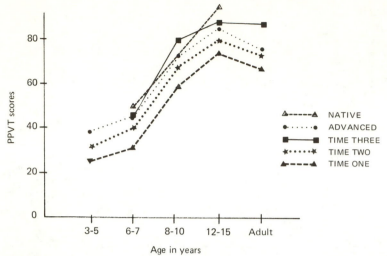

FIGURE 7   Median scores on the PPVT

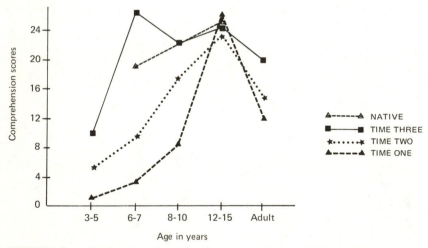

FIGURE 8   Median number of points correctly retold in the Story
Comprehension test

poor, was: 12 to 15, adult, 8 to 10, 6 to 7, 3 to 5. Spontaneous Pronunciation showed a linear increase with age. At times 2 and 3 the size of the age differences had decreased, though they remained significant for all tests except Pronunciation at time 2 and 3 and Auditory Discrimination at time 2. The 8- to 10-year-olds had surpassed the adults in Auditory Discrimination, Sentence Repetition, Sentence Judgment, Story Comprehension, and Spontaneous Speech Fluency by time 2 and in Morphology and Sentence Translation by time 3. The 6- to 7-year-olds had also surpassed the adults on Spontaneous Speech Fluency and Auditory Discrimination by time 3. On the PPVT, the 6- to 7-year olds were significantly better than the 3- to 5-year-olds and the 12- to 15-year-olds and

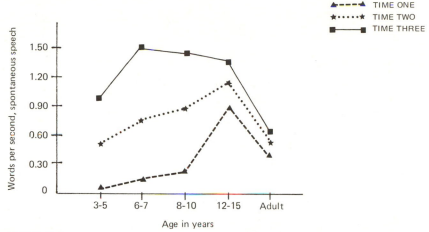

FIGURE 9 Median number of words produced per second in the Dutch Storytelling task

adults were significantly better than the 8- to 10-year-olds at all test sessions. All the tests, then, except Pronunciation, on which the age differences disappeared very quickly, showed a similar pattern: most rapid learning by the 12- to 15-year-olds and adults during the first few months of acquisition, those preceding the first test session, and by the 6- to 10-year-olds during the last three-quarters of the first year. The adults, despite their initial rapid acquisition, fell increasingly behind because their subsequent improvement was very slow. The teenagers had achieved almost native performance extremely quickly, within a few months of starting to speak Dutch. They maintained superiority on most tests because their initial advantage was so great; they were, however, surpassed on Story Comprehension and Spontaneous Speech Fluency by the 6- to 10-year-olds.

The crucial findings of relevance for evaluating the CPH were that the 3- to 5-year-olds scored consistently worse than the older groups on all the tests and that the 12- to 15-year-olds showed the most rapid acquisition of all the skills tested. These findings are basis for rejecting the hypothesis that the period 2 to 12 years constitutes an optimal time for language acquisition.

The notion that younger children are better than older children or adults in second language learning must also be rejected on the basis of scores within those families that contributed subjects in more than one age group. In Table 1 it is indicated whether the scores on the various tests match the prediction of the CPH for each family at time 1. A plus indicates the ordering predicted by the CPH, that the younger family members scored better than the older ones. Any individual case of a younger family member scoring better than an older one is indicated as a plus, even though the other family members might not be ordered in a way consistent with the CPH. Comparisons were made on the basis of the individual ages, even when two children fell into one age group. Only for cases of two adults was no specific effect of age predicted, nor was a plus scored if a

Table 1 Intrafamily Age Comparisons on 10 Tests of Second Language Ability

Family	Pronunciation			Sentence				PPVT	Story		Combined probability
	Imitation	Spontaneous	Auditory discrimination	Morphology	Repetition	Translation	Judgment		Comprehension	Telling	
1*	−	−	0	0	−	0	0	−	−	0	.031
2*	−	−	+	0	−	−	+	−	−	−	.019
3*	−	−	−	0	−	+	+	−	−	0	.14
4*	−	−	+	−	−	−	−	−	−	−	.011
5†	−	−	−	−	−	−	−	−	−	−	.0009
6†	−	−	+	−	−	−	−	−	−	−	.011
7‡	+	+	−	−	−	−	−	+	−	+	.0024
8‡	+	+	−	−	−	−	−	−	−	−	.00002
9‡	−	−	−	−	−	−	−	−	−	−	.00001
10§	+	−	+	−	+	−	+	−	+	0	.0032
Combined probability	.012	.0020	.20	.00002	.00013	.00015	.0037	.00013	.00013	.0055	

− + = ordering within the family confirmed the CPH, for at least one pair of subjects; − = ordering within the family completely disconfirmed the CPH; 0 = too few data were available to make any comparison possible.

*Two family members; the chance of disconfirming the CPH for one test was .50.

†Three family members; the chance of disconfirming the CPH for one test was .50.

‡Three family members; the chance of disconfirming the CPH for one test was .17.

§Five family members; the chance of disconfirming the CPH for one test was .04.

Table 2 Means of the Second Language Learners Expressed as Percentages of the Native Speakers' Means

Test	Age	Beginners			Advanced
		Time 1	Time 2	Time 3	
Auditory*	6–7	7.6	10.2	19.8	46.1
Discrimination	12–15	30.0	33.0	47.4	48.6
Morphology	6–7	.0	22.0	57.0	93.0
	12–15	55.8	66.7	80.4	76.8
Sentence*	6–7	39.8	78.2	95.4	97.0
Repetition	12–15	88.7	95.7	97.9	100.0
Sentence	6–7	38.9	50.0	100.0	53.8
Judgment	12–15	2.2	3.0	4.0	4.0
PPVT	6–7	59.5	81.6	92.2	91.2
	12–15	75.9	83.9	91.5	91.7
Story comprehension	6–7	14.6	48.6	140.5	81.0
	12–15	102.9	94.7	98.0	N.A.†

*Since these scores represented errors, the entries were calculated by dividing the native speakers' mean by the second language learners' means, then multiplying by 100.
†Too few advanced 12- to 15-year-olds performed this task to make any meaningful comparison.

parent scored worse than a teenage child, since this was to be predicted from the total results. A 0 indicates that not all the family members could be scored on that test or that all scored so badly that no comparison would be meaningful. It can be seen that in the vast majority of the cases the CPH was not supported. The probability of finding the number of pluses observed or fewer, given the number of orderings possible within families, is indicated per family and per test. For only one family and one test was $p > .05$. These findings were based on a very conservative estimate of chance within the three families where both parents were included, since either parent could produce a minus by scoring better than a child, but both parents were counted as one in calculating the number of possible orderings. The intrafamily analysis strongly supports the conclusion from the analysis of all the data that the CPH must be rejected as far as second language acquisition is concerned.

It might be argued that the results found here are an artifact of the test construction, that is, that the nature of the tests favors the older subjects. It is, of course, very difficult to design tests which are equally usable with 5-year-olds and with adults. We approached this problem by choosing test content appropriate to the youngest subjects, with the result that most of the test material was quite childish for the older subjects. An indication that the conclusion drawn about the CPH is correct comes from a comparison of the second language learners with the two groups of Dutch native speakers tested. The scores for the second language learners are presented as percentages of the native speakers' scores in Table 2, on the assumption that the native speakers' scores can be taken as the ceiling for the equivalent age groups of second language learners. It can be seen from Table 2 that the 12- to 15-year-old second language speakers approached the native speakers' scores faster (i.e., were closer at time 1, after their first 6 weeks of exposure to Dutch) than the 6- to 7-year-olds in all cases except Sentence Judgment and that they continued throughout the first year to score higher in all cases except Story Comprehension and PPVT. The rather peculiar results for Story Comprehension are very likely an artifact of the attractiveness of the story content; it was an enjoyable story for 6- to 7-year olds but too easy and boring to be retold in detail by the older children (as indicated by the decline in performance on this task for the older children). The Sentence Judgment test is the only one, then, on which the younger second language learners performed better in comparison with native speakers of the same age than older second language learners. The finding that older second language learners are disadvantaged at acquiring the skills associated with giving linguistic judgments, despite their superior linguistic performance, suggests that knowledge of a language comprises several components which are not necessarily related.

A further possibility for explaining the results found is that they represent positive transfer from the first language, English, to the second language, Dutch. Older second language learners would, of course, benefit more from positive transfer than younger ones because their knowledge of English is better. A number of analyses suggest that positive transfer cannot explain the superiority of the older subjects. First, while it is true that English and Dutch are historically closely related, it is not the case that they are highly similar in syntax, morphology, or phonology. The closest relationship, and thus the expectation of greatest positive transfer, exists for vocabulary. Analysis of two word lists commonly used to determine language relatedness (the 100-word list of Rea, 1958, and the 200-word list of Gudchinsky, 1956) reveals that approximately 65 percent of commonly used words are cognates in the two languages. One would expect, then, a relatively great positive effect of age in the area of vocabulary, whereas it is on the tests of syntax and morphology that the younger children score relatively worse.

Furthermore, if the older subjects were relying to a large degree on transfer, one would expect them to perform much better in those aspects of Dutch morphology and syntax that happen to be isomorphic to English grammar than in those that do not. For example, main clauses in Dutch show the subject—verb—direct object order typical of English sentences, but subordinate clauses show the order subject—direct object—verb. It was not the case that older subjects were more likely to produce main clauses correctly and subordinate clauses incorrectly than younger subjects; subjects of all ages tended, in fact, to overgeneralize the verb-final order to all clauses. Very similar patterns of morphological and syntactic acquisition were observed at all ages, as indicated by the following analysis of the order of difficulty of various items and structures for the different age groups on the tests of Morphology, Sentence Repetition, Sentence Translation, and Sentence Judgment.

Morphology. Knowledge of six different sets of morphological rules was tested: those for the formation of the plural, the diminutive, the agentive, the simple past tense, the past participle, and the singular from the plural. The order of acquisition of these six sets of rules was determined for each age group of Beginners by rank ordering their mean scores for the subtest at time 3. Spearman rank-order correlation coefficients calculated for all pairs of age groups showed moderate to high positive correlations (ranging from .13 to .79). The highest correlations were found between adjacent age groups, but the correlations between the adults and all the other groups were in the range .53 to .60, suggesting no sharp differences in the order of acquisition between the youngest groups and the adults.

Sentence repetition. The order of difficulty of the items in the Sentence Repetition task was calculated per age group for the Beginners at time 3 and for the 6- to 7-year-old native speakers. Each sentence was scored 2 points if it was completely correct, 1 point if only minor errors such as deletion of an adjectival suffix or third person ending were made, and 0 if more serious errors were made. The total score per sentence per group was then used to assign ranks. Spearman rank-order correlation coefficients were calculated among the groups. The correlations for the various groups of beginners were all positive and highly significant (ranging from .47 to .80), as were those for the English speakers with the Dutch native speakers (.71 to .83), suggesting that the same items caused difficulties for the native speakers and second language learners of all ages.

Sentence translation. The Sentence Translation test was scored on 24 different grammatical variables, for example, modal auxiliary, tense auxiliary, indefinite article, word order in subordinate clause. For each age group, the percentage of correct answers was determined for each of the 24 variables at time 3, and all 24 were then ranked. Spearman rank-order correlation coefficients were calculated for all pairs of age groups. These correlations were all very high and significant (ranging from .72 to .91), indicating that the same aspects of the grammar of Dutch caused difficulties for all the age groups.

Sentence judgment. The Sentence Judgment test items tested choice of correct subordinating conjunctions and of correct prepositions following various verbs and adjectives. Order of difficulty of the items was determined for each age group of Beginners at time 3 and for the 6- to 7-year-old native speakers (the 12- to 15-year-old native speakers made too few mistakes to analyze). Spearman rank-order correlation coefficients for the difficulty of the items across the age groups showed a general pattern of moderately high and significant positive correlations among all the groups (ranging from .30 to .78), though the adult Beginners showed the lowest correlations with the other age groups and with the native speakers. The fact that the correlations across age on the Sentence Judgment test were generally lower than on the Sentence Repetition or Sentence Translation tests may reflect differences across age groups in ability to acquire metalinguistic skills, related to the relatively poorer performance of the older subjects on this task. However, a firm conclusion about differences between the tasks would require that strictly comparable items be used. This was not the case in the current study.

DISCUSSION

The results of this study fail to support the CPH. The fastest second language acquisition occurred in subjects aged 12 to 15 years, and the slowest occurred in subjects aged 3 to 5 years. Furthermore, subjects of all ages were very similar in the aspects of Dutch they found difficult and those they found easy. At least as far as second language acquisition is concerned, then the conclusion must be drawn that a critical period extending from age 2 to age 12 does not exist.

The primary evidence cited by Lenneberg (1967) in support of the CPH is the fact that complete recovery from acquired aphasia is possible for children but not for adults. Although it is true that children show better recovery from traumatic aphasia than adults, aphasia resulting from vascular disorders rarely shows recovery even in young children (Guttman, 1942; Van Dongen and Loonen, 1976), and aphasia associated with a convulsive disorder often fails to recover as well (Gascon, Victor, Lambroso, and Goodglass, 1973; Van Dongen and Loonen, 1976; Worster-Drought, 1971). Goorhuis-Brouwer found lasting deficits in four of the nine prepubertal traumatic aphasics she studied (1976). Alajouanine and Lhermitte (1965) found similar incidence of recovery in children aged 6 to 10 and in children aged 11 to 15, whereas the CPH would predict better recovery in the younger group. Thus, the evidence concerning recovery from aphasia, like the observations concerning postpubertal first language acquisition (Fromkin et al., 1974) and the evidence presented here about second language acquisition, all fail to support the hypothesis of a critical period for language acquisition extending to the age of puberty.

The results of the present study are compatible with two hypotheses concerning the relationship between brain development and language acquisition: (1) that cerebral dominance becomes established during the period from birth to 5 years (Krashen, 1973; Krashen and Harshman, 1972), and (2) that cerebral dominance is present from birth and the observation of developing lateralization is an artifact of children's growing tendency to use linguistic strategies in various psychological tests (Kinsbourne, 1975). The first hypothesis implies a critical period for first language acquisition ending at 5 years but predicts no necessary differences in speed or ease of second language acquisition among subjects older than 5. The period up to age 5 may be characterized by slower second language acquisition (1) because the effort needed to learn a first language is disadvantageous to second language acquisition, (2) because having already learned a language makes the task of learning a second one easier (Ervin-Tripp, 1974), or (3) because the already established specialization of the dominant hemisphere for language facilitates acquisition. An observation suggesting that the 3- to 5-year-olds were different from all the other groups concerns the effect of second language acquisition on the first language ability. Data concerning fluency in English were collected during the English part of the Storytelling tests and from the subjects' decision whether to retell the story in Dutch or English during the Story Comprehension test. With one exception (a 7-year-old girl), it was only among the 3- to 5-year-old Beginners (and among the 6- to 7-year-old Advanced subjects, who had learned Dutch while 3 to 5 years old) that growing control of Dutch was associated with breakdown of control of English. Although a few subjects in all age groups showed some degree of negative interference, mostly at the lexical level, from Dutch into English, large decreases in English fluency and a preference for speaking Dutch were observed only among the youngest subjects. Under the second hypothesis, that cerebral dominance is present from birth, the critical period would have to be redefined as the period during which transfer of function to the nondominant hemisphere is possible. Observable effects of the critical period would be expected for recovery from injury to the dominant hemisphere, but no negative effect of age on second language acquisition would be predicted since second language acquisition does not involve interhemispheric transfer of function.

In addition to age differences, considerable individual differences were found in the patterning of second language skills achieved by the subjects. All the 6- to 15-year-old subjects had achieved sufficient control of Dutch by the third test session to be described as good bilinguals. Nonetheless, these subjects differed considerably in the degree to which they had achieved complete control of pronunciation, morphology, grammar, vocabulary, fluency, and metalinguistic skills. Eleven subjects could be tested a fourth time, 1½ years after their first exposure to Dutch, and the scores achieved at this fourth session clearly indicate that some subjects had stopped improving in certain tests before achieving a perfect score. One 7-year-old subject, for example, showed no improvement after session 2 in the Imitation condition of the Pronunciation test, and his spontaneous pronunciation remained poorer than that of all the other nonadults at session 4, despite the fact that his scores on the other tests were relatively high. Conversely, a 12-year-old achieved almost perfect pronunciation very early but continued to score poorly, even getting worse between sessions 2 and session 4, on Sentence Judgment and Morphology, the two tests which require the most metalinguistic ability. It is entirely possible that such individual differences in the patterning of language abilities are also present in one's first language. For example Moscowitz (1973) found large individual differences among a group of English-speaking children in knowledge of English phonological rules and also among another group in the ability to learn a non-English phonological rule. We found considerable differences within the group of native speakers on the Morphology and Auditory Discrimination tests. Large differences among adult native speakers have also been reported for ability to give syntactic judgments (Snow, 1975; Snow and Meijer, 1977) and semantic interpretations (Gleitman and Gleitman, 1970). If administering a large battery of language tests to native speakers revealed individual differences in patterns of ability similar to those we have found for second language speakers, this would constitute a basis for questioning the usefulness of the concept "native speaker competence," a concept which is, of course, theoretically very closely related to the CPH. Evidence concerning such variation is important to an assessment of the CPH because if native speakers who have had all the advantages of full critical-period exposure to the first language do not achieve equal skill, then the fact that post-critical-period learners show a range of skill is not surprising.

NOTES

1. This research was supported by the Netherlands Foundation for the Advancement of Pure Research (Z.W.O.). Preliminary reports of portions of the data have been presented to the Dutch Association for Applied Linguistics and the International Association for Applied Linguistics.

2. Ekstrand, L. H. Age and length of residence as variables related to the adjustment of migrant children, with special reference to second language learning. Paper presented at the International Association of Applied Linguistics, Stuttgart, August 1975.

REFERENCES

Alajouanine, T., and Lhermitte, F. Acquired aphasia in children. *Brain*. 1965, 88 (4), 653–662.

Asher, J., and Price, B. The learning strategy of the total physical response: some age differences. *Child Development*, 1969, 38, 1219–1227.

Berko, J. The child's learning of English morphology. *Word*, 1958, 14, 150–177.

Buddenhagen, R. G. *Establishing Vocal Verbalisations in Mute Mongoloid Children*. Champaign, Ill.: Research Press, 1971.

Buffery, A. The neuropsychology of language development: an essay on cerebral dominance. In N. Waterson and C. E. Snow (eds.), *The Development of Communication: Social and Pragmatic Factors in Language Acquisition*. London: Wiley, 1978.

Cook, V. J. The comparison of language development in native children and foreign adults. *International Review of Applied Linguistics,* 1973, 11, 13–28.

Curtiss, S., Fromkin, V., Rigler, D., Rigler, M. and Krashen, S. An update on the linguistic development of Genie. In D. Dato (ed.), *Developmental Psycholinguistics: Theory and Applications*. Washington, D.C.: Georgetown University Press, 1975.

Dulay, H., and Burt, M. Natural sequences in child second language acquisition. *Working Papers in Bilingualism,* 1974 (4), 71–98.

Ervin-Tripp, S. Is second language learning like the first? *TESOL Quarterly,* 1974, 8, 111–127.

Fathman, A. The relationship between age and second language productive ability. *Language Learning,* 1975, 25, 245–253.

Fromkin, V., Krashen, S., Curtiss, S., Rigler, D., and Rigler, M. The development of language in Genie: a case of language acquisition beyond the "critical period." *Brain and Language,* 1974, 1, 81–107.

Gascon, G., Victor, D., Lombroso, C., and Goodglass, H. Language disorder, convulsive disorder, and electroencephalographic abnormalities. *Archives of Neurology,* 1973, 28, 156–162.

Gleitman, L., and Gleitman, H. *Phrase and Paraphrase*. New York: Norton, 1970.

Goorhuis-Brouwer, S. Enkele opmerkingen over afasie bij kinderen. *Logopedie en Foniatrie,* 1976, 48, 69–77.

Gudchinsky, S. C. The ABC's of lexicostatistics (glottochronology). *Word,* 1956, 12, 175–210.

Guttman, E. Aphasia in children. *Brain,* 1942, 65, 205–219.

Kinsbourne, M. The ontogeny of cerebral dominance. In D. Aaronson and R. W. Rieber (eds.), *Developmental Psycholinguistics and Communication Disorders*. New York: New York Academy of Sciences, 1975.

Krashen, S. Lateralization, language learning, and the critical period: some new evidence. *Language Learning,* 1973, 23, 63–74.

Krashen, S. The critical period for language acquisition and its possible bases. In D. Aaronson and R. W. Rieber (eds.), *Developmental Psycholinguistics and Communication Disorders*. New York: New York Academy of Sciences, 1975.

Krashen, S., and Harshman, R. Lateralization and the critical period. *UCLA Working Papers in Phonetics*, 1972, 23, 13–21.

Lenneberg, E. *Biological Foundations of Language.* New York: Wiley, 1967.

Lenneberg, E. On explaining language. *Science*, 1969, 165, 635–643.

Manschot, W., and Bonnema, J. *Experimentele Nederlandse normering van de Peabody Picture Vocabulary Test.* Amsterdam: Swets & Zeitlinger, 1974.

Moscowitz, A. B. On the status of vowel shift in English. In T. E. Moore (ed.), *Cognitive Development and the Acquisition of Language.* New York: Academic Press, 1973.

Rea, J. A. Concerning the validity of lexicostatistics. *International Journal of Applied Linguistics*, 1958, 24, 145–150.

Scovel, T. Foreign accents, language acquisition and cerebral dominance. *Language Learning*, 1969, 19, 245–253.

Seliger, H., Krashen, S., and Ladefoged, P. Maturational constraints in the acquisition of a native-like accent in second language learning. *Language Sciences*, 1975 (36), 20-22.

Snow, C. E. Linguistics as behavioral scientists: toward a methodology for testing linguistic intuitions. In A. Kraak (ed.), *Linguistics in the Netherlands, 1972-73.* Amsterdam: Van Gorcum, 1975.

Snow, C. E., and Hoefnagel-Höhle, M. Age differences in the pronunciation of foreign sounds. *Language and Speech*, 1977, 4, 357–365.

Snow, C. E., and Meijer, G. On the secondary nature of syntactic intuitions. In S. Greenbaum (ed.), *Acceptability in Language.* The Hague: Mouton, 1977.

Taylor, B. P. The use of overgeneralization and transfer learning strategies by elementary and intermediate students of ESL. *Language Learning*, 1975, 25, 73–107.

Van Dongen, H. R., and Loonen, M. C. B. Neurological factors related to prognosis of acquired aphasia in childhood. In Y. Lebrun and R. Hoops (eds), *Recovery in Aphasics.* Amsterdam: Swets & Zeitlinger, 1976.

Worster-Drought, C. An unusual form of acquired aphasia in children. *Developmental Medical Child Neurology,* 1971, 13, 563–571.

III

SHORT-TERM STUDIES OF OLDER AND YOUNGER CHILDREN

In Section II, studies comparing rate of acquisition for children and adults were presented. We concluded, in the introduction to Section II, that the results of these studies were consistent with the hypothesis that adults are *faster* in the early stages of second language acquisition. As mentioned in Section II, however, the same studies also show that older children are generally faster than younger children.

In this section, we add several empirical studies that deal exclusively with the younger child–older child comparison. They vary with respect to both target language and acquisition situation: Fathman examines English as a second language in the United States, while Ekstrand's studies deal with English as a foreign language in Sweden and Swedish as a second language for immigrant children in Sweden. As in previous sections, length of exposure varied, but all studies included here can be considered short-term, the longest being Fathman's subjects, who had been in the United States from 1 to 3 years.

10

THE RELATIONSHIP BETWEEN AGE AND SECOND LANGUAGE PRODUCTIVE ABILITY

Ann Fathman
Stanford University

This study examines the relationship between certain aspects of the second language acquisition process and age. An oral production test was developed to assess the ability of nonnative English-speaking children to produce standard English morphology and syntax. The test was administered to approximately 200 children (ages 6 to 15) who were learning English as a second language in American public schools. The results of this testing were used to examine the relationship between age and (1) the rate of acquisition of certain English grammatical structures and (2) the order of acquisition of these grammatical structures.

The results indicated that there was some relationship between age and rate of learning. Among children exposed to English the same amounts of time, the older children scored higher on the morphology and syntax subtests, whereas the younger children received higher ratings in phonology. There were, however, no major differences observed in the order in which children of different ages learned to produce the structures included in the test. These results suggest that there is a difference in the rate of learning of English morphology, syntax, and phonology based upon differences in age, but that the order of acquisition in second language learning does not change with age.

Some recent studies in second language learning have attempted to identify similarities between first and second language acquisition (Ravem, 1970; Milon, 1972; Ervin-Tripp, 1974; and Dulay and Burt, 1973, 1974). The work done in first language acquisition research has provided new perspectives for research dealing with second language acquisition processes.

It has been noted frequently that there are changes in the acquisition of language with age. The ability to learn a first language seems to be limited after a certain age. Lenneberg (1967) has suggested that there is a critical period for language learning, since there appear to be definite changes in the ability to acquire language after the early teens.

It has also been noted that young children possess a special ability to learn a second language (Donoghue, 1968; Andersson, 1969). They seem capable of learning a foreign language without elaborate training and without retaining much interference from their native language. A number of years ago the Modern Language Association (1956) adopted a statement saying that the apparent optimum age for second language learning was between 4 and 10 years of age. Based upon this widely held belief, the early teaching of second languages has been encouraged in schools.

Recently, with new insights gained from language theory and research in first language acquisition, some second language studies have become less applied and have focused instead on learner abilities and strategies. Some of this research has suggested that the young child is not necessarily a better second language learner than the adult. Work done by Asher and Price (1967) has suggested that adults are superior to children in listening comprehension. Politzer and Weiss (1969) have suggested that initial pronunciation and retention of vocabulary increase with age. Ervin-Tripp (1974) has reported that in her study older children learned number, gender, and syntax more rapidly than younger children.

Thus research has indicated that there seem to be changes in the second language acquisition process with age, but that younger children are not necessarily better second language learners than adults in all respects.

The present study has been conducted to further examine the relationship between age and the second language acquisition process. Two aspects of the process have been considered: changes in the rate and changes in the order of acquisition of English structures with age.

METHOD

Subjects

The subjects for this study were 200 children (ages 6 to 15) from diverse language backgrounds who were learning English as a second language in public schools in the Washington, D.C. area. These children were all from families of lower socioeconomic status who spoke their native language at home. They had had no previous English training before entering the American schools, and all had been in the United States less than 3 years.

From the pool of approximately 200 students tested, a sample of 140 subjects was drawn: 70 who had been in the United States for 1 year, 40 who had been in the United States for 2 years and 30 who had been in the United States for 3 years. These children were all learning a second language by immersion each day in the verbal environment of the school. The types of language programs in the schools varied to some extent. In some of the schools from which the population was drawn, there were special English classes offered where students received 1 hour per day of instruction in English as a second language (ESL). Other schools, however, offered no formal ESL programs. This variable of type of language program as well as differences in age and length of stay in the United States have been considered in the analysis of results.

Instrument

An oral production test was developed to assess the ability of these nonnative English-speaking children to produce standard English morphology and syntax. The test consisted of 20 subtests, with three items per subtest. Each subtest was based upon a particular morpheme category or syntactic pattern. Table 1 lists the subtests in the order in which they appeared in the test. These structures were selected since they were considered basic to learning English as a second language, and many have been studied extensively in first language acquisition research (Berko, 1958; Brown, 1973).

Table 1 Subtests of the Oral Production Test

1	AFFIRMATIVE-DECLARATIVE	11	NEGATIVE
2	ARTICLES	12	PAST PARTICIPLE-IRREG.
3	PRESENT PARTICIPLE	13	SUBJECT PRONOUNS
4	POSSESSIVE	14	OBJECT PRONOUNS
5	PRESENT TENSE-3RD REG.	15	POSSESSIVE PRONOUNS
6	COMPARATIVE	16	PLURAL-IRREG.
7	SUPERLATIVE	17	IMPERATIVE
8	PRESENT TENSE-3RD IRREG.	18	YES/NO QUESTION
9	PREPOSITION	19	WH-QUESTION
10	PAST PARTICIPLE-REG.	20	PLURAL-REG.

The items within each subtest have been selected to represent certain phonetic, syntactic, and semantic variants within each category. For example, the three phonologically conditioned allomorphs /-s, -z, -əz/ were included within the present tense, possessive, and plural subtests. The sixty questions on this test were similar in structure to those found in Berko's morphology test (1958). Most items consisted of two pictures on a page. The test was administeed by first pointing at one of two pictures on a page and giving a stimulus utterance concerning this picture. The examiner would then point to the second picture on the same page and have the child complete the description of this picture by supplying omitted words, phrases, or sentences. For example, to elicit prepositions a picture of a cat by a box and a cat in a box were shown.

Pointing at the first picture, the examiner said, "Here the cat is by the box" and pointing at the second picture, the examiner said, "Here the cat is _____" (requiring the child to complete the description with "in the box").

The score given a response was based only upon the structure which that particular item was testing. The responses were rated as correct or incorrect and given either a one or a zero score. Variant types of responses were considered and rated individually.

In addition to answering the 60 items on the oral production test, each child was asked to give a general description of a composite picture. These descriptions were tape-recorded and later evaluated by two linguists. Ratings were given on a five-point scale for correctness of grammar, pronunciation, and general fluency.

RESULTS

The results of this testing were used to examine the relation between (1) age and the rate of acquisition of the English structures tested, and (2) age and the order of acquisition of the English structures tested. The analysis was done by dividing the children into two age groups: a younger group from 6 to 10 years and an older group from 11 to 15 years.

The results indicated that there is some relationship between age and rate of learning. An analysis of variance (ANOVA) was performed to determine the effect that age, years in the United States, and language program have on oral language performance, as measured by the total scores received on the Oral Production test. The groups included children in the two age groups (6 to 10 and 11 to 15 years); children in the United States for the three different periods of time (1 year, 2 years, and 3 years); children from the two different types of language programs (ESL programs and no ESL program).

The means from this ANOVA are shown in Table 2. These are the mean scores received by each group on the total test. The older children, 11 to 15 years, performed significantly better ($p<.001$) on the morphology and syntax subtests of this oral production test than did the younger children, 6 to 10 years. These results suggested that the group of older children learned the structures tested at a faster rate than the group of younger children.

Table 2 Mean Total Test Score for Each Group

Age	Program	Years in U.S.		
		1	2	3
6–10	ESL	25.2	38.6	49.6
	No ESL	26.0	39.6	51.8
11–15	ESL	34.2	43.0	50.1
	No ESL	28.0	51.4	56.9

There were, however, no significant differences found for the rate of learning of children from schools where there were ESL programs compared with the rate of learning of children from those schools where there were no structured ESL programs. The ANOVA also indicated that there were no significant interactions between age, language program, and number of years in the United States.

The ratings given each child on pronunciation during the composite picture description were also analyzed. A *t* test indicated that the group of younger children, aged 6 to 10 years, were given significantly higher ratings ($p<.05$) than the older children, aged 11 to 15 years, all of whom had been exposed to English the same period of time. This suggested that the group of younger children may be learning English phonology at a faster rate than the group of older children.

Thus from this analysis it appeared that age seemed to have some effect on the rate at which a child learned to produce certain structures. The older children performed better in the production of correct morphological and syntactic structures; whereas the younger children were superior in the use of correct English pronunciation.

In terms of the order of acquisition, the testing results indicated that there were no major differences in the order in which the children of different ages learned the structures being tested. The order of acquisition was based upon the mean scores received by each group on the twenty subtests of the Oral Production test, listed in Table 1.

As indicated in Figure 1, the order of acquisition for the 6- to 10-year-old and the 11- to 15-year-old children was strikingly similar. The order of acquisition of structures tested also remained constant for all children independent of whether they were in structured ESL classes or not, as indicated in Figure 2. The Imperative (subtest 17) and Affirmative-Declarative (subtest 1) ranked consistently highest with ordinate values from 2.5 to 3.0; whereas the

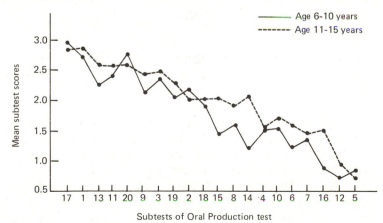

FIGURE 1   Mean scores on each subtest for children of different ages: 6 to 10 and 11 to 15 years

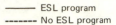
ESL program
No ESL program

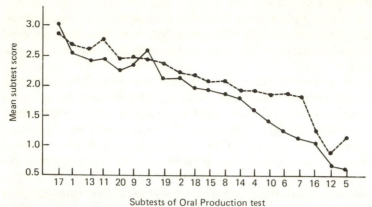

FIGURE 2   Mean scores on each subtest for children in different language programs: ESL and no ESL

Past Participle (subtest 12) and Present (subtest 5) were the lowest with ordinate values of 1.5 to 0.5, as shown in Figures 1 and 2.

The rank order correlation for the sequences obtained for children of the older and younger age groups was $+.88$ ($p<.005$). Thus there was a high correlation between the sequences of learning for the children of these two age groups.

The rank order correlation coefficient for children from the different language programs was $+.95$ ($p<.001$), indicating a high correlation between the sequence of learning despite differences in school program.

Thus the order of acquisition seemed to remain quite constant and independent of the age of the child or of the school program in which the child was involved.

DISCUSSION

The results of this study suggested that certain aspects of the second language acquisition process change with age (i.e., the rate of learning); however, other aspects remain constant independent of age (i.e., order of acquisition).

There appeared to be a difference in the rate of learning of English phonology, morphology, and syntax based upon differences in age. The younger children, aged 6 to 10 years, received significantly higher ratings on their English pronunciation, suggesting that preteen children are more successful at learning the phonology of a new language. These results support those of Asher and Garcia (1969), Oyama (1973), Seliger, Krashen, and Ladefoged (1975). The children aged 11 to 15 years received significantly higher scores on the oral production test, indicating that they were more successful in learning the morphology and syntax of a second language. This agrees with results reported by Asher and Price (1967) and Ervin-Tripp (1974).

These data alone do not prove that there is necessarily a critical period for second language learning, but they do suggest that the ability to learn certain aspects of a second language may be age-related.

The reasons for these differences may be related to maturational, physiological, or environmental factors. There may actually be different critical periods which are optimal times for learning different aspects of a second language. The preteen years may encompass a period during which the ability to discriminate, to interpret, or to imitate sounds is manifested most fully; whereas after puberty the ability to learn rules, to make generalizations, or to memorize patterns may be more fully developed.

The process did appear to remain constant, however for children of different ages in terms of order of acquisition. Despite individual age differences and differences in learning environments, there seemed to be a consistency in the order in which the English structures tested were learned. These findings support those of Dulay and Burt (1973) and Madden, Bailey, and Krashen (1974), whose findings suggested that there appeared to be similarities in the order of acquisition of structures for all second language learners.

Thus the results of this study suggest that the second language acquisition process changes with age in terms of success in learning, but remains constant in terms of order of learning.

CONCLUSION

This study alone should not be used as an argument in favor of a specific kind of language program or as an argument for beginning language instruction at a particular age. However, it might provide insights into new directions for second language acquisition research. More detailed study is needed to determine what other aspects of the second language acquisition process change with age, what kinds of errors learners make, and what types of strategies they use. More controlled study is needed to determine the effect that individual differences and different learning situations have upon this process.

Further study may well tell us more about language learning in general. It is possible that by identifying and controlling the external circumstances and the individual characteristics of the learners we may be able to further answer questions concerning the universal and creative aspects of the language learning process.

REFERENCES

Andersson, T. *Foreign Languages in the Elementary School.* Austin, Texas: University of Texas Press, 1969.

Asher, J., and Garcia, R. The optimal age to learn a foreign language. *The Modern Language Journal.* 1969, 53, 334–41.

Asher, J., and Price, B. The learning strategy of the total physical response: some age differences. *Child Development.* 1967, 38, 1219–1227.

Berko, J. The child's learning of English morphology. *Word*. 1958 14, 159–177.

Brown, R. *A First Language*. Cambridge: Harvard University Press, 1973.

Donoghue, M. *Foreign Languages and the Elementary School Child*. Dubuque: William C. Brown Publishers, 1968.

Dulay, H., and Burt, M. Should we teach children syntax? *Language Learning*. 1973, 23, 235-252.

Dulay, H., and Burt, M. Natural sequences in child second language acquisition. *Language Learning*. 1974, 24, 37–53.

Ervin-Tripp, S. Is second language learning like the first? *TESOL Quarterly*, 1974, 8, 111–127.

Hatch, E. Studies in second language acquisition. Paper presented at the Third International Congress of Applied Linguistics, Copenhagen, 1972.

Lenneberg, E. *Biological Foundations of Language*. New York: Wiley & Sons, 1967.

Madden, C., Bailey, N., and Krashen, S. Acquisiton of function words by adult learners of English as a second language: evidence for universal strategies. Proceedings of the Fifth Meeting of the NorthEast Linguistics Society, 1974.

Milon, J. A Japanese child learns English. Paper presented at TESOL Convention, San Francisco, 1972.

Modern Language Association of America. Childhood and second language learning. *Foreign Language Bulletin* 49, 1956.

Oyama, S. A sensitive period for the acquisition of a second language Ph.D. dissertation. Department of Psychology and Social Relations, Harvard University, 1973.

Politzer, R., and Weiss, L. Developmental aspects of auditory discrimination, echo response and recall. *The Modern Language Journal*. 1969, 53, 75–85.

Ravem, R. The development of wh-questions in first and second language learners, Occasional Papers, University of Essex, Language Learning Center, Colchester, 1970.

Seliger, H., Krashen, S., and Ladefoged, P. Maturational constraints in the acquisition of a native-like accent in second language learning. *Language Sciences*. 1975, 36, 20–22.

11

AGE AND LENGTH OF RESIDENCE AS VARIABLES RELATED TO THE ADJUSTMENT OF MIGRANT CHILDREN, WITH SPECIAL REFERENCE TO SECOND LANGUAGE LEARNING

Lars Henric Ekstrand

School of Education, Malmo, Sweden

BACKGROUND AND PROBLEM

Age and second language acquisition: theory

The idea that children learn a second language better the younger they are is very old. It was brought forward by the Quousque Tandem movement (Elfstrand, 1915) but is probably much older.

More recently, attempts to explain this assumed optimum have been made. Many authors, like Donoghue (1964), claim that the optimal age is also the best time for introducing a foreign language in the elementary school. Her arguments for an early optimum, and an early training, are:

1. Neurological reasons, notably those of Penfield and Roberts.
2. Psychological reasons: young children cannot and need not rely on reading and writing. They retain and repeat audio-orally. Their imitative ability seems to be better than later in life.

In order to minimize harmful effects of brain operations, neurosurgeons have tried to avoid areas of vital importance for a normal life, that is, areas of various speech functions. Penfield and Roberts (1959) discuss such functions in connection with brain damage. Their theories of foreign language learning do not, however, seem to be obvious conclusions of their neurological findings and reasoning. Nevertheless the opinions of such distinguished scientists must be taken seriously. They are: "Before the age of nine to twelve, a child is a specialist in learning to speak. At that age he can learn two or three languages as easily as one." (p. 235) "For the purposes of learning languages, the human brain becomes progressively stiff and rigid after the age of nine." (p. 236) "The physiological reason for the success in the home is that the child's brain has a specialized capacity for learning language—a capacity that decreases with the passage of years." (p. 240) "There seems to be little if any relationship between general intellectual ability and the ability of a child to imitate an accent. Capacity for imitation is maximum between 4 and 8. It steadily decreases throughout later childhood." (p. 243) These very exact predictions allow us to construct a theoretical learning ability curve with an optimum, that is, 100 percent learning capacity, between 4 and 8. It starts decreasing around the age of 9 to 12 and levels out around puberty to, let us say, 50 percent of the maximum capacity as a reasonable guess.

Such a curve is rather unlikely from other theoretical starting points. Piaget's theory predicts increasingly developed and differentiated intellectual functions with increasing age. Developmental studies (see, for example, Bayley, 1955) show that intellectual functions go on increasing until around the age of 30. It seems unlikely that language learning ability should be negatively correlated with other intellectual functions.

Lenneberg (1967) discusses the learning of L1 along the same lines as Penfield and Roberts discuss the learning of L2: recovery from brain damage and anatomical and physiological parameters of brain development. Recovery from brain damage, however, is a bit doubtful as an indication of learning capacity per se. Recovery may well take place after puberty. Lenneberg himself states (p. 143): "Aphasias acquired . . . after the age of eighteen may recover within a three-to-five months period. Symptoms that have not cleared up by this time are irreversible." But he adds: "There are a few clinical exceptions to this picture." He furthermore concludes: "The language disorder is not a learning impairment. A patient with aphasia has not lost other, more general abilities to learn. There are reasons to believe that recovery is due to physiological restoration of function rather than a learning process." His own conclusion (p. 153) does not seem completely logical: "Notice that the earlier the lesion is incurred, the brighter is the outlook for recovery. Hence we infer that language learning can take place . . . only between the age of two to about thirteen." As we shall see later, there is evidence (Jenkins, 1972) that some language learning (L1) takes place before as well as after these age limits.

The development of various brain parameters leads Lenneberg to the conclusion that "puberty is a milestone for the facility in language acquisition" (p. 168). The opposite conclusion is in fact, however, possible as far as the learning of L2 is concerned: Language learning takes place most efficiently when all brain parameters are fully developed.

Carroll (1963) suggests that the ability to acquire a nativelike accent deteriorates toward puberty. He carefully adds that this is when specific instruction is not given.

Strevens (1972) considers age to be the most important among a number of causes for variations in pronunciation proficiency and gives a list of variables which he assumes to lead to a diminished pronunciation learning ability. But he admits "that a small number of adults retain these faculties." He furthermore believes that adults possess certain qualities which may counterbalance the assumed disadvantages. On the basis of these two sets of variables he formulates the antagonistic principles of Innocence and Sophistication and ends up with the following conclusion: "People who learn a second . . . language *can* learn a good pronunciation, at any age."

Age and foreign language acquisition: research

Kirch (1956) claims superiority in German pronunciation of grade 1 pupils over grade 3 and 6 pupils and college students, but gives no actual figures.

Dunkel and Pillet (1957) compared pupils of grade 3 and 4, learning French, with each other and with college students. The college students were superior to the grade 3 and 4 children, who in turn showed no marked differences, on tests of reading and listening comprehension, oral reading, vocabulary, grammar, and writing. The authors stress the fact that the age distributions to a great extent overlap and for this and other reasons tend to disregard the tendencies found.

Among the earliest research, directly aimed at investigating age effects experimentally, seems to be that of the Swedish Board of Education. The evaluation part of the experiment was reported in two unpublished reports by Ekstrand (1959, 1964). About 1200 pupils in grades 1 to 4 were taught English by means of a purely audiovisual course, that is, with the teacher factor under control. The course extended over one semester. Pupils in areas of different dialect and degree of urbanization took part in the experiment. When quarter of year of birth was plotted against pronunciation and listening comprehension, no optimum could be traced. A straight line was the best fit. The slope was such that the older children did significantly better than the younger ones.

Brega and Newell (1965) compared two high school French groups of pupils, one with a preceding FLES program in French, the other one without such a program. They found that the first group was superior to the second on the four MLA tests. Unfortunately the first group was also intellectually superior, which was not corrected for.

Bland and Keislar (1966) compared four preschool with six grade 5 children on a completely individualized program in French. The children could run a card with a recorded phrase through a machine as many times as they wished. The time used to reach a 25-item criterion, including listening comprehension, oral production, and pronunciation, was measured. The grade 5 children used 4.5 to 11 hours and the preschool children used 12.5 to 17.5 hours. This approach is theoretically important, though the number of Ss in this particular experiment is very small.

Asher and Price (1969) compared pupils of 8, 10, 14, and 18 to 20 years of age as to their ability to learn to respond to Russian commands, during four sessions with a duration of a few minutes each. The adults were much superior to the 14-year-olds, who in turn were superior to the 10-year-olds, and so on.

Asher and Garcia (1969) tested the pronunciation of 71 Cuban and 30 American children of different ages. The group that was 1 to 6 years old when entering the United States had the best pronunciation. Next came the group who were 7 to 12 and last the group who were 13 to 19 years of age at the time of migration. This inverse relationship with age is obscured, however, by the fact that pronunciation also became better with longer stay. The probable correlation between age and length of residence, as well as sex differences and proportions, was not controlled.

In Denmark, English was introduced in grades 4, 5, and 6 and the results were compared after 80 and 320 hours of instruction (Florander and Jansen, 1969; Mylov, 1972). Grammar, vocabulary, and reading comprehension were tested with 300 to 400 pupils. The grade 6 pupils were significantly better on both occasions, but the difference diminished considerably between testing occasions.

Olson and Samuels (1973) taught German speech sounds over ten 20-minute periods to three groups of students, aged 9.5 to 10.5, 14 to 15, and 18 to 26 years. Overall and group differences were small, but statistically significant, except between the two older groups.

Jenkins (1972) reports some age effects on the perception and production of synthetic speech sounds. Studies with 2-, 6-, and 10-month-old children, using the orientation reflex (heart-rate change) and its extinction as indices of learning, showed that while the 2-month-olds showed no reliable discrimination, the 6- and 10-month-olds showed good discrimination. The learning of speech sound differences thus starts at a very early age. Further research showed that learning to perceive new, that is, artificial speech sound categories is very difficult, but possible, with 10-year-olds and adults. No formal comparisons between age groups were performed.

Toukomaa (1975), studying Finnish immigrant children in Sweden, has found that they learn Swedish better the older they are by the time of migration. As Toukomaa clearly recognizes the importance of length of residence (LOR)—"Time may be the directly most important variable" (p. 27)—he tries various methods to control the rather strong correlation between age and LOR in his material. As he uses Finnish and Swedish tests of verbal intelligence, not tests of functional language, and uses different tests on different age levels, his comparisons are somewhat uncertain. He ascribes the age effects to the pupils' better mastery of their native language.

The majority of the research reviewed points in a definite direction: second language learning capacity increases with age, with a few exceptions.

Length of residence (LOR), its impact on the linguistic, social, and emotional adjustment of migrant children: theory and research

With regard to L2 learning, no special theory seems to have been laid out. It is generally taken for granted that the new language is learned with time; see, for example, Toukomaa (1975, p. 27). Swedish experiences (M. Ek, adviser of the Swedish Board of Education, personal communication) are that migrant children who are given no or inadequate instruction may spend years literally in silence, however.

When studying the impact of LOR, Toukomaa (1975) finds that L1 seems to deteriorate faster than L2 is acquired, in spite of instruction in both languages. The language shift, that is, the point when L2 becomes the better language, seems to be between 4 and 5 years from the time of migration. Also the research of Asher and Garcia (1969) suggests that LOR is an important variable.

With adults, the impact of LOR on adjustment of other kinds is studied extensively, which does not seem to be the case with children. With regard to emotional and social adjustment, several theories are relevant. The concept of "culture shock" suggests that the confrontation with a new culture may lead to emotional disturbance. Looking closer into the possible mechanisms of this, it seems that psychodynamic as well as learning-theory-based theories of neurosis agree on at least one point: neurotic behavior is typically created either by a traumatic event or by a conflict of a lasting character. Migration is hardly a traumatic event in the true sense of the word, but it may well create a lasting conflict situation. Emotional adjustment may then in some cases be expected to grow worse, or at lease not improve, with time. This prediction gains support from the theory and research on stress. Furthermore, all behavior has a communicative significance (Hall, 1959). Much confusion and conflict is created by mutual misinterpretation of behavior. Hence, we would expect adjustment to be a slow, sometimes negative process, to a great extent independent of language.

Problem

The research on age and LOR carried out so far typically suffers from one or more of the following limitations, in some cases imposed for experimental reasons: restricted time of instruction, short duration of experiment, limited contents, restricted method, questionable validity of tests, limited number of variables tested, questionable selection of variables, limited number of Ss, and instruction carried out without the support of an authentic linguistic and cultural milieu. This study tries to answer the question: What happens when age and LOR are studied as independent variables with a large group of students in an authentic environment and when a number of other independent variables, like teaching techniques, amount of teaching, teacher personality, and teacher competence, are allowed to vary freely under field conditions?

METHOD

Subjects

The population studied consists of all immigrant pupils in school ages who in the spring of 1966 were registered in the Swedish comprehensive school and regarded as needing special tuition in Swedish, and consequently were given such tuition. This definition automatically rules out all pupils not registered or whose need of tuition had not been discovered. No resources to trace such children were at our disposal at the time of data collection.

The data-collection procedures and various statistics regarding the population studied are accounted for elsewhere (Ekstrand, 1974). There were about 2400 pupils fitting the definition. Data for 2189 such pupils (90 percent) were obtained.

Instruments

Various data about the pupils, like age, length of residence, nationality, sex, and grade, were obtained by means of a questionnaire to the teachers. They were also asked to express freely their views on the pupils' progress in school, in Swedish, and in their social and emotional adjustment. These judgments were then quantified into a five-grade scale, where 1 is bad progress or adjustment and 5 is excellent progress. The tests belong to either of three domains: pure language tests (functional Swedish), intelligence tests, and tests of reading skill (oral reading).

The language tests consist of six subjects, which were constructed for this study:

Pronunciation: Imitation, recorded on tape, of 12 standard phrases, read from a sound tape. The recordings are rated with respect to overall quality.

Dictation: A piece, consisting of 11 phrases, is read from a tape, 3 times a phrase.

Listening comprehension: 51 phrases are read from a tape. A series of 5 pictures belongs to each phrase (255 pictures). Pupils choose the picture they think best illustrates the phrase. They do not need to be able to read and write.

Reading comprehension: The same series of pictures are used again, with a phrase printed below each series. The phrases differ from the LC test. No writing is needed.

Free oral production: The pupil is to describe the contents and happenings of 3 pictures. The answers were recorded and rated by 3 judges.

Free written production: The pupil is to describe a picture. The sketch is rated.

Thus, 4 out of the 6 tests measure active skills on the part of the pupils. The intelligence tests consist of a nonverbal test for each of the Thurstone R, N, and S factors, called DBA 4, 7, and 8, respectively, and standardized on Swedish pupils. The reading skill tests consist of 3 individual subtests, each consisting of a short piece to be read aloud. The time limit is 2 minutes for each test. Number of words read, time, if less than 2 minutes, and number of errors are scored.

RESULTS

Checks on missing data

For most questions in the teacher questionnaire, there is a varying percentage of "No information given," as the teachers did not in every case know the answer. In order to study whether the missing background data were systematically related to the measurements in a way that might invalidate the results, the dichotomy data/no data in each background variable was correlated with the tests and teacher judgments point biserially. Out of 506 coefficients, 492 were between ±.10 and the rest (14) were between ±.20. As these coefficients are so low that they may be regarded as negligible, there does not seem to be any bias in the background data of importance for this particular study.

The tests have been completed to a varying degree. There are many reasons for this. The DBA tests can be used from grade 4 only. Free oral production and pronunciation were, for economical reasons, administered to samples of pupils only. Some tests are impossible to carry out with too young or too newly arrived children. Whatever the reasons, the question of interest is whether the drop-out is systematic in a way which invalidates the results or not.

To test for this, point biserial correlations were run between the dichotomy "test completed/not completed" for each test, against the values for each of the other tests. A high correlation indicates that the missing results are systematically related to good or bad performance in other variables. Out of 576 coefficients, 5 percent were not possible to calculate (too few cases), 2 percent fall between ±.37, 18 percent between ±.30, and 75 percent between ±.10. These data suggest that no systematic selection affects the variables under study.

Intercorrelations between age, LOR, and some other background variables

χ^2 and contingency coefficients C were computed between age, LOR, nationality, father's occupation in Sweden and in the native country, mother's occupation in Sweden and in the native country, number of children in the family, grade, type of class, teaching materials used, and previous knowledge of Swedish.

Age is strongly correlated with grade only. The product moment correlation is .93, which means that the pupils on the whole were placed in the proper, or at least an adjacent, grade with respect to their age.

LOR is strongly related to "Previous knowledge of Swedish" only, which is a perfectly natural correlation. In all, the lack of substantial correlations with other background variables means that they need not be controlled in order to study age and LOR, which is the purpose of this paper.

Effects of age

The pupils were grouped in 26 groups according to third of year of birth. 1 = born 1949 or earlier, 2 = born January to April 1950 (16: 1 to 4 years at the time of testing), 3 = born May to August 1950 (15:9 to 16:0), etc.

The median of LOR in the population studied is 10.5 months. Fifty percent fall between $Q_1 = 6.8$ months and $Q_3 = 17.8$ months. The mean of age is 11.6 years, $s = 2.6$ years. As age and LOR are uncorrelated, each variable can be treated separately.

The results of the analyses of variance of age differences in all measurements are given in Table 1. The ω^2 gives the proportion of variance explained by age. It is conventional to disregard differences, even if significant, if the ω^2 is less than .05 (5 percent).

The teacher judgments of adjustment are not at all related to age. Except DBA 4, DBA 7, and Free oral production, all other variables are significant, on the .1 percent level (pronunciation 5 percent). When extreme age groups (8 to 10 versus 12 to 17 years) are compared, also DBA 4 and 7 become significant on the .1 percent level, while Free oral production is still nonsignificant.

A few examples of plots of means of the age groups are given in Figure 1. Test scores, transformed to a 9 grade scale with a mean of 5 and a standard deviation of 1.96, are given on the ordinate, thirds of year of birth on the abscissa.

It should be noted that the teachers tend to judge the pupils' behavior as a unity and that their judgments of progress in Swedish are more strongly correlated with emotional and social adjustment than with the language tests.

Thus language learning ability improves with age, as does intellectual functioning, while social and emotional adjustment seems to be nonrelated to age.

Effects of length of residence (LOR)

Analyses of variance are given in Table 2. The ω^2 values are, with one exception, very low. Free oral production becomes considerably better with time, but not with age, as noted above. The only variables otherwise related to LOR are Listening comprehension and Free written production.

As predicted, the adjustment variables are not related to LOR. Astonishingly, most language variables are very weakly related to LOR. This is probably because only 8.3 percent of the pupils have a longer LOR than 2 years and language learning as a function of time is a slow process.

Intellectual functions are practically not at all related to LOR. For reasons of space, no plots can be given.

DISCUSSION AND CONCLUSIONS

The age effects found in this study go straight against the basic theory of second language acquisition. No optimum is found. On the contrary, language learning ability is growing monotonously and almost linearly with age. The reasoning of

Table 1 Analyses of Variance for Age Differences (Third of Year of Birth), d.f. between Groups = 25

Variable	d.f. within	SS between	SS within	MS between	MS within	F	P	ω^2
1. Progress in school	1796	− 57.1	1604.5	2.3	.9	2.6	.01	.034
2. Social adjustment	1822	− 24.7	1371.3	1.0	.8	1.3	NS	.018
3. Emotional adjustment	954	− 18.2	634.5	.7	.7	1.1	NS	.028
4. Progress in Swedish	1254	+ 27.4	1037.6	1.1	.8	1.3	NS	.026
5. Listening comprehension	1310	+ 6319.4	67739.4	252.8	51.7	4.9	.001	.085
6. Reading comprehension	1275	+ 47869.3	157253.3	1914.8	123.3	15.5	.001	.233
7. RLS 1 time	1244	− 366733.4	1543216.3	14669.3	1240.5	11.8	.001	.192
8. RLS 1 words	1254	+ 20572.0	80139.9	822.9	63.9	12.9	.001	.204
9. RLS 1 errors	1254	− 1960.4	26198.2	78.4	20.9	3.8	.001	.070
10. RLS 2 time	1243	− 751025.0	2519952.0	30041.0	2027.3	14.8	.001	.230
11. RLS 2 words	1251	+ 3875.2	22507.2	155.0	18.0	8.6	.001	.147
12. RLS 2 errors	1249	− 1458.5	16855.2	58.3	13.5	4.3	.001	.080
13. RLS 3 time	1194	− 1001275.6	2270866.0	40051.0	1901.9	21.1	.001	.306
14. RLS 3 words	1201	+ 22134.3	69405.2	885.4	57.8	15.3	.001	.242
15. RLS 3 errors	1200	− 3897.1	38471.3	155.9	32.1	4.9	.001	.092
16. DBA 4	Not computed because of no cases in one or more cells							
17. DBA 7	240	+ 137.7	971.4	5.5	4.1	1.4	NS	.124
18. DBA 8	710	+ 11571.3	73938.5	462.9	104.1	4.4	.001	.135
19. Dictation	1131	+ 72218.9	797676.6	2888.8	263.2	11.0	.001	.195
20. Free written production	1034	+ 585.8	3349.2	23.4	3.2	7.2	.001	.149
21. Pronunciation	289	+ 133383.6	820286.5	5335.3	2838.4	1.9	.05	.140
22. Free oral production	289	+ 10643.3	95772.0	425.7	331.4	1.3	NS	.100

A sign in the column for SS *between* indicates if the variable is negatively or positively correlated with age.

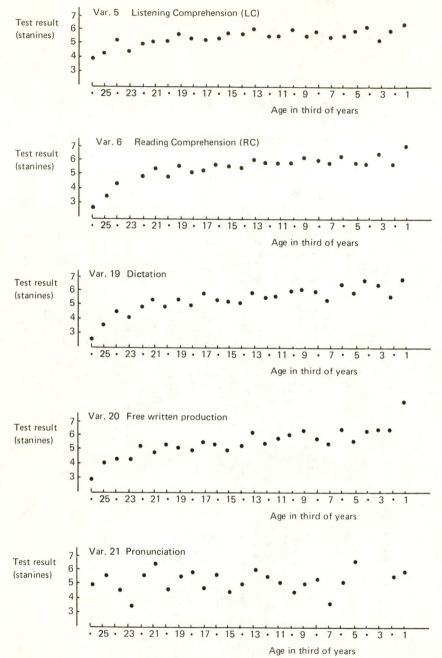

FIGURE 1   Examples of plots of test results as functions of age

Table 2 Analyses of Variance for Differences in Length of Residence (0 to 8 months against 2 Years or More), d.f. between Groups = 1

Variable	d.f. within	SS between	SS within	MS between	MS within	F	P	ω^2
1. Progress in school	874	+ 1.0	823.8	1.0	.9	1.1	NS	.001
2. Social adjustment	889	+ .3	680.1	.3	.8	.4	NS	.001
3. Emotional adjustment	479	− .3	286.8	.2	.6	.4	NS	.001
4. Progress in Swedish	586	+ .5	494.6	.5	.8	.6	NS	.001
5. Listening comprehension	618	+ 2097.9	35694.6	2097.9	57.8	36.3	.001	.056
6. Reading comprehension	597	+ 3197.3	95003.8	3197.3	159.1	20.1	.001	.033
7. RLS 1 time	581	− 11469.5	643850.1	11469.5	1108.2	10.3	.01	.018
8. RLS 1 words	587	+ 42.1	47547.0	42.1	81.0	.5	NS	.001
9. RLS 1 errors	587	− 325.2	11528.1	325.2	19.6	16.6	.001	.027
10. RLS 2 time	580	− 23755.5	1131132.5	23755.5	1950.2	12.2	.001	.021
11. RLS 2 words	585	− 5.9	13672.3	5.9	23.4	.3	NS	.000
12. RLS 2 errors	585	− 186.7	8246.8	186.7	14.1	13.2	.001	.022
13. RLS 3 time	558	− 33812.1	1326640.6	33812.1	2377.5	14.2	.001	.025
14. RLS 3 words	563	+ 101.0	41517.5	101.0	73.7	1.4	NS	.002
15. RLS 3 errors	563	− 607.2	20180.6	607.2	35.8	16.9	.001	.029
16. DBA 4	98	+ 11.7	5356.1	11.7	54.7	.2	NS	.002
17. DBA 7	106	− .8	509.5	.8	4.8	.2	NS	.002
18. DBA 8	325	− 1383.4	39411.1	1383.4	121.3	11.4	.001	.034
19. Dictation	523	+ 3087.7	169362.4	3087.7	323.8	9.5	.01	.018
20. Free written production	476	+ 83.9	1656.1	83.9	3.5	24.1	.001	.048
21. Pronunciation	142	+ 18740.6	482257.8	18740.6	3396.2	5.5	.05	.037
22. Free oral production	142	+ 10066.8	35189.1	10066.8	247.8	40.6	.001	.222

A sign in the column for SS *between* indicates if the variable is negatively or positively correlated with age.

133

Penfield and Roberts and also of Lenneberg must be reversed: the more developed the brain is, the better it is suited for second language learning, in the span of 8 to 16:4 years.

Besides biological factors, the general development of perceptual, intellectual, and motor factors probably contributes to language learning ability. Toukomaa (1975) considers the development of L1 to be of the greatest importance for the learning of L2. His own correlations, however, show that L1 explains only between 10 and 25 percent of the variance in the L2 variables studied.

The results of this study, with Ss learning L2 in an authentic linguistic milieu and experiencing all the communicative needs that a new social and cultural environment creates, support the results of the majority of age studies with Ss learning L2 in their native country. Whether other milieu factors may play a part, interacting with age, will be subjected to further analyses.

The social and emotional adjustment, as judged by the teachers, does not seem to be related to age. There is no well-founded theory or very much research to be compared with this finding.

Most language variables are very weakly related to LOR. A comparison of ω^2 values shows that age is a much better predictor of L2 acquisition than LOR. One possible explanation is that the L2 acquisition is such a slow process that a time span much larger than in this study is needed to give any effects. Another hypothesis is that, contrary to common belief, the time spent in a foreign environment is of secondary importance. Quantity and quality of instruction, motivation and energy of the individual, and not least important, the pattern of verbal and nonverbal contact and communication with the native population may be far more important factors.

There is one clear exception to this finding. It is interesting to note that the only language variable which is unrelated to age, Free oral production, is also the only variable that is strongly related to LOR. This implies, among other things, that conversation can best be learned in an authentic milieu, a point that language teachers have argued for centuries.

In accordance with theoretical predictions, social and emotional adjustment does not improve with LOR. Intellectual variables seem not to be affected by LOR.

Finally, some practical consequences of these findings. Early second language teaching cannot be based on the prevailing theoretical foundations. It may still be a good idea with early L2 teaching, but it should be based on administrative and other practical considerations. In Sweden, most pupils learn two or even three foreign languages in primary and secondary school. Language learning has to start early. On the other hand, the findings of this study should prove positive for adult education.

The instruction in L1 and L2 for migrant children, as well as the supervision of their emotional and social adjustment, must be given much larger resources than is done at the moment. This study (data from 1966) and Toukomaa's (data from 1972) both suggest that the linguistic and socioemotional adjustment processes are slow and may need speeding up. Teaching techniques and materials, as well as the training of teachers, psychologists, counselors, and others, must be developed and improved.

REFERENCES

Asher, J., and Garcia, R. The optimal age to learn a foreign language. *Modern Language Journal.* 1969, 5.

Asher, J., and Price, B. S. The learning strategy of the total physical response: some age differences. *Child Development.* 1969, 53.

Bayley, N. On the growth of intelligence. *American Psychologist.* 1955, 10.

Bland, M., and Keislar, E. A self-controlled audio-lingual program for children. *French Review.* 1966, 40.

Brega, E., and Newell, J. Comparison of performance by FLES program students and regular French III students on Modern Language Association tests. *French Review.* 1965, 39.

Carroll, J. B. Research on teaching foreign languages. In N. L. Gage (ed.), *Handbook on Research on Teaching.* Chicago: Rand McNally & Co., 1963.

Donoghue, M. R. A rationale for FLES. *French Review.* 1964, 38.

Dunkel, H. B., and Pillet, R. A. A second year of French in the elementary school. *Elementary School Journal.* 1957, 58.

Ekstrand, L. H. Utvärdering av metodik och resultat på grundval av inspelade prov från elever i 1:a, 2:a, 3:e och 4:e klass i Västerås, Linköping och Hallstahammar. / Evaluation of teaching technique and results on the basis of recorded tests from pupils in grades 1, 2, 3, and 4. / Stenciled, National Board of Education, 1959.

Ekstrand, L. H. Språkfärdighet och språkmetodik. / Language skill and teaching technique. / Thesis for the degree of licentiate of philosophy. Stenciled, University of Stockholm, 1964.

Ekstrand, L. H. Adjustment among immigrant pupils in Sweden. Paper presented to the 18th International Congress of Applied Psychology, Montreal, 1974.

Elfstrand, D. Tjugofem års erfarenhet med den induktiv-imitativa språkundervisningsmetoden. / Twenty-five years of experience with the inductive-imitative language teaching technique. / Address to the 21st meeting of high school teachers of Sweden, Jönköping, 1915.

Florander, J., and Jensen, M. Skoleforsøg i engelsk 1959–1965. Stenciled, Denmark's Institute of Education, 1969.

Hall, E. T. *The Silent Language.* New York: Doubleday & Co., 1959.

Jenkins, J. J. Effect of age, native language and instruction on speech sound discrimination. Final report. U.S. Department of Health, Education and Welfare, 1972.

Kirch, M. S. At what age elementary school language teaching? *Modern Language Journal.* 1956, 53.

Lenneberg, E. *Biological Foundations of Language.* New York: Wiley, 1967.

Mylov, P. Skoleforsøg i engelsk. / School experiments in English. / Copenhagen: Munksgaard, 1972.

Olson, L. L., and Samuels, S. J. The relationship between age and accuracy of foreign language pronunciation. *Journal of Educational Research.* 1973, 66.

Penfield, W., and Roberts, L. *Speech and Brain Mechanisms.* Princeton: Princeton University Press, 1959.

Strevens, P. The rival virtue of innocence and sophistication. Paper delivered to the TESOL Convention, Washington, D.C., 1972.

Toukomaa, P. Om finska invandrarelevers sprokutveckling och skolframgong i den svenska grundskolan. / On the language development and school progress of Finnish immigrant pupils in the Swedish comprehensive school. / Paper presented to the Scandinavian Seminar on Language Policy, Helsinki, 1975.

12

ENGLISH WITHOUT A BOOK REVISITED: THE EFFECT OF AGE ON SECOND LANGUAGE ACQUISITION IN A FORMAL SETTING

Lars Henric Ekstrand
School of Education, Malmo, Sweden

PROBLEM

Introduction

Since World War II, two major experiments in early second language teaching have been launched in Sweden, both with the English language. The first experiment was done during the period 1958–1968, the second during the period 1969–1979. The first project was called "English without a book" (EuB) and the second has been called "EPÅL," which means "English in the preparatory school" (Engelska *PÅ L*ågstadiet).

A practical result of the first project was that, in Sweden, English was moved from grade 5 to grade 4 and later to grade 3. The result of EPÅL may well be that English is moved to grade 2 or even to grade 1. EPÅL will be reported within the next 2 or 3 years. The experimental children have reached grade 8, and the experiment is not finished until they have passed through grade 9.

The aim of this paper is to give an account for the rationale and results of the first part of the first experiment. Although 10 years have elapsed since the first experiment was terminated and almost 20 years since the first part was finished, the experiment and the outcome are still of great interest. This is so because early second language teaching is again in focus in many countries. For instance, in Braunschweig in West Germany experiments with early English teaching are being conducted (Doyé and Lüttge, 1975), and in Sweden a debate on starting English in grade 2 or even grade 1 has been reopened.

There is also a controversy in the area of teaching languages to the children of immigrants. Some authors, such as Malmberg in Sweden (1971, 1977) and Toukomaa and Skutnabb-Kangas in Finland (1977), strongly argue that early L2 learning is harmful and should be postponed until "L1 is established," which according to the authors is about age 12 to 13.

The method "EuB" was described by the inventors, Gorosch and Axelsson (1964), but the results were reported only within the Swedish National Board of Education. They have been briefly referred to by several authors, for instance, Stern (1963) and Burstall (1975). The detailed results and data, e.g., the age curves, were reported in stenciled papers in Swedish only (Ekstrand, 1964). It seems, therefore, as if an international presentation of the detailed results is called for in spite of the time which has elapsed. Comparisons with some very recent data will be made, however, and the discussion has been brought up to date.

Rationale

There were in fact two kinds of rationale for the "English without a book" experiments. The first kind was a variety of the optimum age theory and the other was set psychology.

The optimum age theory was specified in three hypotheses (Gorosch, 1960):

Listening to sounds uttered in given situations, and then imitating these sounds, is the natural, genetic way of learning a new language. A direct association is thus established between sound and situation.

The ability to perceive and imitate sounds seems to be greatest before the age of 10-12 years and then to deteriorate successively. This seems to be especially true of intonation (pitch), stress and duration. Perhaps the most important feature is intonation.

The pupils' pronunciation is affected by already existing associations between written symbols and the speech sounds of the native language, which inhibit the acquisition of a good pronunciation.

The last hypothesis was later dropped, for reasons unknown (Gorosch and Axelsson, 1964). The three hypotheses may be referred to as "the natural learning hypothesis," "the optimum imitation ability hypothesis," and "the interference hypothesis."

The other rationale was the concept of "set," or "preparatory set" or "learning set." The psychologists of the National Board of Education in Sweden were, on the basis of evidence from developmental psychology, reluctant to accept too literal an interpretation of the early optimum theories. The notion of set, however, suggested that there might be a good chance of creating a foreign language learning set in young children, producing a facilitation in L2 learning later on the regular school situation.

The theoretical basis for the set concept was laid out by Hebb (1949), who pointed out that learning in early years is very slow, but nevertheless a condition for later, more efficient learning to develop. The mechanism proposed was roughly that learning arranges interconnections between nerve cells so that certain cells later tend to act as groups of cells, which need less and less stimulation in order to function. Attention thus becomes directed toward familiar events so that these are more readily perceived than others. Similarly, associative processing of familiar events becomes speeded up.

Harlow (1949) in a series of experiments with monkeys and children, defined learning set as a facilitation of problem solving. When the individual has solved a large number of similar problems, the later problems are solved much more quickly than the first. This learning to learn takes the shape of an ordinary learning curve which is very stable. As language obviously contains a good deal of problem solving, such as inferring exactly which referent a speaker is referring to or choosing the most adequate words and then putting them together in an appropriate way, the learning set approach would seem appropriate.

Thus, when Gorosch and Axelsson suggested that experiments should be conducted in grades 1 to 4 with a purely audiovisual course, the proposal was met with positive interest from the National Board of Education. It was decided that Gorosch and Axelsson were to create the teaching materials and the Board of Education was to perform the scientific evaluation.

METHOD

The teaching materials

There were at least two important reasons for making completely audiovisual materials with no teacher participation in the process. The most obvious reason was lack of teachers with competence in English teaching. The second, not less important, reason was the need for scientific control of the teacher factor. Therefore, the role of the teacher during the teaching sessions was to handle the apparatus. The teacher was not allowed to interfere in the process, i.e., to teach, even if he or she in a few cases was highly qualified.

For the first phase of the experiment, 18 sets of still films and sound tapes were produced. Each set was shown twice a week to the pupils. Each show lasted about 10 minutes. The first time the pupils just listened to the sound tape and watched the pictures. The next time the pupils were instructed to repeat the words aloud. Every new lesson started with a short repetition of the preceding one. Translation to Swedish, comments on how to shape the sounds or grammatical instructions did not occur, with a few rare exceptions.

Later, further sets were created. They were grouped in 4 parts with 12 sets of films and tapes in each part. The parts were intended as progressive materials for each of grades 1 to 4.

Subjects and design

Teaching with the first 18 sets was introduced in the spring semester of 1958 in 10 classes in each of grades 1 to 4, i.e., in 40 classes or roughly around 1000 pupils. Thus age is manipulated systematically and constitutes the independent variable. All other circumstances are kept constant with this design. For instance, the pupils are 8 to 11 years in the spring semester in grades 1 to 4 and thus in the period of concrete operations. Exposure to the language stimuli is the same.

In a later phase of the experiments, pupils were given one part of the course in each grade. Testing took place at the end of grade 5, i.e., after 1 year of regular teaching. Pupils with and without the early, preparatory teaching were then compared.

The 40 classes from phase 1 were distributed with 16 classes from a city in one dialectal area of Sweden, 8 classes from a city of about same size in another dialectal area, and 16 classes from towns and villages in the rural surroundings of the second city. Thus dialect and urbanization degree are introduced as independent variables.

Testing

Sixteen words and sentences from the combined sound and picture material were sampled and played back to the pupils, who were to imitate the spoken items aloud. The pupils were tested one at a time.

The next test was a playback of eight combined items, sampled from the stimulus material. The pupils were asked to translate the English sentences into Swedish. The third test was a sample of five items from the sound tape. They were played back to the pupils, who were asked to translate them.

All the answers, together with the spoken stimuli, were recorded with a professional tape recorder and a microphone with selective sensitivity in classrooms with varying acoustic properties.

Data treatment

The first step of the data treatment was to reduce the amount of data by random sampling. Every third pupil was chosen for testing, which gives a sample described in Table 1. Pronunciation was measured in two ways. The first

Table 1   Composition of Sample of Pupils for Whom Testing and Data Treatment Was Carried Out

Region	Grade (age)				Total
	1 (8)	2 (9)	3 (10)	4 (11)	
City 1 (Linköping)	36	33	41	39	149
City 2 (Västerås)	17	18	17	21	73
Surroundings of city 2	32	27	37	37	133
	85	78	95	97	355

method consisted of category rating of each of the 16 items for every pupil by three Swedish judges with good knowledge of English. A seven-point scale was used. It was anchored so that 1 = no pronunciation or a completely distorted pronunciation and 7 = a very good pronunciation, similar to that of the English voice.

The second method was applied to a still smaller sample of 192 pupils, distributed with 78 pupils from city 1 and 74 pupils from city 2 and surroundings, evenly spread over the four grades. The first step was to make a narrow, complex, and allophonic transcription of the pupils' and the Englishmen's pronunciation of each sentence. This was done by the present author.

Second, the degree of similarity between each speech sound of a pupil and the corresponding sound of the English voice was rated by means of category rating on a five-point scale. As many kinds of mispronunciation were made in a large variety of directions from the master sound, a psychophysical concept was applied. Similarity was conceived of in terms of physical distance. This made the task much easier for the single judge who was involved in the second method.

In both methods, ratings for each sentence were added up to give a grand total for each pupil. To improve metric properties, the totals were converted into a nine-grade standard scale with $\bar{x} = 5.0$ and $s = 2.0$, approximately.

In summary, with method 1 each whole sentence was rated, and with method 2 each speech sound was rated; i.e., intonation is included in method 1 only.

With listening comprehension, it turned out that translation of items with sound and picture was invalidated by the pictures. The picture often triggered a translation or sometimes an imitation in English *before* the voice was heard. Therefore, only the items without pictures were used.

The first step was to make a written transcription of the pupils' recorded translations. Each pupil was then given a raw score, consisting of the number of correctly translated words. Finally, the raw scores were transformed to nine-grade standard scale points.

Although reliability estimates are of less importance in research work than in practical applications (Ekman, 1957), it may be of interest for the reader to note the remarkably high reliability that may be obtained with rating methods. A detailed study is reported by Eriksson and Ekstrand (1962), later reviewed by Ekstrand (1978a).

RESULTS

Pronunciation, method 1

Means and standard deviations are given in Table 2. A test of significance was done by means of analysis of variance (Table 3). As is shown by Tables 2 and 3, older pupils in the age range of 8 to 11 acquire a better pronunciation in a foreign language, having received the same amount of audiovisual teaching twice a week during 18 weeks, and with the teacher factors controlled.

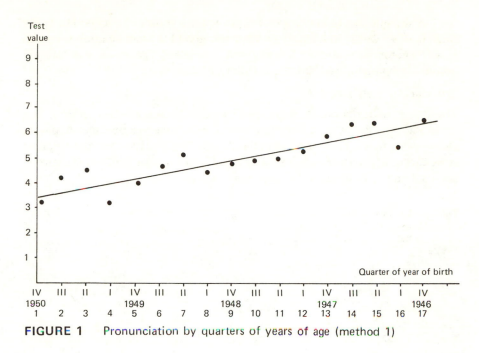

FIGURE 1   Pronunciation by quarters of years of age (method 1)

Table 2   Results of Pronunciation (Method 1) by Grade. Higher values better

Grade	n	$\overline{X}$	s
1	85	3.81	1.88
2	78	4.79	1.73
3	95	5.14	1.85
4	97	6.06	1.69
Total	355	5.00	1.96

Table 3   Analysis of Variance. Pronunciation (Method 1) by Age

Source of variation	Degrees of freedom	Sums of squares	Mean square	F ratio p and ω^2	
Between groups	3	234.44	78.15	F	24.13
Within groups	351	1136.56	3.24	p	< .001
Total	354	1371.00		ω^2	.178

As the tendency seems to be systematic, a curve was fitted to the data. In order to reveal the precise nature of the relationship, the age variable was rather finely graded in quarters of a year. The result is shown in Figure 1.

141

A straight line, obtained with a least-squares solution, is a good fit to the data. In other words, the ability to acquire a good L2 pronunciation seems to grow monotonously, almost linearly with increasing age in the age interval tested. No optimum can be traced within this age range.

Pronunciation, Method 2

The amount of deviations from the ideal speech sounds is given in Table 4. The same tendency to better pronunciation with increasing age becomes apparent also with method 2. Even the size of the steps between grades seems similar, or close to one step between grades 1 and 2 and 3 and 4, and 1/3 of a step between grades 2 and 3, in terms of the nine-point scale.

Table 4   Distance of Pupils' Pronunciation from Ideal. Lower values better

Grade	n	$\overline{X}$	s
1	36	6.00	1.75
2	33	5.21	1.75
3	39	4.87	1.73
4	44	4.07	1.85
Total	152	4.98	1.91

As the overall difference between grades obviously is significant also with method 2, the significance of the differences between grades was tested by means of t-tests (see Table 5). As is seen from Table 5, adjacent grades are significantly, or almost significantly different in pronunciation, if .05 is chosen as the criterion. The difference between grades 2 and 3 is the only exception. Differences between nonadjacent grades are always significant.

Table 5 t Tests between Grades.
Pronunciation (Method 2) by Age

Grade	t	Level of significance		
1/2	1.83	$.10 >$	p	$> .05$
1/3	2.75	$.01 >$	p	$> .001$
1/4	4.70	$.001 >$	p	$>$
2/3	.81		p	$> .10$
2/4	2.73	$.01 >$	p	$> .001$
3/4	2.02	$.05 >$	p	$> .02$

Again, a curve was fitted to data by means of the method of least squares, as shown in Figure 2. As shown by Figure 2, method 2 gives a result similar to that of method 1. The distance from the "ideal" speech sounds becomes less with increasing age.

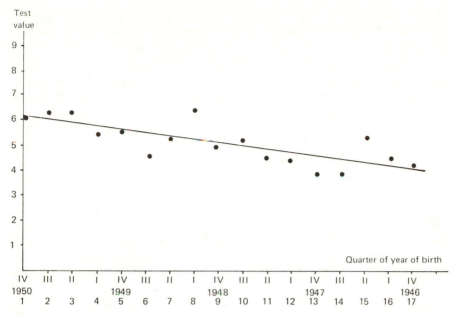

FIGURE 2 Distance from ideal speech sounds. Lower values better

Effects of native dialect and degree of urbanization on pronunciation

While it seems natural and in fact inevitable that native dialect should affect second language pronunciation, the question is if some dialects are more favorable than others for the acquisition of a good pronunciation. As the two cities which took part in this study belong to distinctly different dialectal areas, it is possible to study this question. The results are given in Tables 6 and 7.

Many results point to the importance of differences in rural-urban environments for the development of intellectual and emotional variables

Table 6   Differences between Dialectal and Urban/Rural Areas. Method 1, Category Rating. Higher values better

Region	$\overline{X}$	s	n	diff.	t	p
City 1 (Linköping)	5.03	2.00	149			
City 2 (Västerås)	5.37	1.85	73	−.34	1.26	.20 < p
Surroundings of city 2	4.76	1.93	133	.61	2.18	.02 < p < .05

Table 7   Differences between Dialectal and Urban/Rural Areas. Method 2, Distance from Ideal Speech Sounds. Lower values better

Region	$\overline{X}$	s	n	diff.	t	p
City 1 (Linköping)	5.21	1.92	75			
City 2 (Västerås)	4.27	1.88	37	1.04	2.47	.01 < p < .02
Surroundings of city 2	5.27	1.79	37	1.00	2.33	.02 < p < .05

143

(Husén, 1951; Parker et al., 1969; Burstall, 1975; Ekstrand, 1977). While it was not believed that pronunciation should be affected, the possibility nevertheless was studied. The results are given in Tables 6 and 7.

As seen from the tables, both methods indicate that urban/rural influences have a measurable effect on the acquisition of L2 pronunciation. As none of the methods was used to assess possible qualitative differences, the differences obtained are purely quantitative. With method 1, there is a tendency toward better pronunciation in city 2. The difference is not statistically significant, however. With method 2, the same tendency reappears, now statistically significant. Again, data were not used to make a truly contrastive analysis, i.e., to study qualitative differences, but to study quantitative differences solely.

Metric properties of the pronunciation measurements

The agreement between raters was computed by means of the coefficient of concordance (W coefficient), as described, for instance, in Siegel (1956). Three samples of pupils were used to estimate an agreement value for the whole group, viz., the 25 pupils first rated, the 28 pupils in the middle of the rating, and the 24 last pupils. The coefficients were .71, .88, and .85, respectively. The W coefficient is a slight overestimate of the average of all possible rank correlations. Nevertheless, there is a very good agreement among raters.

The product-moment correlation (r) between method 1 and method 2 was computed and found to be .73. Thus, there is a very high degree of agreement between methods.

Comprehension

The results of the listening comprehension test are shown in Figure 3. A test of significance (analysis of variance) is reported in Table 8. From Figure 3 and Table 8 it is clear that listening comprehension ability is increasingly better with higher age, with the same amount of teaching, with the teacher factor, mode of presentation, and all other factors controlled, and with an age range within the period of concrete operations.

Table 8   Analysis of Variance. Listening Comprehension by Grade. Higher values better

Source of variation	Degrees of freedom	Sums of squares	Mean square	F ratio p and ω^2	
Between groups	3	275.35	91.78	F	27.4
Within groups	351	1176.10	3.35	p	.001
Total	354	1451.45		ω^2	.196

Pronunciation, method 3

In addition to the two methods of assessing pronunciation, described above, a third, less formal evaluation was performed. An experienced radio teacher

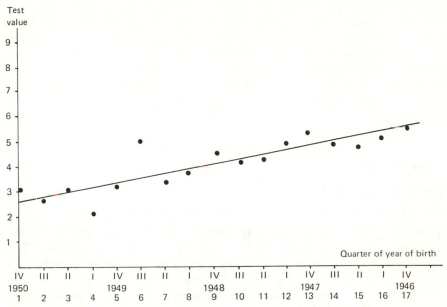

FIGURE 3   Listening comprehension by quarters of year of birth

listened to the pupils' spoken sentences and rated them as pass or fail. In doing so, he marked the sound which he found not acceptable. Making use of these markings, we can classify speech sounds as rated pass or fail. By adding the number of not acceptable sounds, each pupil could be given a total score, reliable enough to allow statistical treatment (Ekstrand, 1959).

As with the other measurements, total scores were transformed to stanine points. The results are given in Table 9 and the tests of significance in Table 10.

Table 9   Results of Pronunciation Ratings, Method 3. Lower values better

Grade	n	$\overline{X}$	s
1	84	5.75	1.94
2	77	5.13	1.58
3	95	5.02	2.03
4	101	4.26	1.89
Total	357	5.00	1.95

Table 10 t tests between Grades. Pronunciation (Method 3) by Grade

Grade	t	Level of significance
1/2	2.22	$.05 > p > .02$
1/3	2.45	$.02 > p > .01$
1/4	5.23	$.005 > p > \text{—}$
2/3	.40	
2/4	3.31	$.005 > p > \text{—}$
3/4	2.69	$.01 > p > .005$

Intercorrelations between the Various Measurements

The coefficients of correlation r are given in Table 11.

145

Table 11   Intercorrelations

Variable	1	2	3	4
1. Listening comprehension	—	.54	.53	—*
2. Pronunciation (method 1)		—	.73	—*
3. Pronunciation (method 2)			--	.62
4. Pronunciation (method 3)				—*

*Not computed

DISCUSSION

Data and the first rationale:
the optimum age and natural learning hypothesis

The first hypothesis is in a way only indirectly tested, as one single method is used and thus no comparisons between different approaches are possible. The method used was, however, tailored exactly according to the words of the first hypothesis: listening to sounds, and then imitating these sounds.

In terms of learning psychology, the emphasis of the materials was on classical conditioning (signal learning) with some additional operant conditioning (the imitation). At least at first glance, no or very few higher processes such as problem solving, seriation, and classification seem to be involved. Still, after only 360 to 400 minutes (6 to 6.5 hours) of this rather passive, simple S-R type of learning, the children had learned a remarkable amount of English. Thus, the first hypothesis gains some support from the outcome of the present experiment.

Later, the idea of a natural way of L2 learning has gained further ground. First, evidence for a strong degree of similarity between L1 and L2 learning is piling up (Garvie, 1973; Asher, 1972; Dulay and Burt, 1972, 1973, 1974a, 1974b; Snow, 1976; Hensen-Bede, 1975; Macnamara, 1975; Rado, 1975). Second, there is evidence that adults use learning strategies, similar to those of children (Bailey et al., 1974; Krashen et al., 1976). Third, no evidence whatever for different biological mechanisms, such as different brain centers for L1 and L2 learning, has ever been advanced. Instead, such students of the biological prerequisites for language as Penfield and Roberts (1959) or Lenneberg (1967) more or less explicitly assume the same neutral substrata for L1 and L2 learning.

It is true that a number of authors, such as Ervin and Osgood (1965), and more recently Ellegård (1971) strongly argue that there are two kinds of language learning and that one may be more natural than the other. Diller (1970) has effectively criticized the compound-coordinate learning concepts and similar notions, pointing out that the definitions are vague, experimental evidence is lacking, and there is no sound theoretical basis. It may be added that the two-type learning theories do not cover all kind of language learning

146

manifestations. Ekstrand (1978b) has suggested that it is much simpler and sounder to assume *one* set of learning mechanisms and that situational and developmental criteria are decisive for the kind of learning that may arise.

The central issue for this paper, however, is the optimum age concept. Penfield and Roberts (1959) advanced the plasticity theory, predictcing an optimum for L2 learning between 4 and 8, because of greater plasticity (ability to shift functions from one brain area to another) in these years. The imitation theory, expressed in our second hypothesis, was advanced by Donoghue (1964), asserting in agreement with Gorosch and Axelsson that audio-oral imitation ability is better in younger years. Lenneberg (1967) advanced the critical period theory, according to which language learning is impossible after puberty. As the strong form of this theory obviously is not tenable for foreign languages, Lenneberg (ibid.) advanced two auxiliary theories. The resonance or automatic acquisition theory states that first as well as second language acquisition before puberty is triggered by exposure to language and certain social settings. The individual who is maturationally ready reacts as a resonator to the environmental stimuli which on the other hand cannot actually *shape* the responses. The matrix theory states that first language acquisition in interaction with innate mechanisms creates a biological matrix which makes second language acquisition possible.

After puberty, the number of language learning blocks rapidly increases, automatic learning disappears, and the second language can be learned only "with a conscious and labored effort" (p. 176). Thus a weak form of the critical period theory is created, assuming two kinds of L2 acquisition, one of which disappears after puberty. Lenneberg's theory may be seen as an elaborated extension of Penfield and Roberts' notion of the mother's method or the direct method versus the school method or the indirect method.

There are, however, important differences. Penfield states that the direct method is possible even in adults, though children are predisposed for it to a higher degree. Penfield, unlike Lenneberg, recognizes the conditioning mechanisms which in interaction with the native bases shape language in the learner. Interestingly, Penfield asserts that there is no association between the ability to imitate an accent and intellectual factors. We will return to that claim when discussing the native dialect impact reported in the present paper.

Andersson (1960) makes a distinction between conditioned and conceptual learning. Explicitly referring to Penfield (Penfield and Roberts, 1959), Andersson states that conditioned learning is equivalent to learning by the direct method while conceptual learning is equivalent to the indirect method. The two types are age-linked, so that, at age 10, conceptual learning outweighs conditioned learning. We will have reason to return to this theory later in the discussion.

Another type of theory are the psychodynamic theories, predicting difficulties in L2 learning after puberty because of too strong superego control.

Authors such as Stengel (1939), Curran (1961), Guiora et al. (1972a, 1972b), Schumann (1975), Peck (1974), Stevick (1975), and others have expanded this type of theory in various ways.

An interesting approach is the thalamus theory (Walz, 1976) which places certain language functions, viz., accent and grammar, in the limbic system, or, more specifically, the thalamus. That there indeed are lateralized thalamic language functions is borne out by clinical experimental research (Penfield and Roberts, 1959; Ojemann and Ward, 1971). According to Walz, the limbic system is "almost fully developed at the age of about four whereas the Non-Limbic System is then still completely underdeveloped" (p. 101). Different parts of language develop separately in different parts of the brain, which will "explain why a child can pick up the accent of a foreign language without difficulty whereas an adult will only do so in exceptional cases" (p. 104).

Oddly enough, very few theories based on developmental psychology seem to have been advanced. One instance is the Piaget-based theory of Rosansky (1975), which states that the restructuring of thought in the formal operations period should be an inhibiting factor for L2 acquisition. Only one hypothesis seems so far to predict an increasing L2 acquisition ability with higher age, viz., that of Toukomaa (1975, 1977), which, however, states that the increasing L2 learning ability is mainly contingent on the L1 development.

The peculiarly unanimous theories of a decline in L2 learning ability are at striking variance with other developmental findings. No studies have ever indicated a decrease in any cognitive capacities around or after puberty. The Piagetian notion of the development of abstract intelligence from early sensory motor experience aims at explaining adult, mature thinking. The last phase of the sequence of periods, from the period of sensory-motor intelligence over the period of perceptual intelligence through the periods of concrete and formal operations, does not constitute a stop for development, nor is it the start of a decline in intelligence. The relationship between child development and adult intelligence is discussed in Chapter 3 of Piaget (1951).

The development of general intelligence as a function of age has been described by Bayley (1955), for the period from birth to 50 years. Intelligence grows rapidly until about 20 years of age. The rate of growth then slows down considerably, but there is still some growth to the age of 50 at least. As Diller (1971) points out, L1 development continues throughout life. This presupposes learning, unless one resorts to the matrix theory of Lenneberg, i.e., development without learning.

Obviously, we must observe the distinction between learning ability and the result of learning, i.e., achievement. Theoretically, as Lenneberg argues in the case of L1, the ability to learn may deteriorate, while something learned during the critical period may continue to develop. However, the ability to learn increases with age for most capacities, i.e., verbal, spatial, logical, or numerical tasks, as shown by a large number of studies, e.g., Northway (1936), Thorndike (1928), McGeoch (1935), Elmgren (1934), McGeoch and Irion (1961), and Newcombe et al. (1977).

Furthermore, as shown by studies by Piaget (1968), Inhelder (1969), and Sinclair-de-Zwart (1969), in addition to the conditioning part, learning has a strong cognitive component which increases with age. For instance, certain reconstruction tasks may be better performed many months after the learning occasion than at the time for learning, without further practice, because of the cognitive development which has taken place between learning and testing. In summary, learning consists of one conditioning component and one cognitive component. The cognitive component changes qualitatively with age. Both components become more efficient with age.

Imitation ability also increases with age, as shown by several studies, many of which have been summarized in a review by Aronfreed (1969). Moreover, perception develops with increasing age, as shown by reviews of experimental evidence (Gibson, 1963, 1969). Thus, in contrast to the second hypothesis of Gorosch and Axelsson and all the related theories, we can forward a developmental hypothesis, stating that L2 learning ability increases with age, unless it be an astounding exception to cognitive, learning, perceptual, and imitative development, in which case it must be either unrelated or negatively related to these abilities.

The present data do not support the second hypothesis and the related optimum age theories. In order to support different varieties, the curves should have a different inflection or a totally different direction from the observed curves. As this is not the case, we must consider the obtained curves as a support for the alternative, developmental hypothesis. This is true for comprehension as well as for pronunciation, for which latter variable the strongest claims for an early optimum have been made.

Further evidence is, however, needed before the developmental hypothesis can be regarded as proved. First, we must see if there are positive relationships between general cognitive and second language variables and between those and learning mechanisms. Second, we need a wider range of starting ages than in the present study. Such evidence is in fact available from different sources. As I have pursued the matter in some detail, I will give some evidence from later studies of my own.

In a later phase of the present study (Ekstrand, 1964, 1978b) we obtained a correlation between intelligence and listening comprehension (picture selection) of $r = .23$ ($N = 192$), intelligence and pronunciation of $r = .40$ ($N = 167$), and comprehension and pronunciation of $r = .47$ ($N = 180$). In a later study of L2 learning in immigrant children (Ekstrand, 1976a), the average intercorrelation between six language tests was $r = .57$ with a range from .43 to .78. In particular, pronunciation intercorrelated with the other five measurements from .50 to .78 (varying Ns from 190 to 1250).

The intercorrelations between these language tests and three intelligence factors (Thuresone's PMA) are given in Table 12 (Ekstrand, 1976a).

The intelligence tests in this study (ibid.) are all nonverbal. From Table 12 it appears that there is a fairly strong nonverbal intelligence component in many language variables. The R-factor test has the strongest relation, on the average, and the S-factor test the weakest. Pronunciation is positively related even to nonverbal measures of intelligence. In contrast to Penfield's notion, pronunciation is positively related to other language variables as well as to intelligence.

Research on the relation between learning and intelligence has also been carried out. For instance, McGeoch and Irion (1961) summarize results from several studies. Meaningful material usually gives rather high (.60-.70) coefficients, while incidental learning and memory span give low (but still positive) coefficients. Intelligence and perceptual-motor learning yield correlations from close to zero to .70, but there are more coefficients below .50 than above (p. 561). Rational learning such as problem solving, reasoning, and inference yields coefficients from very low to .70 or .80. Multiple correlations between intelligence and pooled learning records tend to give more stable correlations. There are large individual variations in learning capacity and rate. No general learning ability can be assumed, but coefficients, whether high or low, are positive, almost without exception. The problems of measurement involved in the assessment of this type of relation tend to combine to yield underestimations of the degree of association.

This general picture seems to be confirmed by somewhat more recent research. Stevenson and Odom (1965) found that verbal learning tasks such as paired associates and anagrams consistently yielded positive coefficients in the range .28 to .57 with verbal as well as nonverbal intelligence for both sexes and various ages, while learning tasks such as concrete or abstract discrimination and concept formation yielded rather low, usually positive coefficients. These

Table 12 Intelligence against Language Variables

	Listening compre- hension	Reading compre- hension	Dictation	Free writing	Pronuncia- tion	Free speaking	$\bar{r}$
DBA 4 (R)	262	256	248	211	116	30	
	.27	.44	.46	.41	.27	.22	.34
DBA 7 (N)	267	261	255	224	46	32	
	.23	.34	.34	.35	.16	.14	.26
DBA 8 (S)	702	399	699	529	146	122	
	.13	.28	.26	.25	.09	.02	.17
$\bar{r}$	.21	.35	.35	.34	.17	.12	
	$\bar{r} = .26$			Range = .02 – .46			

data from more isolated, short-lasting laboratory-type learning studies thus check very well with the complex, long-lasting learning results from field conditions that were given in Table 9.

At the 4th AILA congress in Stuttgart, I presented age curves for the above-mentioned six L2 learning tests and the three nonverbal intelligence tests (Ekstrand, 1976b). With age at testing as age index, I found that L2 learning ability increased in the age range 8 to 17, i.e., far beyond the age where this ability should have decreased, according to all the optimum age theories. If data of birth is used as age index, it will be an index of the age when the testing is done, which also may be expressed as age in years and months. With an extended period of exposure for L2, however, the time for the start of this exposure may be a more sensitive index of a possible optimum.

Various age indices for one typical variable, Dictation (No. 19), are given in Figure 4. All other variables have a similar shape and are presented in Ekstrand (1978b).

As seen in the figure, which shows means of thirds of a year, or years, ± one standard deviation, the first index (A, age at testing) gives a curve which rises all the way from 8 to 17. It is true that the rise is steeper between 8 and 11 (2.5 scale steps) than between 11 and 17 (1 step), but there is no decline around puberty. These are the curves presented in Ekstrand (1976,b).

Age in years on arrival in Sweden for the same pupils gives a somewhat different picture. There seems to be an optimum at age 5 with a decline around age 6 and 7. At age 9, however, this ground is recaptured, and those who arrived at later ages do somewhat better than those who arrived at 4 or 5. This picture is fairly typical for most language and oral reading variables.

However, in these age groups (4 and 5) there are children with a very long period of residence only. Although length of residence has relatively small impact on L2 learning (Ekstrand, 1976b), it cannot be excluded that all of, or part of, this optimum is due to this overrepresentation of children with long residence. Hence, it may be an artifact, and should not be paid heed to until the problem has been further studied (Ekstrand, 1979). The Ramsey and Wright data (1974), which seem strongly to suggest the idea of an optimum before the age of 6, have been refuted by Cummins (1979a, 1979b). A reanalysis showed very long periods of residence in pupils that had arrived at age 6 or earlier. This finding considerably strengthens the hypothesis that long periods of residence may produce tangible effects and therefore must be controlled carefully.

To sum up, general cognitive development, second language learning, basic learning mechanisms, perception, imitation, and social learning all improve with age. They are also positively interrelated. *Thus, there is simply no room for all optimal age and critical period theories which predict a drastic decline in L2 learning ability.* All facts support a developmental theory. On the basis of now existing evidence, I believe that we must accept a developmental theory for second language acquisition. This general trend may be somewhat modified, so that there may be several periods of more powerful language

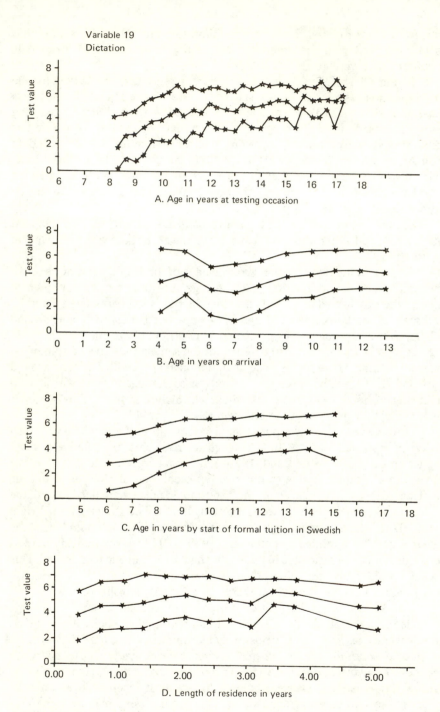

FIGURE 4   Comparisons between various age indexes in L2 acquisition

acquisition with intermittent plateaus. These, so far hypothetical, variations may be related to the brain and mind growth periods as described by Epstein (1974a, 1974b) or to Piagetian periods. The strong forms of the optimum and critical age theories must probably be regarded as belonging to history.

The second rationale

Is the learning set concept applicable on language learning? It seems that this is so: as Clark (1976) has pointed out, referential communication demands a good deal of problem solving from the listener. It seems obvious that the speaker also faces several kinds of problems: the choice of the appropriate thing to say, the choice of which words to use, the choice of the proper grammatical form, etc.

The first phase of the "English without a book" experiments does not really test learning set formation. In an educational setting, the most obvious and technically simplest way to do this is to see if early learning is an advantage for the pupils in later learning situations. In a second phase of this experiment, there were a few differences in favor of the experimental pupils when they were compared with pupils without early L2 experience after 1 year of regular English teaching in grade 5 (Ekstrand, 1964). The differences were small, however, and in other variables there were no differences or even an occasional negative difference. This seemed very disappointing at the time, and the analyses were not pursued further.

After that, a large number of studies of the possible advantages has been launched (see Ekstrand, 1976b, 1978a). The majority of results, especially from the best-designed studies, have confirmed my result from 1964. Early L2 teaching does not seem to yield substantial or lasting positive effects. This is in agreement with all the research on the futility of early training of children and animals (review in Borger and Seaborne, 1966) and the failures of enrichment programs for socioeconomically deprived children (Little and Smith, 1971). It is at variance with the well documented effects of deprived environments on the development of intelligence and language in children (reviews in McCarthy, 1954, and Jones, 1954), with the impact of schooling on intelligence (Husén, 1951b) or with the success of the Milwaukee project (Heber et al., 1972; Garber and Heber, 1974).

We seem to be caught in a paradox. Contributing to this paradox are also the findings of the importance of early learning of learning psychologists (Hebb, 1949) and developmental psychologists (Piaget, 1971) in contrast to the findings of Harlow (Zimmerman and Torrey, 1965) that the formation of learning sets becomes more efficient with age. Perhaps the paradox can be solved when we can identify the critical parameters and specify under which conditions they operate. Possibly compensatory teaching and L2 learning should start very early indeed.

Native dialect and L2 learning

The results concerning the effects on native dialect on pronunciation are unfortunately obscured by the discovery of the comparatively strong cognitive component in pronunciation (cf. p. 16). City 1 (Linköping) belongs to a dialectally characteristic area. It is not at all unlikely that this dialect is a disadvantage for the pronunciation of English. Method 2, which is a contrastive analysis by means of psychophysical ratings, yields a statistically significant indication, while the same tendency fails to reach significance with method 1.

With both methods a statistically significant rural/urban difference appears. As the mean intelligence is lower in rural areas, because of overrepresentation of occupations of a low educational level and also other factors (Husén, 1951b), the possibility that differences between cities 1 and 2 are due to intelligence differences cannot be excluded. This is not likely, however. The contrastive method is more sensitive to the differences between urban dialectal areas than the category rating method, which suggests that dialect is the major differentiating variable. It is furthermore unlikely that there would be major intellectual differences between the city samples.

No checks were done at the time, however. More definite conclusions would require careful analyses of rural/urban and dialectal differences with the pronunciation measures as well as with comprehension and with a design which takes care of intelligence as well as possible interactions, e.g., a two-way analysis of covariance. For the time being we will have to leave it at that, unfortunately.

The interesting thing is that the need for a control of cognitive factors is due to a fairly strong cognitive component in the acquisition of pronunciation. This is at variance with the claim of Penfield and Roberts (1959), but in agreement with the conclusions of Jenkins (1972) that the acquisition of pronunciation is a complicated procedure, far more complex than simple S-R conditioning.

REFERENCES

Andersson. T. The optimum age for beginning the study of modern languages. *International Review of Education*. 1960, 6, 298–306.

Aronfreed, J. The problem of imitation. In Lipsitt, Hayne, and Reese (eds.), *Advances in Child Development and Behavior*. New York: Academic Press, 1969, 210–319.

Asher, J. J. Children's first language as a model for second language learning. *Modern Language Journal*. 1972, 56, 133–139.

Bailey, N., Madden, C., and Krashen, S. D. Is there a "natural sequence" in adult second language learning? *Language Learning*, 1974, 24, 235–243.

Bayley, N. On the growth of intelligence. *American Psychologist*. 1955, 10, 805–818.

Borger, R., and Seaborne, A. E. *The Psychology of Learning*. Harmondsworth, Middlesex, England: Penguin Books, 1966.

Burstall, C. Factors affecting foreign-language learning: A consideration of some recent research findings. *Language Teaching and Linguistics Abstracts*, 1975, 8 (1), 5–25.

Clark, H. H. Inferring what is meant. Paper presented at the 21st International Congress of Psychology, Paris, 1976.

Cummins, J. Age on arrival and immigrant second language learning: a reanalysis of the Ramsey and Wright data. Unpublished manuscript, 1979a.

Cummins, J. The cross-lingual dimensions of language proficiency: implications for immigrant language learning and bilingual education. Unpublished manuscript, 1979b.

Curran, C. A. Counseling skills adapted to the learning of foreign languages. *Bulletin of the Menninger Clinic*, 1961, 25, 78–93.

Diller, K. C. "Compound" and "coordinate" bilingualism: a conceptual artifact. *Word*. 1970, 26, 254–261.

Diller, K. C. *Generative Grammar, Structural Linguistics, and Language Teaching*. Rowley, Mass.: Newbury House, 1971.

Donoghue, M. R. A rationale for FLES. *French Review*, 1964, 38, 525–529.

Doyé, P., and Lüttge, D. Der Braunschweiger Schulversuch "Frühbeginn des Englischunterrichts" (FEU). In Kieslich and Klages (eds.), *Englisch im Primarbereich*. (manuscript, 1975.

Dulay, H. C., and Burt, M. K., Goofing: An indicator of children's second language learning strategies. *Language Learning*, 1972, 22, 235–252.

Dulay, H. C., and Burt, M.K. Should we teach children syntax? *Language Learning*. 1973, 23, 245–248.

Dulay, H. C., and Burt, M. K. Natural sequences in child second language acquisition. *Language Learning*. 1974a, 24, 37–53.

Dulay, H. C., and Burt, M. K. Errors and strategies in child second language acquisition. *TESOL Quarterly*. 1974b, 8, (2), 129–136.

Dulay, H. C., and Burt, M. K. A new perspective on the creative construction process in child second language acquisition. *Working papers on bilingualism,* no. 4, 1974c, ERIC: ED 123 877.

Ekman, G. *Testmetodik*. /Test methodology./ Stockholm: Almqvist & Wiksell, 1957.

Ekstrand, L. H. *Prov i Engelska utan bok*. / Testing English without a book. / Stockholm: National Board of Education, 1959. Stenciled.

Ekstrand, L. H. *Språkfärdigheter och språkmetodik*. / Language skills and teaching techniques. / Stockholm: University & Board of Education, 1964. Stenciled.

Ekstrand, L. H. Adjustment among immigrant pupils in Sweden. *International Review of Applied Psychology*. 1976a, 25 (3).

Ekstrand, L. H. Age and length of residence as variables related to the adjustment of immigrant children, with special reference to second language learning. In Nickel, G. (ed.), *Proceedings of the Fourth International Congress of Applied Linguistics*. Stuttgart: Hochschul-Verlag, 1976b.

Ekstrand, L. H. Social and individual frame factors in second language learning: comparative aspects. In Skutnabb-Kangas, T. (ed.), *Papers from the first Nordic conference on bilingualism*. Helsingfors: Universitetet, 1977.

Ekstrand, L. H. Bilingual and bicultural adaptation. University of Stockholm: Institute of International Education, 1978. Reprinted in *Educational and Psychological Interactions* (Malmö, Sweden: School of Education), no. 66, 1978a.

Ekstrand, L. H. *Towards an integration of the optimal age and developmental theories in second language acquisition*. Paper presented at the XIX:th International Congress of Applied Psychology, Munich, 1978b.

Ekstrand, L. H. Replacing the critical period and optimum age theories of second language acquisition with a theory of ontogenetic development beyond puberty. Educational and Psychological Interactions (Malmö, Sweden: School of Education), no. 69, December 1979.

Ellegård, A. *Språk, språkvetenskap och språkinlärning*. / Language, language science and learning learning. / Stockholm: Aldus/Bonniers, 1971.

Elmgren, J. *Minnets funktion, struktur och utveckling*. / Functioning, structure and development of memory. / Gothenburg: Gumperts, 1934.

Epstein, H. T. Phrenoblysis: special brain and mind growth periods. I. Human brain and skull development. *Developmental Psychobiology*, 1974a, 7, (3), 207–216.

Epstein, H. T. Phrenoblysis: special brain and mind growth periods. II. Human development. *Developmental Psychobiology*, 1974b, 7, (3), 217–224.

Eriksson, K.-H., and Ekstrand, L. H. Språkpedagogik och psykofysik. / Language teaching and psycho-physics. / *Nordisk tidskrift för pedagogik*, 1962, 6 (4), 90–124.

Ervin, S. M., and Osgood, C. E. (eds.) Second language learning and bilingualism. In Osgood, C. E., and Sebeok, T. A. *Psycholinguistics*. Bloomington: Indiana University Press, 1965, 139–146.

Garber, H., and Heber, R. *The Milwaukee Project*. Paper presented at the 18th International Congress of Applied Psychology, Montreal, 1974.

Garvie, E. M. The Urdu-speaking immigrant's learning of English morphology. A comparison of first language acquisition and second-language learning. Paper presented at the 3rd AILA Congress, Copenhagen, 1973.

Gibson, E. J. Perceptual development. In Stevenson, H. W., Kagan, J., and Spiker, C. (eds.), *Child Psychology*. Chicago: University Press, 1963, 144–195.

Gibson, E. *Principles of Perceptual Learning and Development*. New York: Appleton-Century-Crofts, 1969.

Gorosch, M. *English without a Book. A Bilingual Experiment in Primary Schools by Audiovisual Means*. Preliminary report. University of Stockholm, 1960. Stenciled.

Gorosch, M., and Axelsson, C.-A. *English without a Book. A Bilingual Experiment in Primary Schools by Audiovisual Means*. Berlin: Cornelsen Verlag, 1962, 1964.

Guiora, A. Z., Brannon, R. C. L., and Dull, C. Y. Empathy and second language learning. *Language Learning*. 1972a, 22, 111–130.

Guiora, A. Z., Beit-Hallahmi, B., Brannon, R. L. C., Dull, C. Y., and Scovel, T. The effects of experimentally induced changes in ego states on pronunciation ability in a second language: An exploratory study. *Comprehensive Psychiatry*. 1972b, 13, 421–2428.

Hansen-Bede, L. A child's creation of a second language. *Working papers on bilingualism*, no. 6, 1975. Ontario Institute for Studies in Education, Toronto. (ERIC: ED 125 257.)

Harlow, H. F. The formation of learning sets. *Psychological Review*. 1949, 56, 51–56.

Hebb, D. O. *Organization of Behavior*. New York: Wiley, 1949. Paperback edition. New York: Science Editions, 1961.

Heber, R., Garber, H., Harrington, S., Hoffman, D., and Falender, C. *Rehabilitation of Families at Risk for Mental Retardation*. Madison, Wisconsin: University of Wisconsin, Waisman Center, 1972.

Husén, T. *Begåvning och miljö*. Stockholm: Gebers, 1951a.

Husén, T. The influence of schooling upon IQ. *Theoria*. 1951b, 17, 61–88.

Inhelder, B. Memory and intelligence in the child. In Elkind, D., and Flavell, J. H. (eds.), *Studies in Cognitive Development*. Oxford University Press, 1969, 337–364.

Jenkins, J. J. *Effect of Age, Native Language and Instruction on Speech Sound Discrimination*. Washington, D.C.: U.S. Department of Health, Education and Welfare, 1972 (mimeographed). (ERIC: ED 067 964.)

Jones, H. E. The environment and mental development. In Carmichael, L. (ed.), *Manual of Child Psychology*, 2d ed. New York: Wiley, 1954.

Krashen, S. D., Sferlazza, V., Feldman, L., and Fathman, A. Adult performance on the SLOPE test: more evidence for a natural sequence in adult second language acquisition. *Language Learning*. 1976, 26 (1), 145–151.

Lenneberg, E. *Biological Foundations of Language*. New York: Wiley, 1967.

Little, A., and Smith, G. *Strategies of Compensation: A Review of Projects for the Disadvantaged in the United States*. Paris: OECD, 1971.

Macnamara, J. Comparisons between first and second language learning. *Working papers on bilingualism*. September 1975. (ERIC: ED 125 265.)

Malmberg, B. *Språkinlärning*. / Language learning. / Stockholm: Aldus/Bonniers, 1971.

Malmberg, B. Språkundervisningen leder till språkförbistring. / The language teaching produces language confusion. / *Sydsvenska Dagbladet*, October 13, 1977.

McCarthy, D. Language development in children. In Carmichael, L. (ed.), *Manual of Child Psychology*, 2d ed. New York: Wiley, 1954.

McGeoch, G. The age factor in reminiscence: a comparative study of preschool children and college students. *Journal of Genetic Psychology*. 1935, 47, 98–120.

McGeoch, J. A., and Irion, A. L. *The Psychology of Human Learning*. New York: David McKay Company, 1961.

Newcombe, N., Rogoff, B., and Kagan, J. Developmental changes in recognition memory for pictures of objects and scenes. *Developmental Psychology*. 1977, 13 (4), 337–341.

Northway, M. L. The influence of age and social group on children's remembering. *British Journal of Psychology*. 1936, 27, 11–29.

Ojemann, G. A., and Ward, A. A. Speech representation in ventrolateral thalamus. *Brain*. 1971, 94, 669–680.

Parker, S., Kleiner, R. J., and Needelman, B. Migration and mental illness. *Social Science and Medicine*. 1969, 3, 1–9.

Peck, E. C. The relationship of disease and other stress to second language. *International Journal of Social Psychology*. 1974, 20, 123–144.

Penfield, W., and Roberts, L. *Speech and Brain Mechanisms*. Princeton: Princeton University Press, 1959.

Piaget, J. *La psychologie de l'intelligence*. / The psychology of intelligence. / Paris: Armand Colin, 1951. Swedish edition: Intelligensens psykologi. Malmö: Natur och Kultur, 1971.

Piaget, J. *On the Development of Memory and Identity*. Barre, Mass.: Clark University Press and The Barre Publishing Company, 1968.

Rado, M. Intra- and interlinguistic contrast: Bilingual education in Australia. *Working Papers on Bilingualism*, no. 7, 1975. (ERIC: ED 125 256.)

Ramsey, C. A., and Wright, E. N. Age and second language learning. *The Journal of Social Psychology*. 1974, 94, 115–121.

Rosansky, E. J. The critical period for the acquisition of language: Some cognitive developmental considerations. *Working Papers on Bilingualism*, no. 6, 1975. Toronto: Ontario Institute for Studies in Education. (ERIC: ED 125 256.)

Schumann, J. H. Affective factors and the problem of age in second language acquisition. *Language Learning*. 1975, 25 (2), 209–235.

Siegel, S. *Nonparametric Statistics*. New York: McGraw-Hill, 1956.

Sinclair-de-Zwart, H. Developmental psycholinguistics. In Elkind, D., and Flavell, J. H. (eds.), *Studies in Cognitive Development*. London: Oxford University Press, 1969, 315–364.

Skutnabb-Kangas, T., and Toukomaa, P. Teaching migrant children's mother tongue and learning the language of the host country in the context of the socio-cultural situation of the migrant family. *Research Reports* (Tampere, Finland: University, Department of Sociology and Social Psychology), no. 15, 1976.

Snow, C. E. Semantic primacy in first and second language acquisition. *Interlanguage Studies Bulletin*, 1976, 1 (2).

Stengel, E. On learning a new language. *International Journal of Psycho-analysis*, 1939, 20, 471–479.

Stern, H. H. *Foreign Languages in Primary Education: The Teaching of Foreign or Second Languages to Younger Children*. Hamburg: UNESCO Institute for Education, 1963.

Stevensen, H. W., and Odom, R. D. Interrelationships in children's learning. *Child Development*. 1965, 36, 7–19.

Stevick, E. W. One simple visual aid: a psychodynamic view. *Language Learning*. 1975, 25 (1), 63–72.

Thorndike, E. L., Bergman, E. O., Tilton, J. W., and Woodyard, E. *Adult Learning*. New York: Macmillan, 1928.

Toukomaa, P. *Om finska invandrarelevers språkutveckling och skolframgång i den dvenska grundskolan*. / On the language development and school progress of Finnish immigrant pupils in the Swedish comprehensive school. / Paper presented at the Nordic seminar on language politics, Helsingfors, 1975.

Toukomaa, P., and Skutnabb-Kangas, T. The intensive teaching of the mother tongue to migrant children at pre-school age. *Research Reports* (Tampere, Finland: University, Department of Sociology and Social Psychology), no. 26 1977.

Walz, H. P. The human brain as the source of linguistic behavior. In Nickel, G. (ed.), *Proceedings of the Fourth International Congress of Applied Linguistics*, Stuttgart: Hochschul-Verlag, 1976.

Zimmerman, R., and Torrey, C. C. Ontogeny of learning. In Schrier, A. M., Harlow, H. F., and Stollnitz, F. (eds.), *Behavior of Non-human Primates*. New York: Academic Press.

IV

SOME GENERALIZATIONS

Our contribution to the question of age and second language attainment and rate is presented here. This paper summarizes the empirical literature available to us, and concludes that in spite of methodological differences, all studies of this issue reach remarkably similar conclusions. These conclusions, as the reader has surely noticed, have influenced the organization of this volume.

1. Adults proceed through early stages of syntactic and morphological development faster than children (where time and exposure are held constant).

2. Older children acquire faster than younger children (again, in early stages of morphological and syntactic development where time and exposure are held constant).

3. Acquirers who begin natural exposure to second languages during childhood generally achieve higher levels of second language proficiency than those beginning as adults.

Our paper takes up some other related issues as well. First, if the above generalizations are valid, younger children must eventually catch up to older children in second language attainment, since both groups are known to reach high levels of second language proficiency (we are not necessarily claiming that all child second language acquirers reach nativelike levels, although many appear to, as described in Seliger et al., section I). Also, children as a group will catch up to, and surpass, most adults. Our paper discusses how long this catch-up process may take, basing its conclusions on the empirical data provided by other reports reprinted in this volume, especially Snow and Hoefnagel-Höhle's work.

We also hypothesize that the catch-up rate for syntax and phonology may be different, a hypothesis that may explain an apparent discrepancy in the literature: Fathman (1975, Section III) found younger children to be superior to older children in pronunciation but not in syntax, while other studies, such as Ervin-Tripp (1974) find older children to be superior in all skills.

We briefly discuss the literature on FLES (Foreign Language in the Elementary School) as it relates to the age issue, specifically the finding that children who begin FLES programs at older ages attain levels similar to those of children who had started earlier. This could also be a manifestation of generalization 2 above.

13

AGE, RATE, AND EVENTUAL ATTAINMENT IN SECOND LANGUAGE ACQUISITION[1]

Stephen D. Krashen
University of Southern California

Michael H. Long
University of Pennsylvania

Robin C. Scarcella
University of Southern California

One popular belief about second language acquisition is that younger is better, that younger acquirers are better at second language acquisition than older acquirers. Recently, certain research reports claim to counter this early sensitivity hypothesis; several of these papers imply that the literature on age and language acquisition is inconsistent, some showing older, others showing younger performers to be superior (Walburg, Hase, and Pinzur Rasher, 1978; McLaughlin, 1977). The purpose of this brief comment is to demonstrate that the available literature is consistent with three generalizations concerning the relationship between age, rate, and eventual attainment in second language acquisition: (1) Adults proceed through early stages of syntactic and morphological development faster than children (where time and exposure are held constant), (2) Older children acquire faster than younger children (again, in early stages of syntactic and morphological development where time and exposure are held constant), (3) Acquirers who begin natural exposure to second languages during childhood generally achieve higher second language proficiency than those beginning as adults.

In other words, adults and older children in general initially acquire[2] the second language faster than young children (older is better for rate of acquisition), but child second language acquirers will usually be superior in terms of ultimate attainment (younger is better in the long run). Distinguishing rate and attainment, then, resolves the apparent contradictions in the literature.

In order to provide support for these generalizations, we examined investigations of child-adult differences in long-term and short-term studies which compare children and adults acquiring second languages in informal, natural environments, as well as formal, classroom environments.

INVESTIGATIONS OF EVENTUAL ATTAINMENT: LONG-TERM STUDIES

There have been surprisingly few studies investigating child-adult differences in eventual attainment in second language acquisition. The available studies all concur, however, that age of arrival in the country where the language is spoken is the best predictor of eventual attainment: (1) those who arrive as children attain higher levels of second language proficiency, and (2) after a certain period (see discussion below) length of residence (where length of residence taps linguistic interaction/input) is not a factor (see Table 1)[3,4]

INVESTIGATIONS OF RATE: SHORT-TERM STUDIES

Comparisons of Adult/Child Differences. The short-term studies comparing children and adults (see Table 2) show adults to be superior to children in rate. Treatment or length of residency in these studies varies from 25 minutes (Asher and Price, 1969), and extremely short exposure time, to 1 year (Snow and Hoefnagel-Höhle, 1978a). (Compare this with Oyama's 1976 study in which the length of residence varied from 5 to 18 years.) Interestingly, in Snow and Hoefnagel-Höhle (1978a), adults, while clearly superior to young children in morphology and syntax, did not do better than the 12- to 15-year-olds. Snow and Hoefnagel-Höhle suggest that the different sorts of linguistic experience the groups received affected the results of their study.

Comparisons of Older and Younger Child Second Language Acquirers. The short-term studies which compare older and younger children consistently show older children to be faster learners of syntax and morphology when the duration of the exposure to the second language is similar, whether the exposure to the second language is in natural (as in Table 3) or formal environments (as in Table 4).

The generalizations given here imply that younger acquirers catch up to older acquirers and, in the case of children compared with adults, eventually surpass them. The literature allows us to make some preliminary generalizations about the amount of time this catch-up process takes. For morphology and syntax, children apparently surpass adults in about 1 year. Snow and Hoefnagel-Höhle (1978b) report that their 8- to 10-year-old subjects surpassed adult acquirers of Dutch after 1 year on nearly all measures of syntax and morphology, and the 6- to 7-year-olds surpassed the adults on some measures, including speech fluency. Younger children may take a little longer to catch up to older children. The 6- to 10-year-olds in Snow and Hoefnagel-Höhle's study had still not caught up to the 12- to 15-year-old group after 1 year. We assume both groups eventually attain native or near-native proficiency with continued interactions in Dutch.[4,5] Also, in Fathman (1975), older children (11 to 15) maintained a slight superiority in syntax over 6- to 10-year-olds even after 3 years in the country. (This difference may not have been statistically significant, however.)[6]

A separate class of studies compares children who begin the study of second languages in formal circumstances at different ages (for example, foreign language in the elementary school, FLES, beginning at age 8 is compared with FLES at age 11). The results of such studies usually indicate that children starting FLES later catch up to those beginning earlier. For instance, Burstall's 1975 study, involving several thousand children studying French in elementary schools, essentially reports no differences in French attainment between those starting French at ages 8 and 11 and those starting French at age 16. Similar results have been reported in other studies, summarized in Table 5.

This finding could be considered consistent with generalization 2 (that older children acquire faster than younger children); the younger children in these studies acquired at a so much slower pace than the older children that extra time counted for very little. Other explanations are also possible. For example, in Oller and Nagoto's (1974) study, those who had early FLES were mixed in with those who had no FLES; thus the early starters may have had to mark time (p. 18) while the others caught up.[7]

DISCUSSION

The literature provides no evidence which is seriously inconsistent with any of the above generalizations. Walburg et al. showed that language proficiency of children of Japanese businessmen was directly related to time in the United States and not the age of arrival, a finding which Walburg et al. consider to be counter to the "optimal age hypothesis." Their study is not even potentially in conflict with generalizations 1 and 3, however, since no adults were actually involved in the study. Subjects' ages at the time of testing ranged from 6 to 15, and most had been in the United States a range from 0 to 12 years.

Although the study by Walburg et al. differs from others in failing to find a superiority for older versus younger children, there are several possible reasons for this. One is the measures used (self-report and teacher report). Karl Diller has pointed out to us that teacher ratings in this study focused on how the subjects compared with American students at their grade level in English (reading, writing, vocabulary, and "the expression of facts, concepts, and feelings"; p. 433). The data are thus consistent with the hypothesis that older children are faster, since they reached grade level in the same amount of time as did the younger children. (See also Walburg et al., footnote 1, p. 436.) Note also that most subjects had been in the United States "three to four years" and some as long as 12 years; there thus may have been enough time for younger children to have caught up to the older children.

To conclude, the available literature is consistent with the generalizations presented earlier. Any hypothesis dealing with the relationship between age, rate, and eventual attainment in second language acquisition needs to account for the data from the variety of studies presented here, as does any general theory of language acquisition. Moreover, any educational decisions pertaining to second language learning and teaching (e.g., FLES, bilingual education) must also consider all the empirical evidence.

Table 1 Child-Adult Differences in Eventual Attainment in Second Language Acquisition

Study	Ages compared[a]	n	L1	L2	Measures	Results
Asher and Garcia, 1969	1–6 7–12 13–19	19 37 15	Spanish	English	Sentence pronunciation task, judged by junior high school students	1- to 6-year-old arrivals were closer to native speaker level; 13- to 19-year-old arrivals were farthest. Those in the United States 1 to 4 years were better than those in the United States 5 to 8 years
Seliger, Krashen, and Ladefoged, 1975	Below 10 10–15 Over 16	91 100 173	Varies	English, Hebrew	Self-report[b]	Below 10: most (85%) report no accent 10–15: 50% report accent, 50% report no accent Over 16: 92% report accent No effect for years lived in country[c]
Oyama, 1976	6–20	60	Italian	English	Read paragraph, tell anecdote (rated for accent)	Correlation for accent and age of arrival in the United States ($r = -.83$[d]) No correlation for accent and years in the United States ($r = -.02$[e])
Oyama, 1978	6–20	60	Italian	English	Sentence through noise task	Correlation for LC and age of arrival ($r = -.57$[f]) No significant correlation for LC and years in the United States ($r = -.17$[g])

Table 1 *(continued)*

Study	Ages compared[a]	n	L1	L2	Measures	Results
Patkowski (Section I)	5–50	67	Varies	English	Syntactic ratings of transcripts of speech	Correlation for ratings and age of arrival in United States ($r = -.74$)

[a]Age of arrival in country, *not* age when tested. (Age when tested = 7 to 19)

[b]Subjects were asked, "Do you think most ordinary Americans (Israelis) could tell now that you are not a native speaker of English (Hebrew)?"

[c]Comparisons done with the "no accent," 10 to 15 group only, mean years = 5; SD = 11.5; "accent group" mean = 20.6; SD = 19.4. (Reported in Krashen and Seliger, 1975.)

[d]Partial correlation, with years in the United States partialed out (paragraph reading score only).

[e]Partial correlation, with age of arrival partialed out (paragraph reading score only).

[f]Partial correlation, with years in the United States partialed out.

[g]Partial correlation, with age of arrival, actual age, partialed out.

Generalizations: 1. All studies agree that those who arrive as children attain higher levels of proficiency than those who arrive as adults.

2. Length of residence is not a factor for long-term stays (over 5 years?).

Table 2   Children vs. Adults in Rate of Second Language Acquisition

Study	Duration	n	L2*	Ages compared	Treatment	Measures	Results
Asher and Price, 1969	25 minutes	134	Russian	Adult (college) 8-, 10-, 12-year-olds	Total physical response (TPR) teaching	TPR	Adults outperformed all child groups
Olson and Samuels, 1973	10 sessions	100	German	Adult (19–26) Junior high (14–15) Elementary (9.5–10.5)	"Phoneme drills"	Pronunciation	Adults = junior high Adults and junior high students superior to elementary students
Snow and Hoefnagel-Höhle, 1978a	1 month–1 year	96	Dutch	3- to 15-year-olds Adults	Natural exposure	Pronunciation, morphology, imitation, translation	12 to 15 best for morphology; adults next best followed by the 8- to 10-year-olds. Differences diminish over time
Snow and Hoefnagel-Höhle, 1977	1 session	136	Dutch	5–31	Imitate 5 nonsense words, repeated 20 times	Pronunciation	Linear increase in pronunciation according to age

*In all cases, L1 = English.

Generalization: Adults are faster than small children, but not always better than 12- to 15-year-olds in early stages of morphology and syntax development.

Table 3 Studies of Child Second Language Acquisition (Older vs. Younger) Informal Environments with Similar Length of Exposure

Study	Time of residence	n	L2	Ages*	Measures	Results
Ekstrand, 1976	Up to 2 years†	2189	Swedish	8–17	Listening comprehension, reading, free writing, pronunciation, speaking	Older children did better than younger children Linear relationship with age
Fathman, 1975	1–3 years	200	English	6–15	SLOPE test, picture description	11- to 15-year-olds superior to 6- to 10-year-olds for morphology and syntax. 6- to 10-year-olds better for pronunciation (see note 5)
Snow and Hoefnagel-Höhle, 1978a	1 month–1 year	Approximately 90	Dutch	3–15	Pronunciation, morphology, imitation, translation	12- to 15-year-olds best for morphology and syntax; 8- to 10-year-olds next best. Differences diminish over time, (strongest at 1–3 months)
Ervin-Tripp, 1974	Maximum of 9 months	31	French	4–9	Comprehension (acting out)	Older children superior for syntax, morphology, and pronunciation; 7- to 9-year-olds superior to 4- to 6-year-olds

*Age at which children were tested, *not* age of arrival in new country.

†"Only 8.3% of the pupils have a longer LOR (length of residence) than two years" (Ekstrand, 1976, p. 190).

Generalization: In all cases, older children acquire early syntax and morphology faster than younger children.

Table 4 Comparisons of Studies of Child Second Language Acquisition (Older vs. Younger)* Formal or Experimental Environments with Similar Treatments

Study	Duration	n	L2	Grades/Ages	Treatment	Measures	Results
Ekstrand, 1978	18 weeks	335	English	Grades 3, 4, 5 (ages 8–11)	"Audiovisual"	Imitation, listening comprehension (LC) translation	Older children better than younger children: Linear relationship between age and second language learning
Asher and Price, 1969	25 minutes	96	Russian	Grades 8, 10, 14	Total physical response (TPR)	TPR	14-year-olds best, tend to be better than 8-year-olds
Olson and Samuels, 1973	10 sessions	80	German	Ages 9.5–10.5; 14–15	"Phoneme drills"	Pronunciation	14 to 15 group superior to 9.5–10.5 group
Florander and Jansen, 1979	80 hours; 320 hours	300–400	English	Grades 4–6	EFL	Grammar, vocabulary, reading, LC	Grade 6 superior to younger groups. Difference lessens after 320 hours
Grinder, Otomo, and Toyota, 1962	1 year	148	Japanese	Grades 2–4	Audiolingual	Vocabulary, LC, pronunciation	Strong relationship between grade (age) and LC, some pronunciation; trend for older students to excel in vocabulary

*See also Snow and Hoefnagel-Höhle, 1977, Table Two.
Generalization: In all cases, older children acquire faster than younger children.

Table 5 Child Second Language Studies: Formal Environments with Dissimilar Amounts of Exposure (Older Children Catch-up Studies)

Study	Ages/Grades Compared	n	L1	L2	Measures	Results
Burstall, 1975	Starting FLES at age 8 vs. starting at age 11	Approx. 17,000	English	French		At age 16, no difference (except in LC)* group starting at age 8 = groups starting at age 11
Bland and Keisler, 1966	Kindergarten vs. grade 5	4, 6	English	French	Oral production	Fifth graders took less time to reach criterion (4.5 hours vs. 12.5–17.5 hours)
Oller and Nagato, 1974	Grades 7, 8, and 9; one group had FLES in grades 1–6; the other did not	233	Japanese	English	Cloze	+FLES superior to −FLES at grade 7; less difference at grade 9; no difference at grade 11
Ramirez and Politzer, 1978	ESL/BE starting in junior high school vs. ESL/BE starting in kindergarten	21, 46	Spanish	English	LC production	After 1/2 year, junior high school students nearly at grade 3 level
Vocolo, 1967	"Second year high school French," tenth graders with 1 year high school French vs. ninth graders with 4 years FLES (grades 5–8)	31, 31	English	French	MLCT	4 years FLES group only slightly better than group with 1 year of high school French

*Abbreviations:
FLES = Foreign Language in the Elementary School
LC = Listening Comprehension
BE = Bilingual Education
MLCT = Modern Language Cooperative Test
Generalization: FLES studies show that older children catch up to children who have had earlier FLES.

NOTES

1. We thank Eugène Brière, Karl Diller, and Melilnda Krasch for their helpful comments.

2. Here, we do not distinguish "learn" and "acquire," making no claim as to whether conscious language *learning* or unconscious language *acquisition* is involved.

3. This generalization is true only if acquirers who begin second language acquisition as children continue to have sufficient exposure to the second language. Karl Diller has pointed out to us that many people use languages as children but have only minimal competence in them in later years, owing to a lack of high-quality exposure.

4. Since the earliest papers to appear in this category dealt with pronunciation, several scholars hypothesized that children are superior to adults only for this aspect of linguistic competence. Oyama's and Patkowski's work, however, makes it clear that this superiority extends to other parts of language. Patkowski's analysis confirms that those starting as children are not ultimately better simply because they have had more input than those starting later in life. Patkowski partialed out the contributions of both amount of informal exposure and formal instruction, and still found a clear negative correlation between syntactic proficiency and age ($r = -.72; p < .001$).

5. But see comments in Snow and Hoefnagel-Höhle (1977), p. 363 (this volume, page 84). They note that in testing their subjects 18 months after first contact with Dutch, "all but one teen-ager still had English accents. This inability to achieve native-like pronunciation was as true of the younger subjects as of the adults. . . .". This assessment agrees with that of the judges in Asher and Garcia (this volume), who did not award a single rating of "no accent" to any of the subjects they heard, despite the fact that many had come to the United States as children and had been there for many years. It disagrees with Seliger, Krashen, and Ladefoged's self-report data (also this volume). Thus, the question of whether children actually do achieve nativelike control of a second language, or how many do, still remains open.

6. Several studies also report that older children acquire phonological competence (pronunciation) faster than younger children (Ervin-Tripp, 1974; Ekstrand, 1976, for example). Snow and Hoefnagel-Höhle (1977) report that the ability to imitate nonsense words in a second language increases linearly with age, using subjects 5 to 31. Fathman (1975), however, reports that her younger subjects were superior to her older subjects. This difference may be due to the different age groups studied (Ervin-Tripp compared 7- to 9- with 4- to 6-year-olds, Ekstrand's sample consisted of 8- to 11-year-olds, while Fathman compared 11- to 15-year-olds with 6- to 10-year-olds) or length of exposure; Fathman's subjects were in the United States from 1 to 3 years while maximum length of exposure for Ervin-Tripp's subjects was 9 months. As we have seen earlier, it may take quite a while for syntax in younger children to catch up to the level attained by older children. Phonological competence, however, may catch up very rapidly. Snow and Hoefnagel-Höhle (1977) report that "age differences (in pronunciation of Dutch as a second language) disappeared by 4 to 5 months after starting to learn the second language . . . by 10 to 11 months . . . the younger children excelled in pronouncing some sounds, though there was still no overall age difference" (p. 357).

Thus, the younger children in Fathman's study may have caught up with and (temporarily) surpassed the older children in pronunciation. In Ervin-Tripp's study, there may not have been enough time for this to have taken place. Asher and Garcia, however, report that their subjects who were in the United States from 5 to 8 years outperformed those in the United States 1 to 4 years on their pronunciation task. This result implies that acquisition of phonology may take somewhat longer. Further research may settle this issue.

7. Two very recent studies appear to provide counterevidence to the hypothesis that older acquirers' rate superiority extends to pronunciation and vocabulary. Yamada, Takatsuka, Kotabe, and Kurusu (1980) tested 30 children, ages 7 to 11, who were native speakers of Japanese, and who had had no previous contact with English. The subjects were asked to learn concrete, one- or two-syllable English nouns in two sessions. Subjects were shown a picture representing each noun two times and then asked to repeat the nouns. They then attempted to produce each word ten times and were told if their attempt was correct. Yamada et al. report that mean learning scores

significantly *decreased* with age; i.e., younger children learned the words faster. Yamada et al. also had the impression that the younger children's pronunciation was superior. Tahta, Wood, and Loewenthal (forthcoming) report similar results in an experiment in which English-speaking children ages 5 to 15 were asked to repeat words in French and Armenian. Each word was presented only once. Younger children were judged to be more accurate in pronunciation. These studies differ from the others cited here in that the exposure time in both cases was extremely brief; in Yamada et al., only four models were presented, and in Tahta et al. only one model was presented for each word. (Note that in the study with the shortest exposure time in Tables 2 to 4, subjects were given 20 different exposures to the stimuli; Snow and Hoefnagel-Höhle, 1977; differences between age groups were evident, however, after the first 10 presentations. See page 84, this volume.) There are several possible reasons for this outcome. One may be that the paucity of input may have prevented subjects from fully utilizing their language acquisition capacities. Thus, Yamada et al. and Tahta et al.'s results may really show us the younger child's superiority for rote memorization and mimicry, rather than true language acquisition. Another possibility is that older children's superiority emerges only when their superior conversational management abilities help them obtain more comprehensible input (Scarcella and Higa, this volume).

REFERENCES

Asher, J., and García, R. The optimal age to learn a foreign language. *Modern Language Journal.* 1969, 8, 334–341.

Asher, J., and Price B. The learning strategy of total physical response: Some age differences *Child Development.* 1969, 38, 1219–1227.

Bland, M., and Keisler, E. A self-controlled audio-lingual program for children. *French Review.* 1966, 40, 266–276.

Burstall, C. Primary French in the balance. *Educational Research.* 1975, 17, June, 193–198.

Ekstrand, L. Age and length of residence as variables related to the adjustment of migrant children, with special reference to second language learning. In G. Nickel (ed.), Proceedings of the Fourth International Congress of Applied Linguistics. vol. 3. Stuttgart. Hochshul-Verlag, 1976, 179–197.

Ekstrand, L. Bilingual and bicultural adaptation. *Education and Psychological Interactions.* Department of Educational and Psychological Research. School of Education, Malmo, Sweden. 1978, 66.

Ervin-Tripp, S. Is second language learning like the first? *TESOL Quarterly*, 1974, 8, 2, 111–127.

Fathman, A. The relationship between age and second language learning productive ability. *Language Learning.* 1975, 25, 2.

Florander, J., and Jansen, M. 1969. Skoleforsøg i engelsk 1959–1965. Ms. Denmark's Institute of Education.

Grinder, R., Otomo, A., and Toyota, W. Comparisons between second, third, and fourth grade children in the audio-lingual learning of Japanese as a second language. *The Journal of Educational Research.* 1962, 56, 4, 463–469.

Krashen, S., and Seliger, H. Maturational constraints in the acquisition of a second language and a second dialect. *Language Sciences.* 1975, 38, 28–29.

McLaughlin, B. Second language learning in children. *Psychological Bulletin.* 1977, 84, 435–457.

Oller, J., and Nagoto, The long term effect of FLES. *The Modern Language Journal.* 1974, 58, 1–2, 15–19.

Olson, L, and Samuels, S. The relationship between age and accuracy of foreign language pronunciation. *Journal of Educational Research.* 1973, 66, 263–267.

Oyama, S. A sensitive period for the acquisition of a non-native phonological system. *Journal of Psycholinguistic Research.* 1976, 5, 261–285.

Oyama, S. A sensitive period and comprehension of speech. *Working Papers on Bilingualism.* 1978, 16, 1–17.

Ramirez, A.G. and Politzer, R. Comprehension and production in English as a second language by elementary school children and adolescents. In E. Hatch (ed.) *Second Language Acquisition.* Rowley, Mass.: Newbury House Publishers, 1978.

Seliger, H., Krashen, S., and Ladefoged, P. Maturational constraints in the acquisition of second language accent. *Language Sciences.* 1975, 36, 20–22.

Snow, C., and Hoefnagel-Höhle, M. Age differences in pronunciation of foreign sounds. *Language and Speech.* 1977, 20, 4, 357–65.

Snow, C., and Hoefnagel-Höhle, M. Age differences in second language acquisition. In E. Hatch (ed.), *Second Language Acquisition.* Rowley, Mass.: Newbury House. 1978a, 333–344.

Snow, C., and Hoefnagel-Höhle, M. The critical period for language acquisition: evidence from second language acquisition. *Child Development.* 1978b, 49, 1114–1128.

Tahta, S., Wood, M., and Loewenthal, K. Age changes in the ability to replicate foreign pronunciation and intonation. Forthcoming.

Vocolo, J. The effect of foreign language study in the elementary school upon achievement in the same foreign language in high school. *The Modern Language Journal.* 1967, 51, 8, 463–469.

Walburg, H., Hase, K., and Pinzur Rasher, S. English acquisition as a diminishing function of experience rather than age. *TESOL Quarterly.* 1978, 12, 4, 427–437.

Yamada, J., Takatsuka, S., Kotabe, N., and Kurusu, J. On the optimum age for teaching foreign vocabulary to children. *IRAL.* 1980, 28, 3, 245–247.

V

SOME EXPLANATIONS

We turn now from the empirical studies[1] to attempts to explain child-adult differences in second language rate and attainment.

Both papers in this section assume the correctness of our generalizations concerning rate and attainment (Krashen, Long, and Scarcella, 1979; Section IV).

Scarcella and Higa, in a quasi-experimental study, examine one proposed explanation for age differences in second language acquisition, that younger acquirers receive "simpler" input than older acquirers. In their study, child and adolescent second language acquirers participated in a block-building task with native speakers of English. Analysis of the conversations confirmed that the younger acquirers did get input that could be considered simpler. For example, when talking to children, native speakers repeated more than they did to the older subjects; they used shorter, less complex, and more grammatical sentences, and they even encouraged them more! This result seems to be at odds with findings that older acquirers proceed faster. Scarcella and Higa resolve this problem by noting that older second language acquirers utilize conversational strategies to a greater extent. They are better at keeping conversations going ("sustaining the talk") and can use several strategies to improve the comprehensibility of the input they receive. They are therefore better at getting the comprehensible input they need for acquisition, despite the fact that input to younger acquirers seems to be simpler.

Krashen's paper derives from his theoretical work in second language acquisition, popularly termed the "Monitor theory of second language acquisition." The Monitor theory posits that adults have two means of developing ability in second languages: they can subconsciously *acquire*, or "pick up" languages, and they can consciously *learn* about language. Subconscious acquisition, it is hypothesized, dominates in second language performance; we use conscious learning only as a Monitor, only as an editor to correct our output after it has been initiated by the acquired system. We acquire only in one way: by obtaining comprehensible input, by listening, or reading, and understanding the message in language that contains structures "a bit beyond" our current competence (for details, see Krashen's papers in references following his paper).

Krashen first reviews the popular "biological" hypothesis for child-adult differences, the idea that the development of cerebral dominance is related to the child's ultimate superiority in second language acquisition. He concludes that most of the available evidence does not support any obvious connection between cerebral dominance and the loss of the ability to acquire second languages. This does not rule out, however, the possibility that other neurological factors underlie age differences.[2]

Krashen then presents the argument that the older acquirer's rate advantage may be related to *cognitive* factors, specifically the ability to perform formal operations, which is posited to underlie our ability to consciously learn grammar. The child's superiority in ultimate attainment is hypothesized to be due to *affective* factors. Krashen hypothesizes that the affective filter (Dulay and Burt, 1977, in Krashen's References) is strengthened at about puberty, which prevents most adults from reaching nativelike levels of proficiency. It does not prevent them from attaining very high levels of proficiency in second languages, however.

Scarcella and Higa's proposed cause for the older acquirer's superior rate of acquisition does not conflict with Krashen's hypothesis. It seems reasonable to posit that the ability to manage conversations and thereby obtain input predicts a rate superiority for older performers in general, i.e., older child–younger child in addition to adult–child. Krashen's cognitive explanation may be limited to adults versus children, since it depends on formal operations, an event that occurs at about puberty.

It is our hope that all these hypotheses will serve as invitations for further testing.

NOTES

1. The division of papers into "empirical" and theoretical is neither totally accurate nor totally satisfactory. Several of the papers in Sections I to IV deal extensively and thoroughly with explanations for child-adult differences, and one of the papers in this section is experimental.

2. See, for example, Seliger (1978), Long (1978), and Jernigan (1979).

REFERENCES

Jernigan, T. Cerebral Atrophy and Cognitive Decline in the Normal Aged. Ph.D. Dissertation, UCLA Psychology Department, 1979.

Long, M. Towards a neurolinguistic explanation for the effect of age on secondary language acquisition. Unpublished paper, 1978.

Seliger, H. Implications of a multiple critical periods hypothesis for second language learning. In W. Ritchie (ed.), *Second Language Acquisition Research*. New York: Academic Press, 11–19, 1978.

14

INPUT AND AGE DIFFERENCES IN SECOND LANGUAGE ACQUISITION

Robin C. Scarcella and Corrine A. Higa
University of Southern California

There is growing evidence that older learners are able to acquire a second language (L2) faster than younger learners, at least in the initial stages of L2 acquisition. (For discussion, refer to Krashen, Long, and Scarcella, 1979.) The purpose of this paper is to explain this age difference. In doing this, we focus on the native speaker input received by younger and older L2 learners.

It is often believed that the simplified input which young children receive facilitates L2 acquisition better than the input received by older learners. This paper challenges that assumption. We argue that simplified input does not necessarily lead to L2 development. Moreover, we suggest that the older learner's greater ability to manage conversations provides tools for obtaining input which is far better at promoting L2 acquisition than the simplified input received by younger learners.

Although much of research has examined Foreigner Talk (FT), the talk which native speakers use when speaking to foreigners (see, for instance, Ferguson, 1971, 1975; Hatch, Shapira, and Gough, 1977; Henzl, 1975; Gaies, 1977; Gaskill, Campbell and VanderBrook, 1977; Katz, 1977; Freed, 1980; Krashen, 1980a; Meisel, 1976, 1980; and Long, 1980), as well as the strategies which L2 learners use when speaking to native speakers (refer to Tarone, 1977, 1979), there has been little investigation of the negotiation work occurring in the conversations between native and nonnative speakers. (For some recent research, however, refer to Hatch, 1979; Long, 1980; Nelson, 1980; and Snow, VanEeden and Muysken, 1981). Further, while some comparative investigation of adult conversations with younger and older children has been reported in the first language (L1) literature (see, for example, Broen, 1972; Snow, 1972; Phillips, 1973; and Garnica, 1977) there have been no controlled experimental studies comparing adult native speaker interaction with older and younger L2 learners. (For interesting discussion and observation, however, refer to Wagner-Gough and Hatch, 1975.) Such investigation might provide some missing links in explaining age differences in L2 acquisition.

In order to bridge the gap in the research, the present study examines differences in input resulting from the negotiation work in adult native speaker (NS) conversations with younger and older L2 learners. Before proceeding to this research, however, it will be useful to establish a definition of negotiation.

When participating in face-to-face interaction, conversationalists co-operate to sustain the conversation and establish understanding (Goffman, 1974). As Garfinkel (1967) points out, this is an ongoing negotiation process. Here we describe it in terms of the "work" involved in its accomplishment. Primarily, it consists of the work involved in helping one another communicate, for example, by jointly expressing messages, filling in lapses in the conversation, indicating gaps in understanding, and repairing communication breakdowns.

One of the most salient features of negotiation work is that it is not always evenly distributed among conversational partners. In specific, the more competent speaker (socially, cognitively, or linguistically) generally assumes a greater responsibility of sustaining the conversation and establishing under-standing.[1] Consider the following example. Patricia, a native English-speaking adult, and Alma, a Spanish-speaking child just beginning to acquire English, are building a tower out of blocks.

(1)
Patricia: Okay. One more. How many more? One more?
Alma: Yeah
Patricia: Okay now = Now you need what? Red. (points to red block)
Alma: Red

Clearly, Alma, the less competent speaker, is doing little conversational work. In fact, Patricia (the NS) does most of it; she keeps the conversation going (by using rhetorical questions and "spoonfed" answers to put words into Alma's mouth) and establishes understanding (by speaking slowly, repeating, and pointing). It is this asymmetrical aspect of negotiation work which is of special interest in our investigation of age differences in L2 acquisition.

THE STUDY

We turn now to our research to date concerning negotiation in native/ nonnative older and younger learner conversations.

Rationale. Our interest in negotiation stems from our belief that the work of negotiation allows L2 acquirers to obtain comprehensible input. If, as Krashen (1978, 1980b) suggests, comprehensible input is essential for language acquisition, an examination of the observable negotiation work underlying its use should be important in explaining age differences in L2 acquisition.

Hypotheses. The main hypothesis is that older L2 learners do more negotiation work than younger L2 learners (of the same low proficiency level) when participating in conversations with native English speakers (that is, they use more conversational management devices which ensure understanding and sustain the conversation). A major subhypothesis examined is that younger learners receive more simplified input than older learners. (Refer to Appendix A for measures of negotiation work and simplification.)

Subjects. The subjects in the experimental group consist of seven adult native English speakers (university students, ages 18 to 21, inexperienced in speaking to foreigners, all middle-class Caucasian, speakers of the American English spoken on the West Coast) and fourteen L2 learners, seven children (aged 8.5 to 9.5) and seven adolescents (aged 15.5 to 16.5). All L2 learners came from Mexico, spoke Spanish as a first language, had lived in the United States less than 6 months, were from low socioeconomic backgrounds, and were low in their ability to use English. Proficiency level was controlled by (1) placement scores on an exam given by Los Angeles City Schools (both adolescents and children took the same test)[2] and (2) teacher informal interview. The control group consisted of 14 native English speakers (again, university students, aged 18 to 21, all middle-class Caucasian, speakers of the American English spoken on the West Coast).

Task. In order to obtain comparable samples of speech data (refer to Long, 1980), the NSs were alternately paired with both child and adolescent L2 speakers. The dyads were asked to participate in a block-building task, more specifically, to use plastic pieces to replicate a simple picture. Conversations occurring during this 10-minute activity were audio-taped and transcribed. Subsequently, the first fluent 7 minutes of the conversations were analyzed in terms of measures described in advance by the investigators. (Refer to Appendix A for definitions and examples of measures.) Samples were chosen randomly from each of the three speech corpora for remeasurement by two investigators. (Refer to Appendix B for definitions of measurements.) Interrater reliability, established for both the transcription and each measure, was considered adequate, ranging from .83 to 1.00 with a mean of .94.

Analysis. Our analysis is divided into two sections. The first section discusses strategies and techniques used to ensure understanding. In the second section, we analyze strategies used to sustain conversation.

ENSURING UNDERSTANDING

Native Speaker "Work"

This section is organized into the following parts: (1) the work which NSs do to get the L2 learner's attention; (2) the ways in which NSs simplify their language; and (3) clarification devices used by NSs to ensure understanding. It is our contention that all three are important aspects of the "work" of providing less competent speakers with comprehensible input.

Securing and Sustaining the Nonnative Speaker's Attention. As Keenan and Schiefflin (1976) point out, in order for communication to take place, conversationalists must secure the attention of the hearer and establish a mutual focus of attention. A variety of devices may be used by the speaker to these ends including the use of repetition, questions and imperatives, and prosodic and paralinguistic features. Interestingly, the NSs used these devices to a much greater extent with the child L2 learner than they did with the adolescent. Over and over in our transcripts, we found the adults directly calling the child's attention to the object being discussed. (See example 2.)[3]

(2)
Ba: But how are you gonna make that hole there? (points) You see that hole?
Gc: With this.

The following discussion demonstrates both the range of the devices used by NSs and the extent to which they were used with child and adolescent L2 learners and other adult NSs.

Repetition. There was a tendency for NSs to repeat the sentences which they themselves had said before, especially when speaking to the child L2 learner, but also when speaking to the adolescent. (.16 or 69/419 of the utterances addressed to child L2 speakers consisted of self-repetitions, whereas .04 or 17/349 of the utterances to adolescent L2 speakers and .04 or 10/269 of the utterances to adult NSs consisted of self-repetitions.)[4] Keenan (1975) points out that these repetitions frequently serve to secure and maintain the listener's attention. In addition, Garnica (1977) suggests that such repetitions give the language learner a "second look at a sentence, and a second chance to process it" (p. 14). Consider examples 3 and 4.

(3)
Sa/c: We need some red ones. Okay. (.3) *Need some* Here *Need some*
(4)
Sa/c: Okay. Wait Wait Wait Wait

Such repetition was notably absent in the NS talk to adolescents.

Inclusive "we". Brown and Levinson (1977) argue that inclusive "we" (the "we" which includes both the speaker and the hearer in the coversation) may be used to make the addressee more actively involved in the conversation. If this is true, we should not be surprised by the extent this subject pronoun was addressed to the child L2 language learners (Refer to Table 1).

Indeed, native English speakers used these pronouns so consistently that they sometimes repaired their utterances midstream in the conversation to switch from *you* to *we* when addressing the child and from *we* to *you* when addressing the adolescent (example 5 and 6).

Table 1 Frequency of Inclusive "we" (in Proportion to Total Utterances) in the Speech to Child
L2 and Adolescent L2 Speakers and Native Speakers

To child L2 speaker		To adolescent L2 speaker		To adult L1 speaker	
Mean	SD	Mean	SD	Mean	SD
.23 (97/419)	.19	.14 (49/349)	.16	.07 (19/269)	.07

$X^2 = 57.17$, d.f. $= 12, p < .001$, for child L2, adolescent L2, adult L1
$X^2 = 25.10$, d.f. $= 6, \quad p < .001$, for child L2, adolescent L2
$X^2 = 15.13$, d.f. $= 6, \quad p < .001$, for adolescent L2, adult L1
$X^2 = 38.23$, d.f. $= 6, \quad p < .001$, for child L2, adult L1

(5)
Ba/c: I know what *you* = what *we* did wrong
(6)
Sa/ad: Why don't we uhm = why don't *you* put some white blocks on like this,
okay?

Questions and Imperatives. Since questions and imperatives normally require a response from the addressee, they involve the hearer's active attention. In fact, in many cases they are explicit directives to notice or attend to some object (Keenan, Schiefflin, and Platt, 1977). It is interesting to note that reports by Holzman (1972); Atkinson, (1974); Ervin-Tripp (1976); and Newport (1974) indicate that many of the interrogatives which young L1 learners receive are not requests for information; rather, they are rhetorical. Similarly, we found that the speech to child L2 learners is also characterized by heavy use of imperative and interrogative constructions, particularly rhetorical questions (Table 2). In fact, the frequency of rhetorical questions in our child L2 data seems characteristic of the speech to younger rather than older learners in general. (See examples 7 and 8; see also Table 3.)

(7)
Sa: Which way does the window go? Which way do you see the window go?
Nc: (mumble)
Sa: Uhuh (.4) Okay. The window goes this way. Which way?
Nc: This way This way
(8)
Ta: Okay What's that right there? Do you know what that's called?
Pc: Window
Ta: It's a window. Uhuh Okay

Frames. One of the most interesting differences between the NS talk to the younger language learner and the NS talk to the older learner concerns the use of utterance boundary markers, or what are sometimes referred to as "frames" (see Forsyth, 1974; Goodenough and Weiner, 1978; "frames" are in italics in examples 9 to 12).

Table 2 Proportion of Questions, Statements, and Imperatives Addressed to Child and Adolescent L2 Speaker and Adult Native Speaker by Adult Native Speaker

	To child L2 speaker		To adolescent L2 speaker		To adult L1 speaker	
	Mean	SD	Mean	SD	Mean	SD
Questions*	.26 (110/419)	.17	.20 (73/349)	.17	.15 (41/269)	.04
Imperatives†	.23 (96/419)	.13	.15 (53/349)	.05	.06 (17/269)	.04
Statements‡	.50 (213/419)	.20	.52 (183/349)	.17	.78 (211/269)	.10

$*X^2 = 112.15$, d.f. = 12, $p < .001$ for child L2, adolescent L2, adult L1
$X^2 = 86.64$, d.f. = 6, $p < .001$ for child L2, adolescent L2
$X^2 = 49.81$, d.f. = 6, $p < .001$ for adolescent L2, adult L1
$X^2 = 23.55$, d.f. = 6, $p < .001$ for child L2, adult L1

$†X^2 = 68.89$, d.f. = 12, $p < .001$ for child L2, adolescent L2, adult L1
$X^2 = 43.12$, d.f. = 6, $p < .001$ for child L2, adolescent L2
$X^2 = 10.85$, d.f. = 6, $p < .001$ for adolescent L2, adult L1
$X^2 = 54.52$, d.f. = 6, $p < .001$ for child L2, adult L1

$‡X^2 = 57.21$, d.f. = 12, $p < .001$ for child L2, adolescent L2, adult L1
$X^2 = 41.24$, d.f. = 6, $p < .001$ for child L2, adolescent L2
$X^2 = 23.99$, d.f. = 6, $p < .001$ for adolescent L2, adult L1
$X^2 = 26.74$, d.f. = 6, $p < .001$ for child L2, adult L1

Table 3 Proportion of Rhetorical Questions to Total Questions in Native Speaker Speech to Child and Adolescent L2 Speaker and Native Speaker

To child L2 speaker		To adolescent L2 speaker		To native speaker	
Mean	SD	Mean	SD	Mean	SD
.47 (52/110)	.18	.30 (22/73)	.29	.24 (10/41)	.26

$X^2 = 296.10$, d.f. = 12, $p < .001$ for child L2, adolescent L2, and adult L1
$X^2 = 128.88$, d.f. = 6, $p < .001$ for child L2, adolescent L2
$X^2 = 190$,   d.f. = 6, $p < .001$ for adolescent L2, adult L1
$X^2 = 136.71$, d.f. = 6, $p < .001$ for child L2, adult L1

Table 4 Proportion of "Framed Utterances" to Total Utterances in Native Speaker Talk to Child, Adolescent, and Adult Native Speaker

To child L2 speaker		To adolescent L2 speaker		To native speaker	
Mean	SD	Mean	SD	Mean	SD
.46 (193/419)	.15	.17 (61/349)	.04	.07 (20/269)	.07

$X^2 = 62.35$, d.f. = 12, $p < .001$ for child L2, adolescent L2, and adult L1
$X^2 = 16.01$, d.f. = 6, $p < .20$ ns for child L2, adolescent L2
$X^2 = 27.37$, d.f. = 6, $p < .001$ for adolescent L2, adult L1
$X^2 = 50.64$, d.f. = 6, $p < .001$ for child L2, adult L1

(9)

Ja/c: *Yeah*. I think it's one of those *isn't it?*

(10)

Ja/c: *Now* you can put that one there? *Okay?*

(11)

Pa/c: *Okay*. You've got the leg. *Okay*.

(12)

Sa/c: *Okay*. Now hold this end down *Okay*.

Utterances framed in this manner frequently followed this regular pattern:

frame	declarative, imperative, or	frame
pause	interrogative construction	pause
		confirmation check

The frames consisted of utterance boundary markers such as "okay," "now," "well," and "so," while the confirmation checks consisted of short tag questions with rising intonation, such as "right?" "isn't it?" and "okay?" We suggest that the use of these "frames" made utterances easy to segment, and thus attend. As evident in Table 4, "framed constructions" were present in the speech to adolescents to a lesser degree than in the speech to children.[5] While 17 percent of the utterances addressed to adolescents were "framed," 46 percent of the utterances addressed to the children were "framed." This difference, while not statistically significant ($p < .20$), represents an interesting trend.

Support. Giving encouragement may be another way of capturing the listener's attention. Brown (1977) suggests that this "expressive-affective" part of language "has as its chief motive the expression of affection with the capturing of the addressee's attention as a secondary goal." (p. 4) Here, our results are very clear. As seen in Table 5, the children received much more positive feedback (such as "good," "right," and "all right") than the adolescents. Furthermore, the children actually received such compliments as the following: "Good job, good job," "Looks good to me," "Way to go! You had the right idea." In sharp contrast, neither the adolescents nor the NSs received any compliments at all.[6]

Exaggerated Intonation and Nonverbal Gestures. Finally, more observationally, we found that the speech to children was characterized by more exaggerated intonation and nonverbal gestures (such as pointing and touching). These often seemed to emphasize exactly what the child needed to attend to in order to get the "gist" of the adult's message. Garnica (1977) points out that such prosodic and paralinguistic features are important cues for the learner to pay attention to what is being communicated.

NS Speech Simplification. Establishing a mutual focus of attention is only a first step toward making one's message to the nonnative speaker (NNS)

Table 5 Proportion of Positive Feedback to Total Utterances in the speech to
Child and Adolescent L2 Speaker and Native Speaker

	To child L2 speaker			To adolescent L2 speaker		
	Mean		SD	Mean		SD
Positive feedback	.60	(253/419)	.15	.42	(146/349)	.28

	To native speaker		
	Mean		SD
Positive feedback	.13	(36/269)	.05

$X^2 = 72.88$, d.f. $= 12, p < .001$ for child L2, adolescent L1, adult L1
$X^2 = 45.89$, d.f. $= 6, \quad p < .001$ for child L2, adolescent L2
$X^2 = 43.28$, d.f. $= 6, \quad p < .001$ for adolescent L2, adult L1
$X^2 = 17.74$, d.f. $= 6, \quad p < .01$ for child L2, adult L1

"comprehensible." The speaker must also make his or her message easy to understand. Brown (1977) suggests that this might be done by simplifying one's speech. He states,

What I think adults are trying to do when they use BT, (Baby Talk, the simplified language addressed to young children), is communicate, to understand and be understood. . . (p. 18).

In this part, we discuss the simplifications used by NSs when talking to adolescents and children. Here, we do not mean to draw a line between NS talk and NNS talk. Rather, it is our intent to gain insights from the research on Foreigner Talk (FT) while at the same time expanding the study of FT to include native/nonnative speaker interaction. For the purposes on hand, we focus on those characteristics of FT most widely discussed in the literature: utterance length, grammaticality, complexity, dysfluency, and vocabulary. Finally, we turn to a characteristic which, though extremely important, has received considerably less attention: the simplification of speech acts. Once again, we compare native/nonnative younger and older learner conversation.

Utterance Length, Complexity, Grammaticality, and Dysfluency. As seen in Table 6, the adult native English speakers used shorter, less complex, and more grammatically correct utterances when addressing the child L2 learners than they did when addressing adolescents. All L2 input language was, then, fairly well formed. The lack of dysfluency observed in the talk to children has been reported to increase the intelligibility of the message (Garnica, 1977). Similarly, the use of less complex grammatical utterances is also believed to improve comprehensibility.

Examples of utterances addressed to the child which might be considered ungrammatical, at least at first glance, include the following:

Table 6 Mean Length of Utterance, Grammatical Complexity, Grammaticality, and Dysfluency in Adult Speaker Talk to Child and Adolescent L2 Speakers and Adult Native Speakers

	To child L2		To adolescent		To native speaker	
	Mean	SD	Mean	SD	Mean	SD
Mean length of utterance*	4.7	2.5	5.5	3.4	5.6	1.6
Grammatical complexity (relative clauses)†	.04 (18/419)	.03	.10 (36/349)	.05	.14 (39/269)	.13
Grammaticality‡	.97 (408/411)	.02	.94 (328/349)	.04	.94 (255/269)	.04
Dysfluency§	.05 (29/419)	.09	.09 (32/349)	.02	.13 (35/269)	.05

* $X^2 = 60.78$, d.f. $= 12$, $p < .001$ for child L2, adolescent L2, adult L1
$X^2 = 1.30$, d.f. $= 6$, $p < .98$ (n.s.) for child L2, adolescent L2
$X^2 = 53.39$, d.f. $= 6$, $p < .001$ for adolescent L2, adult L1
$X^2 = 48.66$, d.f. $= 6$, $p < .001$ for child L2, adult L1

† $X^2 = 42.39$, d.f. $= 12$, $p < .001$ for child L2, adolescent L2, adult L1
$X^2 = 11.92$, d.f. $= 6$, $p < .10$ (n.s.) for child L2, adolescent L2
$X^2 = 34.53$, d.f. $= 6$, $p < .001$ for adolescent L2, adult L1
Expected frequency levels too low for X^2 analysis for child L2, and adult L1

‡ n.s. for all comparisons using X^2 analysis.

§ $X^2 = 22.52$, d.f. $= 12$, $p < .001$ for child L2, adolescent L2, adult L1
$X^2 = 1.79$, d.f. $= 6$, $p < .95$ (n.s.) for child L2, adolescent L2
$X^2 = 16.40$, d.f. $= 6$, $p < .02$ for adolescent L2, adult L1
$X^2 = 19.70$, d.f. $= 6$, $p < .01$ for child L2, adult L1

(13)

Sa: Then we put another one.

(14)

Ca: Put some white ones.

(15)

Pa: Now press down it.

However, it is important to note that such "ungrammatical" utterances also appeared in the NS conversations and may be more characteristic of the language of block building than FT.

What did the child have to do to receive this input? Not much. In fact, it appears that the children may not have even interacted with the adults enough to reveal their language proficiencies (refer to Table 7). While the adolescents produced more utterances than their native speaker conversational partner (54 percent of all utternaces), the children produced only 28 percent of the utterances. We found, as did Snow (1972) in her study of BT, that the more competent speaker (in our case, the NSs) dominated the conversation, hardly allowing the child to get a word in edgewise. The following is typical of the adult/child data.

(16)

Ja: Now can you put that one there? Okay push down on that so its snaps on. Push down on your side and I'll push down on mine. Got it? Okay What's next now? This is the third green one? We're up to here (pointing) A white one. Let's see. Right there. . .

However, it is necessary to interpret these findings with caution. First, it is questionable whether the children were actually responding as naturally and spontaneously as the adolescents. After all, the children probably had less experience participating in conversations with middleclass native English-speaking adults (who were complete strangers) than the adolescents. Second, the task may have been more difficult for the children than for the adolescents. Thus, the children's concentration on the task may at least partially account for their lack of verbal interaction.

Nonetheless, the fact that the NSs simplified their speech for the child despite the lack of verbal feedback is, for us, of significant consequence: *It lends*

Table 7 Proportion of Child and Adolescent Utterances to
Native Speaker Utterances

Child L2 utterances to native speaker utterances	Adolescent L2 utterances to native speaker utterances
.28	.54

$X^2 = 39.07$, d.f. = 6, $p < .001$

further support to the hypothesis that simplification is triggered more by age than by linguistic competence (see, for example, Snow, 1972; Newport, Gleitman, and Gleitman, 1977).[7]

Vocabulary. Compared with the adult native English speaker control group, child and adolescent L2 learners received "simpler" vocabulary. Vocabulary was simplified by employing more frequent words as well as by replacing more difficult lexical items with more frequently occurring terms, as in examples 17 and 18.

(17)
Jad: Let's start with the *base* then. At the *bottom*.
(18)
Aad: Okay okay 'n then you need a *double*. *Two*.

In addition to using more difficult terms, such as "parallels," "destroy," and "perpendicular," the native English-speaking controls never explained the meaning of the lexical items they used.

Speech Acts: Directives. Simplification of speech acts was also apparent. The preponderance of directives in the data made their analysis ideal. Several findings were made. First, children received more imperative directives than adolescents. These directives were frequently accompanied by gestures. Thus, it appears that the NSs reverted to the use of earlier, more primitive request forms when addressing children (for discussion, see Halliday, 1975; Gruber, 1973; Dore, 1973; Carter, 1974; and Bates, 1976; for a review, refer to Ervin-Tripp, 1978). Second, as mentioned earlier, children's directives were more frequently "framed," making them easily identifiable as requests. Third, the NSs did not always wait for the child to respond to their directives. Instead, they carried out their own requests in much the same way that they answered their own rhetorical questions. Fourth, adolescents received many more hints than children. In fact, 39 percent of all utterances directed to adolescents consisted of hints (refer to examples 19 and 20). Many of these were elliptical, requiring the adolescent to draw inferences about the desired object or action requested.

(19)
Aa: It's suppose to be only one row of white.
(20)
Ba: Think the red one goes across.

Here it seemed as though the NSs were avoiding the use of explicit requests with older learners of more equal status (cf. Ervin-Tripp, 1978; Brown and Levinson, 1977).

In sum, we come to the view that requests to children were more readily identifiable and easier to understand (simpler in form and more direct in meaning) than requests to adolescents. For a complete analysis of directives, refer to Table 8.

Table 8   Adult Native Speaker Directives to Child and Adolescent L2 Speaker and Adult Native Speaker

	To child L2 speaker		To adolescent L2 speaker		To adult L1 speaker	
	Mean	SD	Mean	SD	Mean	SD
Simple imperatives*	.17 (72/419)	.13	.10 (36/349)	.05	.05 (14/269)	.04
Let's imperatives†	.06 (24/419)	.03	.05 (17/349)	.05	.01 (3/269)	.01
Need statements‡	.08 (34/419)	.04	.03 (11/349)	.03	.03 (7/269)	.03
Hints§	.12 (52/419)	.10	.39 (137/349)	.21	.28 (75/269)	.14

* $\chi^2 = 68.91$, d.f. = 12, $p < .001$ for child L2, adolescent L2, adult L1
$\chi^2 = 51.07$, d.f. = 6, $p < .001$ for child L2, adolescent L2, adult L1
$\chi^2 = 25.81$, d.f. = 6, $p < .001$ for adolescent L2, adult L1
$\chi^2 = 29.23$, d.f. = 6, $p < .001$ for child L2, adult L2

† $\chi^2 = 20.40$, d.f. = 6, $p < .01$ for child L2, adolescent L2; other comparisons not possible because of low expected frequencies

‡ $\chi^2 = 45.60$, d.f. = 12, $p < .001$ for child L2, adolescent L2, adult L1; other comparisons not possible because of low expected frequencies

§ $\chi^2 = 36.64$, d.f. = 12, $p < .001$ for child L2, adolescent L2, adult L1
$\chi^2 = 52.06$, d.f. = 6, $p < .001$ for child L2, adolescent L2
$\chi^2 = 69.26$, d.f. = 6, $p < .001$ for adolescent L2, adult L1
$\chi^2 = 74.01$, d.f. = 6, $p < .001$ for child L2, adult L1

NS Clarification Devices. Before concluding this section, we turn to an additional technique the NSs employed to help the NNSs understand the conversation. This technique is the use of confirmation checks (such as "okay?" "right?" and "huh?") As seen in example 21, when the NSs were not certain whether the NNSs attended or understood their talk, they sometimes elicited feedback by using confirmation checks.

(21)
Ma: We need more red <u>huh</u>?
Gc: Uhuh

The response to these checks provided the NS with information concerning the comprehensibility of the message and, as illustrated in example 22, sometimes triggered "repairs." (Refer to Sachs, Schegloff, and Jefferson, 1977, for a discussion of the repair system.)

(22)
Ba: ... This is a long one <u>right</u>? (.4) We have = Two shorts make long right?

Here, the NS explains the term "long" when his NNS conversational partner does not respond to his request for feedback.

Confirmation checks occurred repeatedly in the data. Table 9 demonstrates that, as expected, adults employed more confirmation checks with the children than with the adolescents.

NNS Work to Ensure Understanding

Just as NSs work to provide their NNS conversational partners with comprehensible input, NNSs work to obtain it. For example, when an L2 learner does not understand what the NS is saying, he or she may bring this to the attention of the NS by either verbal or nonverbal means. This feedback may be all that is necessary for the NNS to identify the source of communicative difficulty and repair his or her utterance in such a way as to make it understood by the L2

Table 9   Proportion of Confirmation Checks to Total Number of Utterances in Native Speaker Speech to Child and Adolescent L2 Speaker and Adult Native Speaker

To child L2 speaker			To adolescent L2 speaker			To native speaker		
Mean		SD	Mean		SD	Mean		SD
.60	(255/419)	.11	.33	(154/361)	.25	.16	(43/269)	.08

$X^2 = 79.84$, d.f. $= 12$, $p < .001$ for child L2, adolescent L2, adult L1
$X^2 = 34.6$, d.f. $= 6$, $p < .001$ for child L2, adolescent L2
$X^2 = 64.84$, d.f. $= 6$, $p < .001$ for adolescent L2, adult L1
$X^2 = 25.5$, d.f. $= 6$, $p < .001$ for child L2, adult L1

learner. The NNS adolescents used wh-questions as well as yes/no questions and expressions such as "huh?" to indicate when they did not understand (see examples 23, 24, 25).

(23)
Sa: Okay. Wait how do you say your name?
Lad: What?
Sa: How do you say your name?
(24)
Sa: (.3) Still trying to figure out what I'm doing here.
Lad: Hmm?
Sa: This is really hard. I was going, "Oh Lord"
(25)
Sa: We're gonna need another one. . .
Lad: We need two?

In addition, they utilized repetition (with rising, question intonation) for this purpose.

(26)
Ba: Well I know there was red first
Jad: Red? Red?

These techniques were, however, virtually absent in the child L2 data.

Table 10   Mean Number of Utterances per Turn in Native
Speaker Speech to Child and Adolescent L2 Speaker

To child L2 speaker		To adolescent L2 speaker	
Mean	SD	Mean	SD
4.7 (639/137)		1.7 (456/264)	

$X^2 = 25.03$, d.f. $= 6$, $p < .001$

Table 11   Mean Number of Words per Turn in Native Speaker Speech to Child and Adolescent
L2 Speaker and Native Speaker

To child L2 speaker			To adolescent L2 speaker			To native speaker		
Mean		SD	Mean		SD	Mean		SD
18.9	(2588/137)	9.7	8.41	(2222/264)	2.6	5.8	(1460/251)	1.7

$X^2 = 19.51$, d.f. $= 12$, $p < .01$ for child L2, adolescent L2, and adult L1
$X^2 = 12.77$ d.f. $= 6$, $p < .05$ for child L2, adolescent L2
$X^2 = 1.14$,   d.f. $= 6$, $p < .95$ (n.s.) for adolescent L2, adult L1
$X^2 = 10.52$ d.f. $= 6$, $p < 10$ (n.s.) for child L2, adult L1

KEEPING THE CONVERSATION GOING

Having discussed native and nonnative speaker work involved in negotiating understanding, we move to another important component of negotiation: sustaining a conversation. It may be this aspect of negotiation which enables NNSs to interact with NSs long enough to obtain sufficient input for language development.

NS Work to Sustain the Conversation

Adult NSs carried a much greater responsibility for the conversation when speaking to children than they did when addressing adolescents. In fact, even a cursory glance at the data reveals that adults dominated the conversation when speaking to the child and controlled the turn-taking system.

Rhetorical Questions. In addition to dominating the conversation, as discussed earlier, adults sustained their conversations with the children by using rhetorical questions (often providing answers to their own questions, as in examples 27, 28, and 29).

(27)
Sa: What is this? Feet
(28)
Sa: How many more do you need? One more.
(29)
Pa: You need what? Red.

Repetition. NSs also used repetition of the L2 learner's previous utterance to make the conversation last. Again and again, we find this use of repetition in the NS speech to child L2 learners (see examples 30 and 31).

(30)
Sa: What color is this? Can you see what color this is?
Cc: Green?
Sa: Green. Okay we're gonna need a big green bottom yeah?
(31)
Ka: We've got the right color?
Mc: wh- (.3) green
Ka: Green again (.2) and (.3)
Mc: White
Ka: White again

NNS Work to keep the Conversation Going

Adolescents assumed much more of the responsibility of sustaining the conversation than children. This is not to say that the children were egocentric or noncommunicators. Rather, our data suggest that the conversational burden placed on the adolescent was greater than that placed on the child; that is, adult

NSs seemed to expect more of older learners. Thus, the older learners were required to communicate even when they lacked the necessary linguistic competence to do so.

Our data, are consistent with two hypotheses: (1) the conversational demands are greater on older L2 learners (cf. Wagner-Gough and Hatch, 1975; Hatch, 1978); and (2) in order to cope with these heavy demands for early conversational performance, older learners utilize conversational strategies which allow them to stretch their linguistic competence (Tarone, 1977, 1979). Here we discuss these strategies.

Stepping in Sideways. One of the primary strategies used by the adolescents to participate in conversations with the NS's was what might be termed "stepping in sideways." Briefly stated, this strategy can be phrased as follows:

Allow the NS to introduce a topic. Then, subsequently, comment on the topic, adding new and relevant information.

(Example 32 illustrates this strategy.)

(32)
As: Okay and then another square
Ead: like that
Aa: goes there

Jefferson and Schenkein (1977) have shown that adult first language speakers often build conversations on prior utterances in this way. Others, such as Bloom (1973), Keenan (1974), and Scollon (1976, 1979), have observed young child first language learners relying on antecedent utterances to collaborate in the building of conversations. Such collaboration has been referred to as "co-operative dialogue" (Keenan, 1974). It is our contention that these cooperative dialogues lighten the task of participating in a conversation; it is easier for L2 learners to "step into a conversation sideways" than it is to initiate a new topic. It is interesting to note that the cooperative dialogues appearing in the data often took the form of expansions (as seen in examples 33 and 34)

(33)
Sa: We need some
Jad: Some of those
(34)
Ba: Then we put another one. One of those.
Gc: One at the end
Ba: And one more

or completions, as in examples 35 and 36.

(35)
As: Okay and this goes like =
Ead: that
(36)
Ja: I can't tell if that's a (.2)
Rad: The black one?
Ja: A black one.

Again, we emphasize that the difference between native/nonnative older and younger learner speech and NS talk lies in the *extent* to which cooperative dialogue is employed and not in its presence or absence (refer to Tables 12 and 13).

Repetition. Another strategy used by the adolescents (but not to the same extent by the children) to keep the conversation going was repetition (refer to examples 37 and 38).

(37)
Aa: Red one.
Ead: Red one
(38)
Aa: Here it's supposed to be only one row of white. Look
Ead: One yeah

Table 12   Mean Number of Cooperative Dialogues in the Speech Data of Native Speakers/Child L2 Speakers, Native Speakers/Adolescent L2 Speakers, and Native Speakers/Native Speakers Conversations

Child L2 speakers/ native speakers		Adolescent L2 speakers/ native speakers		Native speakers/ native speakers	
Mean	SD	Mean	SD	Mean	SD
52	1.34	94	5.68	26	5.4

$\chi^2 = 17.84$, d.f. $= 12$, $p < .20$ (n.s.) for child L2, adolescent L1
$\chi^2 = 11.18$, d.f. $= 6$, $p < .10$ (n.s.) for child L2, adolescent L2
$\chi^2 = 4.45$, d.f. $= 6$, $p < .70$ (n.s.) for adolescent L2, adult L1
$\chi^2 = 8.89$, d.f. $= 6$, $p < .20$ (n.s.) for child L2, adult L1

Table 13   Mean Number of Cooperative Dialogues Initiated by Nonnative Speakers

Child L2 speaker/native speaker		Adolescent L2 speaker/native speaker	
Mean	SD	Mean	SD
2.9	1.34	5.4	5.7

$\chi^2 = 19.78$, d.f. $= 6$, $p < .001$

These partial and complete repetitions of the speaker's previous utterance appeared to serve two purposes: (1) to check on the comprehensibility of the message, and (2) to fill in one's turn at talk.

Topic Initiation and Topic Shift. In addition, unlike children, adolescents often initiated new topics. Consequently, during lags in the conversation, they were able to begin the talk anew. Moreover, the adolescents frequently changed the subject. This was a particularly useful strategy for L2 learners who did not understand the vocabulary being used (consider example 39; see Table 14).

(39)

Sa: Wait we need da = dark blue

Lad: <u>We need time for do this</u>

Sa: Huh?

Lad: You need time

Sa: Yeah (.1) Well (.1) you think it's black? or blue? Black yeah.

Lad: Black.

Perhaps the adolescents initiated more topics than NSs because they were using topic initiation as a means of keeping the conversation focused on familiar subjects which they could easily understand.

Conversational Fillers. Finally, curiously enough, while the adolescents used a wide variety of fillers such as "ya know," "let's see," and "uhm" to hold and take their turn at talk while simultaneously keeping the conversation going

Table 14 Mean number of Topics Initiated by Child and Adolescent L2 Speakers and Native Speakers

Child L2 speakers			Adolescent L2 speakers			Native speakers		
Mean		SD	Mean		SD	Mean		SD
.25	(27/108)	.21	.43	(84/194)	.17	.28	(74/269)	.27

$X^2 = 216.31$, d.f. = 12, $p < .001$ for child L2, adolescent L2, adult L1
$X^2 = 98.51$,   d.f. = 6, $p < .001$ for child L2, adolescent L2
$X^2 = 20.84$,   d.f. = 6, $p < .001$ for adolescent L2, adult L1
$X^2 = 54.32$,   d.f. = 6, $p < .001$ for child L2, adult L1

Table 15 Proportion of Pause Fillers to Utterances in the Speech of Child and Adolescent L2 Speakers and Native Speakers

Child L2 speakers			Adolescent L2 speakers			Native speakers		
Mean		SD	Mean		SD	Mean		SD
.09	(19/108)	.20	.43	(84/194)	.26	.23	(62/269)	.15

$X^2 = 284.84$, d.f. = 12, $p < .001$ for child L2, adolescent L2, adult L1
$X^2 = 159$,   d.f. = 6, $p < .001$ for child L2, adolescent L2
$X^2 = 85$,   d.f. = 6, $p < .001$ for adolescent L2, adult L1
$X^2 = 130.78$, d.f. = 6, $p < .001$ for child L2, adult L1

(and frequently buying time to think of just the right word or phrase to use next), these fillers were rarely used by the children.[8] (Refer to examples 40 and 41; see also Table 15.)

(40)
Ga: Should we take the little pieces first? That's the bottom of his foot.
Mad: Let's see.
Ga: Oh they're green. Okay I don't think there are enough pieces here.
Mad: Let's see.
(41)
Sa: What's next?
Jad: Uhm = (.1) Maybe his shoes

CONCLUSION

In concluding, we would like to return to the original motivation of this study: explaining age differences in L2 acquisition. In investigating the negotiation work involved in participating in native/nonnative speaker conversation, one clear-cut finding emerges: Adult native English speakers do much more negotiation work in conversations with younger L2 learners than they do with older learners. *They provide larger quantities of simple input, a more supportive atmosphere, and a constant check to see that the input the child receives is both attended to and understood.*

This leads us to an interesting paradox. Krashen, in a series of papers (1978, 1980a, 1980b), describes "optimal" input for language acquisition. Drawing evidence from both first and second language research, he hypothesizes that good input is (1) sufficient in quantity, (2) given in a nonthreatening atmosphere, (3) both attended to and understood by the language learner, and (4) at an appropriate level (just a little beyond the learner's current linguistic competence). These characteristics of "optimal input" appear to accurately describe the input which the *child* L2 learner in our study received. If, indeed, younger learners receive "better" input than older learners, we would expect them to have a big advantage over older learners in acquiring an L2.[9] Yet the literature indicates that the exact reverse happens: older learners are better than younger learners in the early stages of L2 acquisition.

How can we explain the older learner's headstart in second language acquisition in view of this apparent "input handicap"? To answer this question, we would like to reexamine input and the work of negotiation. First, in order for conversational participants to communicate, they must attend very closely to the ongoing discourse. This active involvement in the conversation is said to facilitate language acquisition, "charging" the input, and allowing it to "penetrate" deeply (refer to Stevick, 1976, 1980a, 1980b; see also Sternfeld, 1978). Second, when NNSs use strategies to get NSs to clarify, they are frequently able to get just those parts of the input explained which they do not understand. Younger learners, on the other hand, who do not employ these strategies to the same extent, may receive more simplified input, but even this simplified input may contain structures and vocabulary which the child does not understand. The older learner's active work in sustaining the talk results in his or her exposure to large quantities of comprehensible "charged input" which is closely attended to. In other words, the simplified input which the child L2 learner receives is not as "optimal" as the input which the older learner receives through the work of negotiation. NSs do not always guess accurately; they are not always able to correctly ascertain the NNSs English proficiency level and adjust their speech accordingly. Thus NNSs who do not negotiate may receive input which is too simple (and perhaps already acquired) or too difficult (and therefore incomprehensible) (Krashen, 1980). Through the work of negotiation, the NNSs can receive challenging input, in advance of their linguistic competence, and make this input comprehensible.

A few caveats before concluding. Clearly, this is no more than a beginning. This study was constrained by the methods which can be successfully used with both older and younger learners. First, confronted with the task of obtaining comparable samples of data, we were forced to use a task which, in addition to eliciting only seminaturalistic data, also constrained the language used.[10] Second, we must also point out that differences in adult-adolescent and child-oriented interactions in this study were also influenced by the status of the child in middle-class Western society. As Freed (1980) suggests,

Vis à vis the adult caretaker, they (children) are. . . . of relatively reduced status. (p. 1)

Further, as Brown (1977) points out,

There is also the universality of infant status. With respect to any other speaker of the language, an infant, and indeed every infant, is less competent linguistically and cognitively and is an object of some affection. (p. 18)

Third, the fact that adolescents use more negotiating devices than children (or that children receive more "simplified" input) cannot in itself explain age differences in L2 acquisition. Further studies are needed if the problem of cause and effect is to be explored. Fourth, admittedly the size of the study was small, examining only 21 conversational dyads. Further studies are needed to confirm these findings. Finally, all along we have been assuming that the input which the child and adolescent L2 learner receive from the outside world is adult. Yet, as Fillmore (1976) and Peck (1978) demonstrate, much of the child L2 learner's input comes from peers who provide input of a different sort. Certainly naturalistic studies are called for here.

The investigation reported here, though a first venture, is one further step toward explaining the role of input in age differences in L2 acquisition. It has shown that the study of age differences and negotiation provides a wealth of information which has only begun to be tapped.

APPENDIX A

Measures of Negotiation Work

I. Native speaker work to provide "comprehensible" input
   A. Attention-getting and attention-holding devices
      1. Self-repetition
      2. Inclusive "we"
      3. Questions and imperatives
      4. Frames
      5. Support
         a. Positive feedback
         b. Compliments
      6. Exaggerated intonation
      7. Nonverbal Gestures
   B. Simplification
      1. Mean length of utterance
      2. Grammatically correct utterances
      3. Dysfluency
      4. Complex utterances
      5. Vocabulary
         a. Replacement
         b. Explanation
      6. Speech Acts: Directives
   C. Clarification devices: confirmation checks

II. Nonnative speaker work to get the native speaker to provide "comprehensible" input
   A. Wh- questions, yes/no questions, "huh?"
   B. Repetition (other-repetition + question intonation)

III. Native speaker work to sustain the conversation
   A. Control of turn-taking system
   B. Rhetorical questions
   C. Repetition (self, complete and partial)

IV. Nonnative speaker work to sustain the conversation
   A. Stepping in sideways
   B. Other repetition (complete and partial)
   C. Topic initiation and topic shift
   D. Conversation fillers

APPENDIX B

*Definitions of Measures**

Compliments: Expressions and utterances used to praise one's conversational partner, excluding positive feedback such as "good" and "right." Examples include "Way to go." and "You're the mastermind."

Confirmation Checks: Short tag questions having rising intonation which follow utterances.
Examples: "Huh?" "Yeah?"

Conversation Fillers: Expressions such as "ya know" and "let's see" occurring anywhere in an utterance as in "Let's see the red one goes here."

Declarative Statements: Utterances which assert or declare. Examples are "I just got hit in the nose." and "This is really complicated."

Directives: Utterances used to direct one's conversational partner. Examples include "Just add 'em on." and "You do that."

Dysfluent Utterances (Broen, 1972): Within utterance revisions, word repetitions and hesitations.
Example: "Holy Moly. *Where's the uhm where's* the door?"

Frames: Boundary markers such as "well," "so," "okay," and "now" which precede or follow utterances.

Hints: Utterances (declaratives or interrogatives) which function as requests and require inference for their correct interpretation.
Examples: A: "The red one should go on top." B: Over here? A: Uhum.

Imperatives: An utterance which expresses a command or request, including simple imperative forms such as "Put the red one there." and "Don't use red." and "let's imperatives" such as "Let's put it there.", but excluding other directive forms (e.g., "Would you put it on top." "I think it goes over there.").

Inclusive "we": The we which includes both the speaker and the hearer in the conversation. *Examples*: "We need green." "Do we have a problem?"

Let's Imperatives: An directive of the form: Let's + simple imperative construction. *Example*: "Let's build it faster."

Need Statement: Directives expressing personal desire or need, always containing verbs *need* or *want*. *Examples*: "We need to build it bigger." "I want a blue one."

Other-repetition: An exact sequential repetition of the preceding speaker's utterance or expression with falling intonation. *Example*: A: It's a red one. B: Red one.

---

*All variables (with the exception of rhetorical questions and cooperative dialogue) were calculated as percentages, number of total occurrences of the variable examined, over total number of utterances. Rhetorical questions were calculated in ratio to total number of questions. Cooperative dialogues were given as total number of occurrences in a seven minute speech sample.

Positive Feedback: Expressions such as "right," "yeah," and "uhuh" which are inserted after the speaker's utterance/s.

Questions: All wh-questions and yes/no questions, excluding tag questions such as "Just like that, all right?"

Relative Clause: A subordinate clause preceded by a relative pronoun or adverb which may be deleted. *Examples*: "I guess it goes on the bottom." "I know that the red one is wrong."

Rhetorical Questions: Any question to which the speaker already had an answer.

Stepping in Sideways (Cooperative Dialogue): Any idea communicated across utterances between speakers. *Examples:* A: And then we put B: another one A: like that B: there.

Self-Repetition: An exact sequential repetition of one's utterance or expression. *Example*: "Here. It's this one. This one. This one.

Simple Imperative: A request consisting of the following: $\left\{ \begin{matrix} You \\ We \end{matrix} \right\}$ Verb X *Examples*: "Build it." "You do it."

Topic (Keenan and Schiefflin, 1976): A proposition (or set of propositions) expressing a concern (or set of concerns) the speaker is addressing. (Each declarative or interrogative utterance has a specific discourse topic.)

Topic Shift (Keenan and Schieflin, 1976): A change in discourse topic. (Note that topics may shift with each new utterance or be sustained across utterances.)

Turn: Calculated in terms of the number of speaker changes. For example, the following constitutes three turns: A: What comes next? B: Blue. A: Sure?

Utterance (Brown, 1973): A complete, grammatical sentence. Judged by intonation contour, pauses, and semantic content.

Mean Length of Utterance (adapted from Brown, 1973) Words per utterance, including repetition, yes/no and single-word responses to questions.

Word (Andersen and Johnson, 1973, p. 151): A standard orthographic unit including proper names, contractions, and exclamatory expressions, but not concatenate forms such as *kinda*, which count as two words.

NOTES

1. For a discussion of the role of communicative distress in such asymmetrical negotiation, refer to Sabsay and Bennett, 1977.

2. More specifically, all subjects took the BINL (Bilingual National Language) examination, and were categorized as "limited" English speakers.

3. To facilitate reading the transcripts, speakers have been identified by first initial. In addition, the following abbreviations are used: a for adult native speaker, ad for adolescent second language speaker, and c for child second language speaker.

4. Statistical analysis was not possible here, since expected frequencies were not sufficiently large.

5. The fact that frames occur to a far lesser degree in Native Speaker Talk (constituting only 7 percent of all utterances) suggests that frames may be a feature of Foreigner Talk.

6. Obviously, the task had a powerful influence on the language used. Indeed, it is difficult to imagine older learners being complimented on their ability to use blocks!

7. Note that second, rather than first, language acquisition is an ideal testing ground for researchers interested in this hypothesis.

8. As seen in Table 15, the adolescent L2 speakers used even more conversational fillers than the adult NSs. Again, this might indicate that the adolescents were relying on conversational fillers as a strategy for keeping the conversation going.

9. In fact, based on the first language literature as well as our findings here, we would expect the child's input to grow progressively toward the adult native model as the child matures. This increasingly complex input should keep pace with both the child's chronological age and his or her linguistic maturity.

10. Thus, we were unable to investigate differences in topic nomination and its influence on conversation. We would expect to see even greater differences in negotiation work had we not controlled for topic.

REFERENCES

Andersen, E. S. Learning to speak with style: a study of the sociolinguistic skills of young children. Unpublished Ph.D. Dissertation, Stanford University, 1977.

Andersen, E. and Johnson, C. Modifications in the speech of an eight-year-old as a reflection of age of listener. Stanford Occasional Papers in Linguistics, 1973, 3, 149–160.

Atkinson, M. Prerequisites for reference. Paper presented at BAAL Annual Meetings, 1974. Also in E. Ochs and B. Schieffelin (eds.), *Studies in Developmental Pragmatics*. New York: Academic Press, 1979.

Bates, E. *Language and Context: The Acquisition of Pragmatics*. New York: Academic Press, 1976.

Bloom, L. *One word at a Time*. The Hague: Mouton, 1973.

Broen, P. The verbal environment of the language learning child. Monograph of American Speech and Hearing Association No. 17, Dec. 1972.

Brown, P., and Levinson, S. Universals in language usage: politeness phenomena. In *Questions and Politeness: Strategies in Social Interaction*. Cambridge Papers in Social Anthropology, 1977, 8.

Brown, R. *A First Language*. Cambridge, Mass.: Harvard University Press, 1973.

Brown, R. Introduction to *Talking To Children*, C. Snow and C. Ferguson (eds.), Cambridge: Cambridge University Press, 1977.

Carter, A. Communication in the sensori-motor period. Unpublished Ph.D Dissertation. Berkeley, California: University of California, 1974.

Chaudron, C. Complexity of teacher speech and vocabulary explanation and elaboration. Paper presented at the 13th Annual TESOL Convention, Boston, 1979.

Dore, J. The development of speech acts. Unpublished Dissertation. New York: City University of New York, 1973.

Ervin-Tripp, S. Is Sybil there?: The structure of some American directives. *Language and Society*. 1976, 5, 25–66.

Ervin-Tripp, S. A psychologist's point of view. In C. Snow and C. Ferguson (eds.), *Talking to Children*. Cambridge: Cambridge University Press, 1977.

Ervin-Tripp, S. Wait for me roller skate! In S. Ervin-Tripp and C. C. Mitchell-Kernan (eds.), *Child Discourse*. New York: Academic Press, 1978.

Ferguson, C. Absence of copula and the notion of simplicity: A study of normal speech, baby talk, foreigner talk and pidgins. In D. Hymes (ed.), *Pidginization and Creolization of Languages*. Cambridge: Cambridge University Press, 1971.

Ferguson, C. Toward a characterization of foreigner talk. *Anthropological Linguistics*. 1975, 17, 1–14.

Fillmore, L. W. The second time around: cognitive and social strategies in second language acquisition. Ph.D Dissertation, Stanford, 1976.

Forsyth, I. J. Patterns in the discourse of teachers and pupils. G. Perren (ed.), *The Space Between: English and Foreign Languages at School*. London: Centre for Information on Language Teaching, 1974

Freed, B. Talking to foreigners versus talking to children: Similarities and differences. In R. Scarcella and S. Krashen (eds.), *Research in Second Language Acquisition*. Rowley, Mass: Newbury House, 1980.

Gaies, S. The nature of linguistic input in formal second language learning: linguistic and communicative strategies in teachers' classroom language. In H. D. Brown, C. A. Yorio, and R. H. Crymes, *On TESOL 1977. Teaching and Learning: Trends in Research and Practice*. Washington, D.C.: TESOL, 1977.

Garfinkle, H. *Studies in Ethnomethodology*. Englewood Cliffs, New Jersey: Prentice-Hall, Inc., 1967.

Garnica, O. Some prosodic and paralinguistic features of speech to young children. In C. Snow and C. Ferguson (eds.), *Talking to Children*. Cambridge: Cambridge University Press, 1977.

Gaskill, W., Campbell, C., and VanderBrook, S. Some aspects of foreigner talk. In C. A. Henning (ed.), *Proceedings of the Los Angeles Second Language Research Forum*, 1977.

Goffman, E. *Frame Analysis*. New York: Harper and Row, 1974.

Goodenough, D. R., and Weiner, S. The role of conversational passing moves in the management of topical transitions. *Discourse Processes*. 1978, 1, 4, 394-404.

Gruber, J. Correlations between the syntactic instructions of the child and the adult. In D. I. Slobin and C. Ferguson (eds.), *Studies in Child Language Development*. New York: Holt, 1973.

Halliday, M. A. Learning How to Mean: Explorations in the Development of Language. London: Edward Arnold, 1975.

Hatch, E. Optimal age or optimal learners? UCLA: Workpapers in Teaching English as a Second Language. 1975, 11, 45–56.

Hatch, E. Discourse analysis and second language acquisition. In E. Hatch (ed.), *Second Language Acquisition: A book of readings*. Rowley, Mass: Newbury House, 1978.

Hatch, E. Simplified input and second language acquisition. Paper presented at the 1979 LSA Conference, Los Angeles, California, 1979.

Hatch, E., Shapira, R., and Wagner-Gough, J. Foreigner talk discourse. *ITL: Review of Applied Linguistics*. 1977, 39–40, 39–60.

Henzl, V M. Linguistic register of foreign language instruction. *Language Learning*. 1973, 23, (2), 207–222.

Holzman, M. The use of interrogative forms in the verbal interaction of mothers and their children. *Journal of Psycholinguistic Research*. 1972, 1, 311–336.

Jefferson, G., and Schenkein, J. Some sequential negotiations in conversation: Unexpanded and expanded versions of projected action sequences. *Sociology*, 1977, 11, 1.

Katz, J. Foreigner talk input in child second language acquisition: its form and function over time. In C. A. Henning (ed.), *Proceedings of the Los Angeles Second Language Research Forum*, 1977.

Keenan, E. O. Conversational competence in children. *Journal of Child Language*. 1974, 1, (2), 163–185.

Keenan, E. O. Making it last: uses of repetition in children's discourse. *Proceedings of First Annual Meeting of the Berkeley Linguistics Society,* Berkeley, California. Also in S. Ervin-Tripp and C. Mitchell-Kernan (eds.), *Child Discourse*. New York: Academic Press, 1975.

Keenan, E. O., and Klein, E. Coherency in children's discourse, *Journal of Psycholinguistic Research*. 1975, 4, 365–378.

Keenan, E. O., and Schiefflin, R. Topic as a discourse notion: A study of topic in the conversations of children and adults. In C. Li (ed.), *Subject and Topic*. New York: Academic Press, 1976.

Keenan, E. O., Schiefflin, R., and Platt, M. Questions of immediate concern. In E. N. Goody (ed.), *Questions and Politeness*. Cambridge: Cambridge Papers in Social Anthropology, 1977.

Krashen, S. Adult second language acquisition and learning: A review of theory and practice. In R. Gingras (ed.), *Second Language Acquisition and Foreign Language Learning*. Washington: Center for Applied Linguistics, 1978.

Krashen, S. The Input Hypothesis, Paper presented at the Georgetown 1980 Roundtable Discussion. Georgetown University Press, 1980a.

Krashen, S. The theoretical and practical relevance of simple codes in second language acquisition. In R. Scarcella and S. Krashen (eds.), *Research in Second Language Acquisition.* Rowley, Mass.: Newbury House, 1980b.

Krashen, S., Long, M. and Scarcella, R. Age, rate and eventual attainment in second language acquisition. *TESOL Quarterly.* 1979, 13, (4), 573–582.

Krashen, S., and Scarcella, R. On routines and patterns in second language acquisition. *Language Learning.* 1979, 28, 283–300.

Long, M. Questions in Foreigner Talk Discourse. Paper presented at the 1980 TESOL Convention, San Francisco, 1980.

Meisel, J. M. The language of foreign workers in Germany. *Grazer Linguistische Studien.* 1976, 3, 107–134.

Meisel, J. M. Linguistic simplification: a study of immigrant worker's speech and foreigner talk. In S. P. Corder and E. Roulet (eds.), *Actes du 5eme colloque de linguistique appliquee de Neu Chatel.* Geneva, 1977.

Meisel, J. M. Linguistic simplification. In W. Felix (ed.), *Second Language Development: Trends and Issues.* Gunter Narr Verlag Tübingen, 1980.

Nelson, J. Language Systems in Adult Informal Second Language Learners. Ph.D. Dissertation. McGill University, Montreal, Canada, 1980.

Newport, E. Motherese and its relation to the child's acquisition of language. Paper presented at the conference on language input and acquisition, Boston, 1974.

Newport, E., Gleitman, H., and Gleitman, L. Mother, I'd rather do it myself: Some effects and non-effects of maternal speech style. In C. E. Snow and C. A. Ferguson (eds.), *Talking to Children.* Cambridge: Cambridge University Press, 1977.

Peck, S. Child-child discourse on second language acquisition. In E. Hatch (ed.), *Second Language Acquisition.* Rowley, Mass.: Newbury House, 1978.

Phillips, J. Syntax and vocabulary of mother's speech to young children: age and sex comparisons. *Child Development.* 1973, 44, 182–185.

Sabsay, S., and Bennett, T. Communicative distress. In E. Ochs Keenan and T. Bennett (eds.), *Discourse across Time and Space.* Southern California Occasional Papers in Linguistics, 1977.

Sachs, H., Schegloff, E. and Jefferson, G. The preference for self-correction of repair in conversation. *Language,* 1977, 53, 361–382.

Scarcella, R. Developing conversational competence through role-play. Paper presented at the 1977 CATESOL conference, San Francisco, 1977.

Scarcella, R. "Watch up": A study of verbal routines in adult second language performance. *Working Papers in Bilingualism,* 1979, 19, 79–88.

Schegloff, E., Jefferson, G., and Sachs, H. The preference for self-correction of repair in conversation. *Language.* 1977, 53, 361–382.

Scollon, R. Conversations with a one year old. Honolulu: University of Hawaii, 1976.

Scollon, R. A real early stage: an unzippered condensation of a dissertation on child language. In E. Ochs and B. Schiefflin (eds.), *Developmental Pragmatics,* New York: Academic Press, 1979.

Snow, C. Mothers' speech to children learning language. *Child Development.* 1972, 43, 549–565.

Snow, C. E., VanEeden, R., and Muysken, P. The interactional origins of FT: Municipal employees and foreign workers. *International Journal of Sociology of language,* 1981, 28–91.

Sternfeld, S. The Italian experiment. Unpublished paper, University of Southern California, 1978.

Stevick, E. *Memory, Meaning and Method.* Rowley, Mass.: Newbury House, 1976.

Stevick, E. *Teaching Languages. A Way and Ways.* Rowley, Mass: Newbury House, 1980a.

Stevick, E. The Levertov machine. In R. Scarcella and S. Krashen (eds.), *Research in Second Language Acquisition.* Rowley, Mass.: Newbury House, 1980b.

Tarone, E. Communication strategies. In *On TESOL '77,* Washington D.C.: TESOL, 1977.

Tarone, E. Communication strategies revisited. Paper presented at the 1979 TESOL Summer Institute.

Wagner-Gough, J., and Hatch, E. The importance of input data in second language acquisition studies. *Language Learning.* 1975, 25, 297–308.

15

ACCOUNTING FOR CHILD-ADULT DIFFERENCES IN SECOND LANGUAGE RATE AND ATTAINMENT

Stephen D. Krashen
University of Southern California

In a recent paper, Krashen, Long, and Scarcella (1979) presented evidence for three generalizations concerning the effect of age on rate and eventual attainment in second language acquisition:

1. Adults proceed through the early stages of syntactic and morphological development faster than children (where time and exposure are held constant).
2. Older children acquire faster than younger children (again, in the early stages of syntactic and morphological development where time and exposure are held constant).
3. Acquirers who begin natural exposure to second languages during childhood generally achieve higher second language proficiency than those beginning as adults.

The aim of this paper is to attempt to present some explanations for at least two of these generalizations (1 and 3). It will examine some explanations that have already appeared in the second language research literature, the "neurological" explanation, the "cognitive" explanation, the "affective" explanation, and the "input" explanation for child-adult differences. At least one version of the neurological explanation, it will be argued, is not well supported by current research. The cognitive explanation is able to account for part of the data, namely, age differences in rate of acquisition, while the affective explanation may be able to account for differences in ultimate attainment.

THE NEUROLOGICAL HYPOTHESIS

A well-known hypothesis is that there are clear neurological differences between child and adult brains, and that these differences are directly responsible for child-adult differences in language acquisition. Lenneberg (1967) provided evidence that seemed to connect the development of *cerebral dominance*, or lateralization, with child-adult differences in language acquisition, an idea first suggested by Penfield (Penfield and Roberts, 1959).

Below, I present a brief definition of cerebral dominance and a discussion of some of the ways it is determined. Following this, Lenneberg's hypothesis is presented. This is, in turn, followed by a summary of research done since Lenneberg's book, *Biological Foundations of Language*, was published, evidence that strongly suggests that Lenneberg's position on the development of cerebral dominance requires some modification.

Cerebral Dominance

It is by now a well-established finding that for most people (practically all right-handers and most left-handers), the two sides of the cortex perform different functions. As Table 1 indicates, the left hemisphere is responsible for most linguistic performance in adults. Recent studies strongly suggest that the left brain is also involved in certain nonlinguistic functions, specifically those related to the perception of *time*. For example, the left hemisphere is superior to the right in judging temporal order or deciding which of two stimuli was presented first (e.g., Carmon and Nachshon, 1971; Papcum, Krashen, Terbeek, Remington, and Harshman, 1974). The "other side of the brain," the right hemisphere, appears to be responsible for spatial relations, so-called "gestalt" perception (exemplified by the ability to estimate rapidly the number of dots on a card after an extremely brief exposure, without actually counting each dot), and "part-to-whole" judgments (for example, matching arcs to circles). At least some aspects of musical perception may also be done by the right hemisphere (Milner, 1962).

The eminent neurosurgeon, Joseph Bogen, in a fascinating series of papers (Bogen 1969a, 1969b; Bogen and Bogen, 1969), has speculated that the two sides of the brain utilize two different cognitive modes, one "propositional"

Table 1   Functions of the Two Hemispheres

Left hemisphere	Right hemisphere
Language	Spatial relations
Time-related functions	"Gestalt" perception
	Part-to-whole judgments
	Music
"Propositional" thought	"Appositional" thought

(analytic, digital) and one "appositional" (analogic, synthetic). Only the intactness of the corpus callosum, the fibers connecting the two hemispheres, allows us the illusion that we have just one mind.

A variety of techniques have been used by researchers to ascertain "where things are" in the brain. At one time, researchers had to depend on "natural experiments," the unfortunate consequences of unilateral brain damage caused by tumor, strokes, and manmade accidents (e.g., gunshot wounds). Correlations were made between the locus of a lesion and the type of impairment the patient suffered. For example, we know that in adults, aphasia is nearly always the result of injury to the left hemisphere (Russell and Espir, 1961, report that 97 percent of their 205 aphasics had left hemisphere damage).

While researchers continue to rely on data from brain damage to a large extent, more recently laterality in normal subjects has been investigated using several harmless techniques. In *dichotic listening*, subjects are presented with competing, simultaneous auditory stimuli (e.g., the right ear hears "ba" while the left ear hears "ga"). A right-ear advantage in response accuracy is thought to reflect left hemisphere processing for the stimulus presented. In adults, dichotic presentation of verbal stimuli typically results in a right-ear advantage (Kimura, 1961), while certain nonverbal stimuli (environmental sounds, musical chords; see Curry, 1967; Gordon, 1970) yield a left-ear advantage. The right-ear advantage for verbal stimuli typically seen in normal subjects is generally quite small, but it is reliable, and when groups of subjects are used, it is usually statistically significant.

Other techniques include the use of EEG and AER (average evoked response). When verbal stimuli are used, subjects typically show a higher evoked response in the left hemisphere, indicating greater processing activity (Wood, Goff, and Day, 1971). In EEG studies, verbal stimulation results in depressed alpha wave activity in the left hemisphere (the presence of alpha waves indicates a resting or meditative state) (Morgan, McDonald, and MacDonald, 1971).

The Development of Cerebral Dominance and Language Acquisition

Lenneberg (1967) related the developmental course of cerebral dominance to the ability to acquire language. In Chapter 4 of his *Biological Foundations of Language*, he hypothesized that the development of cerebral dominance was complete by around puberty ("firmly established"). According to Lenneberg, the infant brain is not firmly lateralized; in case of damage to the left hemisphere, or in case of removal of the left hemisphere ("hemispherectomy"), the right hemisphere is able to assume the language function. Lenneberg presented evidence that suggested that this ability of the language function to "transfer" hemispheres lasts until puberty, a conclusion that appeared to be consistent with reports of better recovery from acquired aphasia in children under age 10 or so. After puberty, the right hemisphere did not appear to be able to assume the language function in case of injury to or removal of the left hemisphere, and

Lenneberg hypothesized that this was due to the fact that lateralization of language to the left hemisphere was now complete. The presence of some of the language function in the right hemisphere in children also might be responsible for their superior recovery from aphasia.

Lenneberg (see also Scovel, 1969) also hypothesized that the end of the development of cerebral dominance coincided with the close of a "critical period" for language acquisition, noting that "foreign accents cannot be overcome easily after puberty" (p. 176) and that "automatic acquisition (of second languages) from mere exposure . . . seems to disappear after this age" (p. 176). Lenneberg therefore proposed a *biological explanation* for child-adult differences in language acquisition attainment, a very serious claim for those of us interested in second language acquisition in adults and one which could imply lowered expectancies on the part of both teachers and students.

Research done since 1967, using a wide variety of techniques, does not, however, support the idea that this "biological barrier" to natural second language acquisition exists.

Simply, it is no longer clear that the development of cerebral dominance is complete at puberty. There are now arguments and data supporting the position that lateralization is "firmly established" much earlier, at least by age 5, and that the preconditions for lateralization may be present even at birth. Below, we briefly summarize the experimental and clinical literature that has appeared on this topic in the last few years. As we shall see, most of the reports support "early" lateralization. There are, however, some apparent inconsistencies, which we discuss below.

1. Dichotic listening: Witelson (1977) has reviewed all known studies using dichotic listening with children and concludes that "of 36 experiments, 30, or about 83%, reported right-ear superiority for their youngest sub-groups, and all found right-ear superiority in at least their older subgroups" (p. 230) (where "younger" indicates from about age 3 to about 7). Studies evaluating developmental trends usually report no increase in degree of lateralization over time (age), supporting the hypothesis that language lateralization is firmly established far earlier than puberty. A few studies, however, do in fact report an increasing right-ear advantage up to about puberty, consistent with Lenneberg's position. What is interesting about these studies (e.g., Satz, Bakker, Teunissen, Goebel, and Van der Vlugt, 1975) is that the stimuli used for dichotic presentation were slightly different from the stimuli used in studies that report no change in degree of lateralization with increasing age. In the "puberty" studies, the children were presented with two or three sets of digits at one time [e.g., the pair "2" (right ear) and "9" (left ear) would be presented, followed by "1" (right ear) and "3" (left ear). The subject is asked to recall as many digits as possible out of the six presented.] In most other studies, one single pair of syllables (e.g., "ba" and "ga") or words were used, a lower short-term memory load. This raises the possibility that there might be two different developmental courses for two different kinds of language processing, one completely lateralized to the left hemisphere by puberty and the other much earlier in life.

2. Motor skills: Early completion of the development of cerebral dominance is also indicated by studies examining the development of unimanual motor skills. Caplan and Kinsbourne (1976), in a paper appropriately titled "Baby drops the rattle," provide an interesting example. The experimenters gave rattles to 21 infants (average 21 months, 21 days) and found that the babies tended to hold the rattles longer when they were placed in their right hands (average duration of grasp = 62 seconds for the right hand and 41 seconds for the left hand), suggesting early lateral specialization of the central nervous system. Witelson (1977) has reviewed many studies of this sort using children age 7 and younger and concludes that "right-hand or right-sided superiority was observed in the large majority of the 34 studies" (p. 236). This supports the hypothesis that there is an early propensity for unimanual performance of motor tasks, which is consistent with the hypothesis that cerebral dominance is established early in life.

3. Brain damage: Studies examining the effects of unilateral brain damage on language in children also imply that lateralization is complete earlier than puberty. In later childhood (age 5 and older), just as in adults, aphasia is primarily the result of *left* hemisphere lesions. It appears to be the case, however, that before age 5 aphasia may result from right hemisphere lesions somewhat more frequently (about 30 percent of the time, as compared with 3 percent in adults and older children). Still, even for very young children, aphasia is associated more often with left lesions than with right lesions (for reviews, see Witelson, 1977; Krashen, 1973a; Hécaen, 1976).

4. Hemispherectomy: The removal of an entire hemisphere, hemispherectomy, is perhaps the ultimate test of laterality. If the left hemisphere is removed, and the patient is able to speak, we can assume that the right hemisphere had at least some part in the language function before the surgery. The literature indicated that early removal of the left hemisphere for lesions incurred before age 5 does *not* generally result in aphasia. This result, like the data from unilateral lesions above, implies at least some right hemisphere participation in the language function in early years (Krashen, 1973a; Witelson, 1977).

According to Krashen (1973a), the hemispherectomy data are clear only up to age 5, as this surgical procedure is rarely used with older children.

5. EEG and AER: Research using EEG and AER techniques suggest that signs of hemispheric specialization are present even at birth. When infants as young as 2 weeks old are presented with verbal stimuli (e.g., the mother's voice), the audiotory evoked response is greater over the left hemisphere; when musical stimuli are presented (e.g., a music box), the AER is greater over the right hemisphere (Molfese, 1976). EEG results are similar: we see left-right differences in infants as young as 5 months old (Gardiner and Walter, 1976).

6. Some researchers have looked for anatomical differences between the two hemispheres. Slight differences do in fact exist in the adult brain (Geschwind and Levitsky, 1968), and it has been confirmed that similar left-right morphological differences exist in the infant and even in the prenatal brain

(Witelson and Pallie, 1973; Wada, Clarke, and Hamm, 1975), suggesting at least the potential or predisposition for hemispheric specialization.

What can we conclude about the development of cerebral dominance from this array of reports? We have seen some evidence for "lateralization by zero" (consistent with EEG, AER, and anatomical studies, as well as some dichotic listening studies and experiments using unimanual motor skills), some for "lateralization by five" (clinical data on brain damage and hemispherectomy), and some for lateralization by puberty (dichotic studies using more difficult stimuli). A possible solution is to posit the following developmental course:

1. Most of us are born with a predisposition for left hemisphere language, and there is thus some specialization right from the start, enough to be detected by EEG and AER, and to influence the development of unimanual motor skills.

2. This degree of lateralization increases until about age 5, by which time most aspects of language processing are lateralized to the left hemisphere at the adult level. This accounts for the brain damage and hemispherectomy data, which show some right hemisphere contribution to the language function before age 5.

3. Certain aspects of language are not entirely lateralized to the left hemisphere until later, perhaps by puberty, These aspects of linguistic competence may be those that are necessary for the perception of longer and more complex stimuli. This accounts for the exceptional dichotic listening studies.[1]

Whether or not this particular schema is the correct one, one clear conclusion that can be drawn from this literature survey is that there is little doubt that most children show left hemisphere dominance for much of the language function well before puberty. There is also no necessary relationship between cerebral dominance and second language acquisition ability. The completion of the development of lateralization may not mean the establishment of an absolute barrier to successful and natural second language acquisition. As we shall see, alternative explanations have been proposed for child-adult differences in second language rate and attainment, explanations that undoubtedly have some neurological correlates but are probably unrelated to cerebral dominance.[2]

THE COGNITIVE HYPOTHESIS

Formal Operations and Conscious Grammar

There have recently been some attempts to relate "linguistic puberty" to an important event in the development of cognition, the onset of what Piaget has labeled "formal operations (Inhelder and Piaget, 1958), which generally occurs at around age 12. At this time, according to Piaget, the child becomes able to think abstractly; that is, he or she is able, for the first time, to relate abstract ideas to each other without recourse to concrete objects. In a sense, the adolescent can now consider abstract ideas themselves to be objects and can mentally manipulate them. The preformal, or concrete, thinker learns or arrives at abstract ideas only from direct experience with the actual empirical data. On the other hand, the formal thinker can have "ideas about ideas" (Ausubel, 1962) and is no longer totally dependent on what Ausubel calls "concrete-empirical props."

In addition, the formal thinker has a meta-awareness of this developing system of abstractions: "the adolescent seems to reflect on the rules he possesses and on his thoughts" (*Developmental Psychology Today*, 1971, p. 336). Also important is the finding that the formal thinker can develop general solutions to problems: "the adolescent organizes his operations into higher order operations, ways of using abstract rules to solve a whole class of problems" (op. cit., p. 336). A classic example of this is the solution to the problem of selecting which items from a group can float; the formal thinker will typically apply a general rule (i.e., objects made out of wood), while the concrete thinker may try out each item. Finally, Elkind (1970) notes that the formal thinker can "conceptualize his own thought, . . . take his mental constructions as objects and reason about them" (p. 66).

The ability to think abstractly about language, to conceptualize linguistic generalizations, to mentally manipulate abstract linguistic categories, in short, to construct or even understand a theory of a language, a grammar, may be dependent on those abilities that develop with formal operations. It is interesting that in the United States instruction in foreign languages generally begins just at the age when formal operations has taken place, in the early teens, in high school. While I do not wish to defend this practice, it does make a certain kind of sense, considering that many widely used methodologies in high school foreign language teaching are those which emphasize the conscious learning of rules (e.g., grammar-translation), as it is only at this age that the student is able to deal with this form of pedagogy. Of course, as I have emphasized elsewhere, there is much more to language proficiency than the conscious learning of rules; conscious learning occupies a surprisingly small place in the total picture of adult second language performance (Krashen, 1978a).

Just as formal operations apparently does not occur in all people (Dulit, 1972; Baxter, 1977), all second language performers do not utilize conscious rule learning (Krashen, 1978).

How does formal operations influence language acquisition and how does it predict child-adult differences? Interestingly, several scholars have argued that cognitive differences between children and adults should predict that the adult is better at second languages than children are. We turn first to these arguments, and then discuss a somewhat different view as to how formal operations might help account for child-adult differences.

Formal Operations and Adult Language Learning/Acquisition

Some linguists maintain that the adult's cognitive superiority should help in second language acquisition. Genessee (1977), while not referring specifically to formal operations, notes that "the adolescent's more mature cognitive system, with its capacity to abstract, classify, and generalize, may be better suited for the complex task of second language learning than the unconscious, automatic kind of learning which is thought to be characteristic of young children" (p. 148). In support of his argument, Genessee cites several studies that indicate superior rate of second language achievement in classroom studies using older learners, concluding "there is a rather noteworthy consensus among these studies concerning the learning rates of students at different ages—older students seem to be more efficient learners than younger students. That is to say, given the same amount of instruction, or even less, adolescents will learn as much or more than younger children" (p. 150). Genessee continues to note that: "This is not a new idea, especially to most practicing educators. Would we expect primary school children to learn mathematical or scientific concepts faster than adolescents? I think not" (p. 150).

Taylor (1974) also says that "it seems logical to assume that the adult's more advanced cognitive maturity would allow him to deal with the abstract nature of language even better than children" (p. 33). Taylor suggests that cognitive differences between children and adults could not account for observed child-adult differences, since adults do not have a cognitive deficiency but rather have a cognitive superiority.

Other scholars suggest that cognitive differences predict that adult language acquisition will be *different* from child language acquisition. Rosansky (1975), referring specifically to formal operations, suggests that, since other "postcritical period learning" may involve behavior that looks the same on the surface as "normal" behavior acquired during the critical period but may have been learned through alternative routes, "adults *do* learn language via an alternate route, namely as 'known', and . . . they most likely require instruction in the 'subject' (the second language)" (p. 99). In other words, the adult may not have access to the child's acquisition device but will employ a more conscious strategy to produce behavior that appears, on the surface, similar to the results of child language acquisition.

The position taken here is that formal operations relates directly to the ability to *learn* language consciously (using *learning* as a technical term in contrast to subconscious language *acquisition*). This hypothesis helps to explain certain child-adult differences, and also clarifies the insights of the scholars cited above. The hypothesis states that the ability to think abstractly about language, to conceptualize linguistic generalizations, to mentally manipulate abstract linguistic categories, in short to construct or even understand a theory of a language, may be dependent on just those abilities that develop with formal operations.

The hypothesis that formal operations allow the development of the conscious grammar predicts certain child-adult differences. First, it accounts for the fact that adult meta-awareness of language is typically greater than that of children. Adults (not all) are better *learners*; they can talk about rules like subject-verb agreement, relative clause formation, and occasionally complex rules such as equi-NP deletion and dative movement. As Hatch (1978) has pointed out, some children do have some degree of meta-awareness of language, but it is typically restricted to the most elementary rules of grammar (e.g., singular-plural differences, gender distinctions) and, as far as we know, is not applied to actual performance.

The formal operations hypothesis also helps to account for the finding that older performers appear to be superior to younger ones with respect to rate of progress, specifically that adults are faster than children. The conscious grammar, used as a Monitor (Krashen, 1976, 1978), allows the adult to operate in a different "mode" which allows for both early performance and more opportunities for the necessary input for language acquisition.

The L1 plus Monitor Mode

The L1 plus Monitor mode of producing utterances allows second language production without acquired competence. I have hypothesized elsewhere (Krashen, 1977) that adults are able to utilize the first language as a substitute utterance initiator, which may take the place of acquired second language competence. This happens especially when performers need to produce utterances very early in their second language experience, before they have had a chance to acquire the needed L2 structures "naturally" via input. Performers simply utilize the surface structure of their first language, and then employ the conscious grammar as a Monitor to make alterations to bring the L1 surface structure into conformity with their idea of the surface structure of the second language.[3]

This mode does allow for early production, and in of itself helps to account for early adult progress in second languages, but it is very limited, since it depends so much on the performer's ability to use the Monitor to make repairs; it requires continuous attention to form, continuous mental gymnastics. It produces very quick results, however. Experienced learners can use such a procedure to produce utterances in a second language within hours, and indeed it is this mode that is implicitly encouraged in second language classes that demand early production.

The L1 plus Monitor mode has an indirect benefit, one that helps the adult get a head start on acquisition. When performers use such a mode to communicate, to engage in conversation, it invites input, and this input, in turn, may stimulate language acquisition, if the input is comprehensible (the input hypothesis, Krashen, 1980b).[4]

The Formal Operations Hypothesis: Conclusion and Summary

The formal operations hypothesis as expressed here is quite consistent with the views of other scholars cited earlier. Indeed, as Genessee claims, adults are able to progress faster in second language performance; the data cited in Krashen, Long, and Scarcella (1979) also support this claim and the use of the L1 plus Monitor mode may account for it. Also, as Taylor suggests, the adult is better able to deal with the abstract nature of language, according to the formal operations hypothesis as stated here. Finally, as Rosansky suggests, the adult has an "alternate route" to language performance, namely; conscious learning. The limits of conscious learning (Krashen, 1977b); Krashen, Butler, Birnbaum, and Robertson, 1978), however, qualify these statements. Initial use of the first language and the conscious grammar may allow an adult to progress faster at *initial stages* in second language performance, but this progress may be severely constrained by the adult's ability to consciously learn (no performer will be able to learn all the rules of the target language) and by the learner's ability to apply these rules in performance (Monitor use is hypothesized to be restricted to situations where the learner has sufficient time and is focused on form). Our model thus predicts that the rate advantage is temporary, that the use of the L1 plus Monitor mode is not as efficient a route as subconscious acquisition, which is available to both the child and the adult.

Cognitive differences between children and adults are thus able to predict some child-adult differences: Hypothesizing a relationship between formal operations and conscious learning successfully predicts the age at which the capacity for extensive meta-awareness develops, as well as the adult advantage in rate of learning. It also predicts that this rate advantage is a temporary one if it depends on the use of the L1 and the Monitor. The cognitive argument, however, says nothing about the fact that children typically outperform adults in second language performance over the long run. To account for this, we turn to a discussion of affective explanations for child-adult differences.[5]

Figure 1 represents the formal operations hypothesis, and shows "what it can do" in accounting for child-adult differences.

THE AFFECTIVE HYPOTHESIS

The idea that child-adult differences in second language performance are due to affective changes is a popular one. Schumann (1975), in a review paper, discusses several scholars' views on this topic. For example, Larsen and

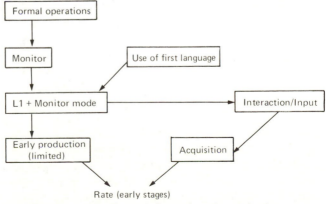

FIGURE 1   The Formal Operations hypothesis

Smalley (1972) suggest that "As puberty approaches and the individual is concerned with the consolidation of his personality, it apparently becomes more difficult for him to submit to the new norms which a second language requires" (Schumann, 1975, pp. 229-230). Also, Curran (1961) feels "that children acquire second languages more easily than adults because they are less threatened by the sounds of the new language and because they are willing to depend on others for support in learning. . . . But when (the adult) attempts to communicate in the new language his normal linguistic securities are undermined, and he finds himself in a dependent state which he may resist" (Schumann, 1975, p. 230). The observed correlations between affective variables and second language acquisition (reviewed in Schumann, 1975, Krashen, 1980a, and below) for adult acquirers, as well as the impressions cited above, lead Schumann to conclude that "language learning difficulties after puberty may be related to the social and psychological changes an individual undergoes at that age" (p. 229).

The case for affective variables is intuitively appealing. There are obvious changes in personality and attitude at around puberty, which is also a clear turning point in second language acquisition and learning. In this section, we will briefly review the literature on the relationship between affective variables and adult second language acquisition, and attempt to draw some generalizations as to how affective variables relate to a general theory of second language acquisition. This review will allow us to make some statements about the hypothesis that affective changes are responsible for child-adult differences. Following this, we will discuss the possible relationship between affective and cognitive variables, the hypothesis that at least some of the affective changes that occur at puberty are related to formal operations. This in turn will allow us to state a more general hypothesis of the cause of child-adult differences in language acquisition and language learning.

Affective Variables and Adult Second Language Acquisition

How do affective variables relate to second language acquisition?[6]

Before reviewing the literature describing which variables have been looked at, and which have been found to be related to second language achievement, it is essential to state what the relationship between affective variables and second language achievement is. It is hypothesized here that affective variables affect progress in second language acquisition in at least two ways: First, performers with "optimal" attitudes (listed and discussed below) will simply obtain more input than performers with less than optimal attitudes—the former group will attempt to communicate more with speakers of the target language, and thereby obtain more of the input necessary for language acquisition. This has been stated before (Oller, 1977; Gardner, Smythe, Clement, and Gliksman, 1976). Second, it is also hypothesized that performers with better attitudes will be more "open" to the input. In Dulay and Burt's (1977) terms, they will have a lower "socio-affective filter." In Stevick's (1976) terms, the input will strike them "deeper." This predicts that given the exact same amount of understandable input, a performer with better attitudes or in an affectively more positive situation will acquire less of the language directed at them, as less input is allowed into the language acquisition device. The filter is a very useful construct, as it will allow us to hypothesize a cause for certain child-adult differences without positing any change in the language acquisition device or in the input directed at the acquirer. The change, we will hypothesize below, is in the filter.

Another important point is the hypothesis that affective variables relate directly to acquisition, and not to conscious learning. This was argued explicitly in Krashen (1977a; 1980a) and is based on the generalization that affective variables appear to relate strongly to second language achievement especially when communicative tests are used as measures and when performers have been exposed to "acquisition-rich" environments (e.g., second language as opposed to foreign language; this is somewhat of an oversimplification; see Krashen, 1980a, for detailed discussion.)[7]

This generalization is also important for our forthcoming discussion of child-adult differences and affective variables, as it will be hypothesized that the child is a superior *acquirer*, not a superior *learner*. Table 2 lists the hypothesized relationships between affective variables and second language acquisition.

Review of Affective Variables

Below we briefly review the research literature pertaining to affective variables and second language acquisition.

Motivation. The concepts of integrative and instrumental motivation (Gardner and Lambert, 1972) are important and have been widely researched and discussed. I will dwell on them here only long enough to state how they might relate to the generalizations given above. Integrative motivation is defined as the desire to be like members of the target language community, while instrumental motivation is defined as the motivation one has when the goal is only to *use* that language for some practical or utilitarian purpose. Table 3 gives

Table 2   Relationships Hypothesized between Affective Variables and Second Language Acquisition

1. Performers with optimal attitudes will
   a. Seek and obtain more input
   b. Have a lower affective filter—will allow more input "into the LAD"

2. Affective variables relate primarily to language acquisition, not language learning (Krashen, 1978b)

Table 3   Motivation Type and L2 Acquisition

Motivation type	Input	Filter	Fossilization will occur when
Integrative	Yes	Weaker	Social needs are met
Instrumental	Yes	Stronger	Communicative needs are met

my hypotheses as to how these two motivation types affect second language acquisition. It states that integratively motivated performers *and* instrumentally motivated performers will seek out input in the second language, but perhaps for different reasons. The integratively motivated performer will have a lower affective filter, however, We might also expect that the instrumentally motivated performer will proceed in L2 acquisition only as far as he or she needs to in order to "get the job done," while the integratively motivated performer will be more open to acquiring those aspects of the target language that are communicatively less important but that may be socially important, certain redundant parts of language (including parts of morphology and pronunciation).

Studies have shown that integrative motivation clearly relates to second language proficiency in certain situations. These include:

1. French as a foreign/second language in Anglophone Canada (Montreal, Toronto). (Gardner and Lambert, 1972; Gardner, 1960; Gardner et al., 1976; Bialystok and Fröhlich, 1977).
2. English as a second language in the United States, using foreign students from several countries and an "indirect" measure of integrative motivation (Spolsky, 1969).

Integrative motivation is somewhat less successful as a predictor of second language achievement in other situations, such as:

1. French as a foreign language in the United States (Gardner and Lambert, 1972).
2. English as a foreign language in Japan (Chihara and Oller, 1978).

Instrumental motivation has been shown to take precedence over integrative motivation in these situations:

1. English as a second language in Bombay, India (Lukmani, 1972).
2. English as a second language in the Philippines (Gardner and Lambert, 1972).

The published literature is thus quite consistent with the generalizations given earlier concerning the relationship between affective variables and second language acquisition. We see stronger effects for integrative motivation in situations where some real language use is at least possible, and weaker effects for more extreme foreign language situations. This is consistent with the idea that this affective variable is related to acquisition. Also, Gardner and Lambert (1972) point out that the relationship between integrative motivation and second language achievement was strongest for "aural-oral" skills, a result confirmed by Gardner et al. (1976) and also reported by Gardner (1960), who concluded that integrative motivation was especially important for "the development of communicative skills" (p. 215). Instrumental motivation appears to be stronger in situations where there is some urgency about second language acquisition and where there is little desire to integrate with members of the target language group. This is consistent with the idea that with instrumental motivation, input is sought after, but the filter is "up."

Self-confidence. Certain personality factors are also associated with success in second language acquisition, according to the professional literature, and these factors appear to be related to self-confidence: lack of anxiety (a characteristic of the acquisition situation as well as the performer), outgoing personality, and self-esteem. The self-confident person, it is hypothesized, will be more able to encourage input and will have a lower filter.

The research literature indicates that the relationship between anxiety and second language acquisition is particularly robust. Some studies demonstrating negative correlations between various types of anxiety and second language acquisition are given in Table 4. These studies show that *low* anxiety is beneficial for language acquisition. Gardner et al. (1976) also report that classroom anxiety correlated with "speech skills" more closely than with "grades," a result consistent with the hypothesis that such affective variables are strongest in Monitor-free situations (grade 7 French as a second language in Canada).

Table 4 also summarizes the literature on outgoing personality and language acquisition. Naimon et al. (1977) provide a potential counterexample but also provide an alternative explanation for their negative results (invalidity of measure).

Self-image has received both direct and indirect support as a predictor of second language success. Heyde (1977) found a high correlation between global self-esteem and teacher ratings of oral production in a pilot study involving 15 ESL students, while Oller, Hudson, and Liu (1977) reported that their subjects who perceived themselves as having traits which they valued positively did better on a cloze test of English as a second language. Also, Naimon et al. reported that teachers of French felt that poor learners in the classroom lacked "self-confidence."

Table 4

Anxiety and second language acquisition:
1. Carroll, 1963 (test anxiety)
2. Gardner et al., 1976 ("classroom anxiety")
3. Naimon, Frohlich, Stern, and Todesco, 1978 (classroom anxiety)
4. Wittenborn, Larsen, and Vigil, 1945
5. Chastain, 1975 (test anxiety)*

Outgoing personality and language acquisition:
1. Chastain, 1975: Outgoing students (Marlowe-Crowne scale) tend to get higher grades in FL classes.
2. Wesche, 1977: Students more willing to "role-play" do better in intensive French as a second language (listening comprehension, speaking skills)
3. Pritchard, 1952: Correlation between "sociability" and French as second language (child L2).

---

*Found for audiolingual but not "traditional" courses; discussion in Krashen, 1979a.

Affective Factors and Child-Adult Differences

To return to our problem, it was hypothesized earlier that cognitive explanations of child-adult differences (i.e., formal operations), were only partially successful in accounting for the data. The formal operations hypothesis may be able to account for adults' faster progress in earlier stages as well as the birth of the ability to do extensive language *learning*. It is not able to account for the finding that children are superior to adults in terms of ultimate attainment in second language acquisition, however. To more fully account for child-adult differences, then, we need to consider affective factors.

In the preceding section, I briefly reviewed the evidence supporting the hypothesis that affective factors relate to second language acquisition, and it was further hypothesized that affective factors relate to language acquisition indirectly; they do not affect the actual functioning of the "language acquisition device." Rather, they affect how much input the acquirer gets, and whether this input "gets in." They thus affect the strength of the "affective filter." If this view is correct, we can account for child-adult differences in attainment by hypothesizing the following:

At around puberty, the affective filter is strengthened.

In hypothesizing this, I am agreeing with scholars who posit that child-adult differences are in fact related to the personality changes that occur at around puberty (e.g., Schumann, 1975). When more carefully examined, however, this hypothesis makes some very specific claims that other positions may not.

First, it claims that no real change in the language acquisition device occurs at puberty. The LAD does not shut off, nor does it even "degenerate." Rather, the necessary input may be kept out. This is, I believe, a conservative position, and all that may be necessary to account for the data. Hypothesizing a change in the LAD, destruction or degeneration, is a very strong hypothesis that is counter to the considerable evidence we have that indicates that adults can *acquire* and do so quite well and in ways quite similar to child language acquirers.

Second, the filter hypothesis relates only to language acquisition and not to language learning. Specifically, it is intended to predict that the child is a better acquirer than the adult over the long run, that the child is superior with respect to ultimate attainment. It should be pointed out, however, that this difference in ultimate attainment is not always a big difference, and that it is true of groups but not necessarily of every individual. The acquirer who begins second language acquisition as a child will have a better chance of appearing to be a native speaker of the language (e.g., Seliger, Krashen, and Ladefoged, 1975) and will outperform the later starter in certain measures (Oyama, 1976, 1978), but this does not imply that the adult beginner cannot attain very high levels of proficiency. The available evidence, along with common observation, indicates clearly that adult starters often do very well in second language acquisition. The result of strengthening the filter may, in many cases, only be that the acquirer is not able to reach the native speaker level, a level that requires the acquisition of many communicatively redundant elements. Thus, the acquisition process is posited to be very powerful in the adult, the LAD intact, with the filter usually preventing only the final stages of second language acquisition for many acquirers.

This position does not exclude the possibility that certain adults may in fact achieve nativelike levels of proficiency despite their late start. We would only predict that such acquirers would have access to sufficient amounts of input, and would possess certain personality characteristics associated with a low affective filter.[8]

Two other points need to be made concerning the filter hypothesis before we proceed. The filter hypothesis does not deny the possibility that children (especially older children) have no filter at all. What is proposed is that the strength of the filter *increases* at around puberty. Also, the filter hypothesis implies that the filter does not necessarily weaken over the years, once strengthened, it may stay strong. A personality change, or an affectively positive acquisition situation (in which the acquirer is not "on the defensive," Stevick, 1976) could weaken the filter, either temporarily or permanently.[9, 10]

The filter hypothesis may thus be able to account for the finding that children are better acquirers over a long period of time, while the formal operations hypothesis accounts for adult advantages in rate of progress in early stages. Interestingly, the two positions may be related. At least some of the affective changes that cause a strengthening of the filter may have their origin in formal operations.[11]

Formal Operations and Affective Changes

According to Elkind (1970), the effects of formal operations may extend into more than just the strictly cognitive domain. Elkind states that the ability to think abstractly, a characteristic of formal thought, leads the adolescent to "conceptualize his own thought... (and) to take his mental constructions as objects and reason about them" (p. 66). Earlier, it was suggested that this new ability underlies the capacity to understand and use a conscious grammar of a second language. Another consequence is that the adolescent can now also "conceptualize the thought of other people" (p. 67).

In thinking about other people's mental worlds, however, adolescents typically make a serious error: they falsely assume that others are concerned with and are thinking about the same thing they are concerned with: themselves. "He assumes that other people are as obsessed with his behavior and appearance as he is himself" (Elkind, p. 67). This error leads to hypersensitivity and self-consciousness, feelings of vulnerability, and a lowered self-image, a result of the feeling that he or she is always the focus of attention and is under "the constant critical scrutiny of other people" (p. 67). In our terms, the result is a stronger affective filter (see also Schumann's concept of "psychological distance," Schumann, 1975).

If the above is a true picture, it implies that formal operations is no friend of adult second language acquisition. Exchanging some of our ability to subconsciously acquire for a conscious grammar that can only serve as a Monitor is a bad trade. As stated elsewhere, there are severe limits on the use of grammar in performance, and subconscious acquisition is far more efficient over the long run. The capacity for abstract thought, however, may be a gift worth exchanging for the ability to acquire a second language naturally and completely. The aims of the development of cognition are related to the ability to do higher mathematics, science, philosophy, and of course, linguistics. The damage it does to language acquisition is a casuality of this progress.

Figure 2 models the effect of affective factors on language acquisition. There are affective changes at puberty, changes that may result from one or both of these factors: biological puberty and/or formal operations. These affective changes are hypothesized to cause an increase in the strength of the affective filter, which in turn renders the performer less "open" to the input necessary for high eventual attainment in second language acquisition.

OTHER FACTORS

The formal operations-filter model goes a long way toward predicting child-adult differences in second language acquisition and learning. Some other factors may play a role, however, although it is not clear how central a role this is.

Scarcella and Higa (this volume) present evidence that strongly suggests that while younger children apparently get simpler input, and more help, from native speakers in second language interaction, older acquirers (adolescents in their study), use more "negotiating devices"; that is, they work harder to get the native speaker to provide comprehensible input. For example, older acquirers tend to provide more feedback, indicating whether or not they have understood what was said to them, and are better at keeping conversations going.

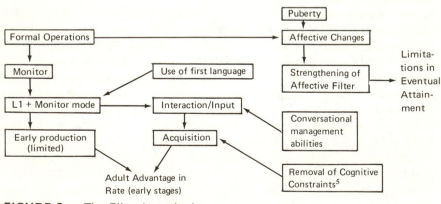

FIGURE 2   The Filter hypothesis

Older performers might thus be better at managing conversations, and hence actually be better at getting comprehensible input, despite the fact, noted by Wagner-Gough and Hatch (1975) as well as Scarcella and Higa, that younger children receive linguistically simpler input (see Hatch, 1977, for similar suggestions). This may be a powerful factor in predicting older acquirers' superiority in rate of acquisition, and probably helps to predict older-younger differences in general. There is no evidence for a sharp cutoff at puberty for the ability to manage conversations. It may simply be an ability that grows with time and experience.[12]

Also, as described earlier (see footnote 5), older performers may have fewer "cognitive constraints," as suggested by Cazden, Cancino, Rosansky, and Schumann (1975). This also predicts more rapid acquisition in adults and older children.

Another explanation for age differences in rate of acquisition has been made recently by Cummins (1980). Cummins distinguishes two aspects of language proficiency. BICS (basic interpersonal communication skills), which covers accent, oral fluency, and sociolinguistic competence, is distinguished from CALP (cognitive/academic proficiency), which covers "those aspects of language proficiency which are closely related to the development of literary skills in L1 and L2" (Cummins, 1980, p. 177). Both general language proficiency and cognitive and memory skills make up CALP, according to Cummins, and it is CALP, and not BICS, that is the major determinant of educational progress (see Cummins' figure 1, p. 179, in Cummins, 1980). BICS and CALP are hypothesized to have slightly different developmental courses, with BICS developing early.

The relevance of the BICS/CALP distinction to age differences in rate of acquisition is Cummins' further hypothesis that "older learners will perform better than younger learners on any measure that loads on a CALP factor" (p. 180). Thus, they can be expected to do better on most standardized tests but may not show a superiority for communicative skills such as oral fluency, phonology, and listening comprehension.

Cummins notes that evidence for age differences in BICS-related skills is "less clear," some studies, such as Oyama (1976, 1978) reporting younger acquirers to be superior for pronunciation and listening comprehension, while others (Snow and Hoefnagel-Höhle, 1978) find older subjects better for these skills. As pointed out earlier, however, and elaborated in Krashen, Long, and Scarcella (this volume), this may be because these studies actually probe two different things. Oyama's studies, which involved subjects who had been in the United States for many years, show that children are superior with respect to ultimate attainment over the long run. It thus remains to be demonstrated that the older-younger difference in rate holds only for CALP-related aspects of second language proficiency.

Older performers' greater "CALP," however, may contribute to observed age differences in rate of acquisition. With greater cognitive development and increased knowledge of the world, older performers may be able to make more sense of the input they hear; more CALP may thus mean more comprehensible input.

The expanded diagram given in Figure 3 attempts to integrate cognitive, affective, and some "other" factors.

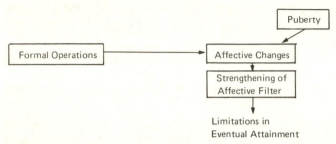

FIGURE 3   Cognitive, affective, and "other" factors and child-adult differences in rate and attainment

CONCLUSIONS

The schema given above is complex. It says, in effect, that child-adult differences in second language acquisition and learning are due to a number of causes, some interrelated and some not. This is in contrast to a number of current positions in the literature that imply that child-adult differences are due to a single factor or that such differences simply do not exist. These positions are able to account for only some of the data, however.

A major weakness of this set of hypotheses, however, is that they are post hoc. They account for previously established results but have not been used to predict new experimental evidence. These predictions could be readily generated and tested. For example, one could predict that nonformal thinkers will have a lower affective filter and will thus be better acquirers (suggested by Gloria Heller) but will perhaps also tend to be "underusers" of the Monitor (Krashen, 1978a).

The major prediction this schema makes, however, and one that I think is satisfied regularly, is that the adult is still an excellent acquirer when he or she is provided with the input he or she needs for acquisition in a situation where the filter is "low." The classroom may be an excellent place to provide such a situation, as long as it satisfies both the acquirer's purely linguistic needs (comprehensible input) as well as his or her affective needs. If the latter needs are not met, if the student is "on the defensive" (Stevick, 1976) and the filter is "up," the best input will be ineffective. If the filter is down, the adult can regain many of the advantages the child enjoys.

NOTES

1. This schema leaves two unresolved problems. First, Molfese (1976) reports no change in degree of AER asymmetry with age for his infant subjects. This may not conflict with the hypothesis that lateralization develops with age; measured laterality in the infant brain may relate quite differently to "true" underlying laterality (see Krashen, 1975, for detailed discussion). Another possible problem is Lenneberg's observation that recovery from aphasia is better for those injured before puberty, a finding that seems to imply right hemisphere participation in the language function until puberty. Here there are two possibilities: First, recovery need not involve the right hemisphere but may be due to undamaged tissue on the left side assuming the language function (e.g., Roberts, 1958). Second, if it is indeed the right hemisphere that is responsible for this superiority in recovery, perhaps these late-lateralized aspects of language (posited in the text of this paper) play some role.

2. It should be emphasized that if the development of cerebral dominance is complete before puberty (e.g., at age 5), this does *not* necessarily imply that the "critical period" for language acquisition ends at 5. My interpretation of such a result is that the process of the development of lateralization and the ability to acquire second languages are independent. Krashen and Harshman (1972) suggest that the development of cerebral dominance may relate to the maturation of mental abilities underlying *first* language acquisition (see also Krashen, 1973b).

3. The evidence for this hypothesis is indirect but consistent: We tend to find first language influence in acquisition-low situations (e.g., foreign language as opposed to second language, in early stages as opposed to later stages), and the domain of L1 influence appears to be similar to those structures that tend to be early acquired (e.g., word order as opposed to bound morphology; see Dušková, 1969; LoCoco, 1975). Children acquiring second language tend to have a "silent period" in early stages, a time during which acquisition is built up via active listening. L1 influence in children is not unknown, however, and it occurs in predictable circumstances: early output demands and less than optimal input for acquisition (see Selinker, Swain, and Dumas, 1975; Ervin-Tripp, 1974).

4. Getting this extra early input may be quite beneficial, but it also has its dangers. Users of the L1 plus Monitor mode may give the impression of having acquired much more than they really have and may invite very complex input from conversational partners; they thus get in "over their heads."

5. Cognitive changes other than the onset of formal operations may account for some age-related differences in language acquisition. In their study of six Spanish-speaking ESL performers, Cazden, Cancino, Rosansky, and Schumann (1975) note that an adolescent was the fastest acquirer of the group, which included children aged 5 and two adults. They speculate as follows: "Juan's superior performance might be explained by the fact that he was old enough so that his learning was not constrained by language related cognitive development, and he was young enough so that whatever constraints are concomitant with puberty were not yet in effect" (p. 57). Cazden et al. are referring here to aspects of cognition that emerge prior to formal operations, aspects that are prerequisite to normal language acquisition. I understand their proposal as follows: First language acquisition may be constrained by cognitive development; that is, the acquisition of certain forms may depend on the previous maturation of certain cognitive abilities. This is the Piagetian view supported by Sinclair-de-Zwart (1969), in which it was shown that language training does not directly lead to cognitive development. This implies that "language reflects, rather than determines, cognitive development" (Dale, 1976, p. 262). The older second language acquirer will thus have fewer "cognitive constraints" on the acquisition of linguistic structure, being more cognitively mature, and he or she may thus be a faster acquirer (not that we are discussing language acquisition exclusively and not language learning). These comments also hold for adult vis à vis young children, and thus may also help to account for faster adult second language acquisition, at least in earlier stages. (Later stages in adults are hypothesized to be constrained by affective factors, discussed below.)

6. Much of the material in this section is a summary of Krashen (1980a).

7. This position modifies the "input hypothesis," which states that language acquisition (not learning) results from the performer's comprehension of input that contains structures "just beyond" his or her current level of competence ($i + 1$, discussed in Krashen, 1980b). The addition of the affective filter implies that understood input at the right level is necessary for language acquisition but not sufficient.

8. Neufeld (1979) confirms that some adults can come very close, even in pronunciation. In his study, native speakers of French judged passages read by native speakers and nonnative speakers of French who had begun their exposure to French as adults. Neufeld reports that several adult second language acquirers did sound convincing to the judges. It should also be pointed out that some performers may achieve the illusion of nativelike proficiency in certain situations without fully acquiring all aspects of the target language. This can be done with the use of certain strategies, such as avoidance, or the use of the conscious grammar to supplement acquired competence (the optimal Monitor user described in Krashen, 1978b).

9. We might also want to posit an "output filter" to handle cases of performers (all of us?) who do not "perform their competence" in second languages. It may be the case, for example, that some performers feel hesitant to really "use their best French accent" for fear of sounding silly. Such reactions may in fact be most common for pronunciation (see Stevick's illuminating discussions in Stevick, 1976). When performers are reluctant to perform their competence, the tendency is to "fall back" on the first language. Thus, L1 influence may be due either to lack of acquisition or to the failure to utilize acquired L2 competence. Weakening the output filter may be the explanation for Guiora, Beit-Hallahmi, Brannon, Dull, and Scovel's (1972) results. In their study, subjects demonstrated better pronunciation of a foreign language after ingesting an "optimal" amount of alcohol. A reasonable hypothesis is that the output filter is also strengthened at around puberty.

10. Of course, affective changes take place one's entire life, and it is probably the case that these changes have both short- and long-term effects on the affective filter as well as the "output filter" (footnote 9). What is claimed here is that the affective change that comes around puberty has a permanent affect on language acquisition, that the changes it causes in the filter are only reversible to a limited degree. (It is an important goal of pedagogy, I think, to bring the filter down as much as possible by providing a low-anxiety situation in which the student is "off the defensive," as Stevick puts it. There is probably a fair amount of individual variation in the extent to which the filter can be lowered.)

11. Affective variables have also been shown to relate to success in child second language acquisition, but the literature is not extensive (e.g., Fillmore, 1976). I would predict that such variables would relate primarily to the amount of input the child gets; the more outgoing child, for example, might interact more and thus receive more input. This predicts faster acquisition but makes no prediction with respect to ultimate attainment. Ultimate attainment here is hypothesized to relate to filter strength, and it can be further hypothesized that in children in general the filter is never strong enough to prevent the attainment of nativelike proficiency in second languages, given enough input and time. Fillmore's subject Nora, for example, "was strongly motivated to be associated with English speaking children (and) sought them out to play with to an extent that none of the other children in the study did" (p. 706). Nora was also described as more self-confident than the other child ESL acquirers in her group, and was more uninhibited in using the language. She thus made much faster progress in English as a second language than the other children did. This does not imply that the less integratively oriented and self-confident children did not eventually acquire English to the same level of proficiency. Unfortunately, we have no follow-up data on Fillmore's children.

12. Older performers may be aided in conversational management by their better short-term memories. With better memories, there is a greater capacity to learn and use prefabricated routines and patterns, which in turn could result in greater linguistic interaction, more comprehensible input, and hence faster language acquisition. (Of course, use of routines and patterns can also result in inviting incomprehensible input. Native speakers, hearing gram-

matically correct and appropriate memorized language, may respond with complex language that is much too difficult for the second language acquirer.) See Hatch (1972), Hakuta (1974), Krashen and Scarcella (1978), and Fillmore (1976).

REFERENCES

Ausubel, D. "Implications of preadolsecent and early adolescent cognitive development for secondary-school teaching. *The Modern Language Journal*. 1962, 45, 268–275.

Baxter, R. The assessment of formal operations in the solution of two paper and pencil tasks by older adolescents and adult graduate students in education. In J. Magary et al. (eds.), *Piagetian Theory and the Helping Professions*. University of Southern California, 1977.

Bialystok, E., and M. Fröhlich, Aspects of second language learning in classroom settings. *Working Papers on Bilingualism*. 1977, 13, 1–26.

Bogen, J. The other side of the brain I. Dysgraphia and dyscopia following cerebral commissurotomy. *Bulletin of the Los Angeles Neurological Society*. 1969a, 34, 73–105.

Bogen, J. The other side of the brain II. An appositional mind. *Bulletin of the Los Angeles Neurological Society*. 1969b, 34, 135–162.

Bogen, J., and Bogen, G. The other side of the brain III: The corpus callosum and creativity. *Bulletin of the Los Angeles Neurological Society*. 1969, 34, 191–200.

Butterworth, G., and Hatch, E. A Spanish-speaking adolescent's acquisition of English syntax. In E. Hatch (ed.), *Second Language Acquisition*. Rowley, Mass.: Newbury House, 1978, 231–245.

Caplan, P., and Kinsbourne, M. Baby drops the rattle: Asymmetry of duration of grasp by infants. *Child Development*. 1976, 47, 532–534.

Carmon, A., and I. Nachshon, Effect of unilateral brain-damage on perception of temporal order. *Cortex*. 1971, 7, 410–418.

Carroll, J. The prediction of success in intensive foreign language training. In R. Glazer (ed.), *Training Research and Education*. University of Pittsburgh: Pittsburgh, 1963.

Cazden, C., Cancino, H., Rosansky, E., and Schumann, J. Second language acquisition sequences in children, adolescents, and adults. Final Report, United States Department of Health, Education, and Welfare, 1975.

Chastain, K. Affective and ability factors in second-language acquisition. *Language Learning*. 1975, 25, 153–161.

Chihara, T., and Oller, J. Attitudes and attained proficiency in EFL: a sociolinguistic study of adult Japanese learners. *Language Learning*. 1978, 28.

Cummins, J. The cross-lingual dimensions of language proficiency: implications for bilingual education and the optimal age issue. *TESOL Quarterly*. 1980, 14, 175–187.

Curran, C. Counseling skills adapted to the learning of foreign language. *Bulletin of the Menninger Clinic*. 1961, 25, 78–93.

Curry, F. A comparison of left-handed and right-handed subjects on verbal and non-verbal tasks. *Cortex*. 1967, 3, 343–352.

Dale, P. *Language Development: Structure and Function*. 2d ed. New York: Holt, Rinehart, and Winston, 1976.

Developmental Psychology Today. Del Mar, California: CRM Books, 1971.

Dulay, H., and Burt, M. Remarks on creativity in language acquisition. In M. Burt, H. Dulay, and M. Finocchiaro (eds.), *Viewpoints on English as a Second Language*. New York: Regents, 1977, 95–126.

Dulit, E. Adolescent thinking à la Piaget: the formal stage. *Journal of Youth and Adolescence*. 1972, 1, (4), 218–301.

Duškova, L. On sources of error in foreign language learning. *International Review of Applied Linguistics*. 1969, 4, 11–36.

Elkind, D. *Children and Adolescents: Interpretive Essays on Jean Piaget*. New York: Oxford Press, 1970.

Ervin-Tripp, S. Is second language learning like the first? *TESOL Quarterly*. 1974, 8, 111–127.

Fillmore, L. *The Second Time Around: Cognitive and Social Strategies in Second Language Acquisition*. Ph.D. Dissertation, Department of Linguistics, Stanford University, 1976.

Gardiner, M, and Walter, D. Evidence of hemispheric specialization from infant EEG. In S. Harnad et al. (eds.), *Lateralization in the Nervous System*. New York: Academic Press, 1976, 481–502.

Gardner, R. Motivational variables in second language learning. Reprinted in Gardner and Lambert (1972).

Gardner, R., and Lambert, W. *Attitudes and Motivation in Second Language Learning*. Rowley, Mass.: Newbury House, 1972.

Gardner, R., Smythe, P., Clement, R., and Gliksman, L. *The Canadian Modern Language Review*. 1976, 32, 198–213.

Genessee, F. Is there an optimal age for starting second language instruction? *McGill Journal of Education*, 1977, 13, 145–154.

Geschwind, N., and Levitsky, W. Human brain: left-right assymmetries in temporal speech region. *Science*. 1968, 161, 186–187.

Gordon, H. Hemispheric asymmetries in the perception of musical chords. *Cortex*. 1970, 6, 387–398.

Guiora, A., Beit-Hallahmi, B., Brannon, R., Dull, C., and Scovel, T. The effects of experimentally induced changes in ego states on pronunciation ability in a second language: an exploratory study. *Comprehensive Psychiatry*. 1972, 13, 421–428.

Hakuta, K. Prefabricated routines and the emergence of structure in second language acquisition. *Language Learning*. 1974, 24, 287–298.

Hatch, E. Some studies in language learning. *UCLA Workpapers in Teaching English as a Second Language*. 1972, 6, 29–36.

Hatch, E. Optimal age or optimal learners? *Workpapers in TESL*. 1977, 11, 45–56.

Hatch, E. Introduction to E. Hatch (ed.), *Second Language Acquisition* Rowley, Mass.: Newbury House, 1978, 1–18.

Hecaen, H. Acquired aphasia in children and the ontogenesis of hemispheric functional specialization. *Brain and Language*, 1976, 3, 111–134.

Heyde, A. 1977. The relationship between self esteem and the oral production of a second language. In H. D. Brown, D. A. Yorio and R. H. Crymes (eds.) *On TESOL '77: Teaching and Learning English as a Second Language*. Wash. D.C.: TESOL.

Inhelder, B., and Piaget J. *The Growth of Logical Thinking from Childhood to Adolescence*. New York: Basic Books, 1958.

Kimura, D. Cerebral dominance and the perception of verbal stimuli. *Canadian Journal of Psychology*. 1961, 15, 166–171.

Krashen, S. Lateralization, language learning, and the critical period. *Language Learning*. 1973a, 23, 63–74.

Krashen, S. Mental abilities underlying linguistic and non-linguistic functions. *Linguistics*. 1973b, 115, 39–55.

Krashen, S. The development of cerebral dominance and language learning: More new evidence. In D. Dato (ed.), *Developmental Psycholinguistics: Theory and Applications*. Georgetown Round Table on Language and Linguistics. Washington: Georgetown University, 1975, 209–233.

Krashen, S. Formal and informal linguistic environments in language learning and language acquisition. TESOL Quarterly. 1976, 10; 157–168.

Krashen, S. The Monitor Model for adult second language performance. In M. Burt, H. Dulay, and M. Finocchiaro (eds.), *Viewpoints on English as a Second Language*. New York: Regents, 1977a, 152–161.

Krashen, S. Some issues relating to the Monitor Model. In H. D. Brown, C. Yorio, and R. Crymes (eds.), *Teaching and Learning English as a Second Language: Trends in Research and Practice. On TESOL '77.* Washington: TESOL, 1977b, 144–158.

Krashen, S. Individual variation in the use of the Monitor. In W. Ritchie (ed.), *Principles of Second Language Learning.* New York: Academic Press, 1978a, 1975–183.

Krashen, S. Adult second language acquisition and learning: A review of theory and applications. In R. Gingras (ed.) *Second Language Teaching and Foreign Language Learning.* Arlington, VA: Center for Applied Linguistics. 1978b.

Krashen, S. Attitude and aptitude in relation to second language acquisition and learning. In K. Diller (ed.), *Individual Differences and Universals in Language Learning Aptitude.* Rowley, Ma.: Newbury House, 1980a.

Krashen, S. The input hypothesis. Paper presented at 1980 Round Table on Languages and Linguistics. Georgetown University, 1980b.

Krashen, S., and Harshman, R. Lateralization and the critical period. *UCLA Working Papers in Phonetics.* 1972, 23, 13–21.

Krashen, S., Butler, J. Birnbaum, R. and Robertson, J. Two studies in language acquisition and language learning. *ITL: Review of Applied Linguistics.* 1978, 39–40: 73–92.

Krashen, S., and Scarcella, R. On routines and patterns in language acquisition and performance. *Language Learning.* 1978, 28, 283–300.

Krashen, S., Long, M., and Scarcella, R. Age, rate, and eventual attainment in second language acquisition. *TESOL Quarterly.* 1979, 13, 573–582.

Larsen, D., and Smalley, W. *Becoming Bilingual: A Guide to Language Learning.* New Canaan, Conn.: Practical Anthropology, 1972.

Lenneberg, E. *Biological Foundations of Language.* New York: Wiley, 1967.

LoCoco, V. An analysis of Spanish and German learner's errors. *Working Papers on Bilingualism.* 1975, 7, 96–124.

Lukmani, Y. Motivation to learn and language proficiency. *Language Learning* 1972, 22, 261–273.

Milner, B. Laterality effects in audition. In V. Mountcastle (ed.), *Interhemispheric Relations and Cerebral Dominance.* Baltimore: Johns Hopkins University Press, 1962, 117–195.

Molfese, D. The ontogeny of cerebral asymmetry in man: auditory evoked potentials to linguistic and non-linguistic stimuli. In J. Desmedt (ed.), *Recent Developments in the Psychology of language: The Cerebral Evoked Potential Approach.* London: Oxford University Press, 1976.

Morgan, A., McDonald, P., and MacDonald, H. Differences in bilateral alpha activity as a function of experimental task, with a note on lateral eye movements and hypnotizability. *Neuropsychologia.* 1971, 9, 459–469.

Naimon, N., Frohlich, M., Stern, D., and Todesco, A. *The Good Language Learner.* Toronto: Ontario Institute for Studies in Education, 1978.

Neufeld, G. Towards a theory of language learning ability. *Language Learning.* 1979, 29, 227–241.

Oller, J. Attitude variables in second language learning. In M. Burt, H. Dulay, and M. Finocchiaro (eds.), *Viewpoints on English as a Second Language.* New York: Regents, 1977, 172–184.

Oller, J., Hudson, A., and Liu, P. Attitudes and attained proficiency in ESL: a sociolinguistic study of native speakers of Chinese in the United States. *Language Learning.* 1977, 27, 1–27.

Oyama, S. A sensitive period for the acquisition of a non-native phonological system. *Journal of Psycholinguistic Research.* 1976, 5, 261–285.

Oyama, S. The sensitive period and comprehension of speech. *Working Papers on Bilingualism.* 1978, 16, 1–17.

Papcun, G., Krashen, S., Terbeek, D., Remington, R., and Harshman, R. The left hemisphere is specialized for speech, language, and/or something else. *Journal of the Acoustical Society of America.* 1974, 55, 319–327.

Penfield, W., and Roberts, L. *Speech and Brain Mechanisms.* New York: Atheneum Press, 1959.

Pritchard, D. F. 1975. An investigation into the relationship of personality traits and ability in modern languages. *British Journal of Educational Psychology*, 22.

Roberts, L. Functional plasticity in cortical speech areas and the integration of speech. *Archives of Neurology and Psychiatry.* 1958, 79, 275–283.

Rosansky, E. The critical period for the acquisition of language: some cognitive developmental considerations. *Working Papers on Bilingualism.* 1975, 6, 10–23.

Russell, R., and M. Espir. *Traumatic Aphasia.* New York: Oxford Press, 1961.

Satz, P., Bakker, D., Teunissen, J., Goebel, R., and Van der Vlugt, H. Developmental parameters of the ear asymmetry: a multivariate approach. *Brain and language.* 1975, 2, 171–185.

Scarcella, R., and Higa, C. Input and age differences in second language acquisition. This volume.

Schumann, J. Affective factors and the problem of age in second language acquisition. *Language Learning.* 1975, 2, 209–235.

Scovel, T. Foreign accents, language acquisition, and cerebral dominance. *Language Learning.* 1969, 19, 245–254.

Seliger, H., Krashen, S. and Ladefoged, P. Maturational constraints in the acquisition of native-like accent in second language learning. *Language Science,* 1975.

Selinker, L., Swain, M.m and Dumas, G. The interlanguage hypothesis extended to children. *Language learning.* 1975, 25, 139–155.

Sinclair-de-Zwart, H. Developmental psycholinguistics. In D. Elkind and J. H. Flavell (eds.), *Studies in Cognitive Development.* New York: Oxford University Press, 1969.

Snow, C., and Hoefnagel-Höhle, M. Age differences in second language acquisition. In E. Hatch (ed.), *Second Language Acquisition.* Rowley, Mass.: Newbury House, 1978, 333-344.

Spolsky, B. Attitudinal aspects of second language learning. *Language Learning.* 1969, 19, 271–283.

Stevick, E. *Memory, Meaning, and Method.* Rowley, Mass.: Newbury House, 1976.

Taylor, B. Toward a theory of language acquisition. *Language Learning.* 1974, 24, 23–36.

Wada, J., Clarke, R., and Hamm, A. Cerebral hemispheric asymmetry in humans. *Archives of Neurology.* 1975, 32, 239–246.

Wagner-Gough, J., and Hatch, E. The importance of input data in second language acquisition studies. *Language Learning.* 1975, 25, 297–308.

Wesche, M. 1977. Learning behaviors of successful adult students on intensive language training. In Henning, C. (ed.), *Proceedings of the Los Angeles Second Language Research Forum,* UCLA.

Witelson, S. Early hemisphere specialization and interhemispheric plasticity. In S. Segalowitz and F. Gruber (eds.), *Language Development and Neurological Theory.* New York: Academic Press, 1977, 213–287.

Witelson, S., and Pallie, W. Left hemisphere specialization for language in the newborn. *Brain.* 1973, 96, 641–646.

Wood, C., Goff, W., and Day, R. Auditory evoked potentials during speech perception. *Science.* 1971, 173, 1248–1251.

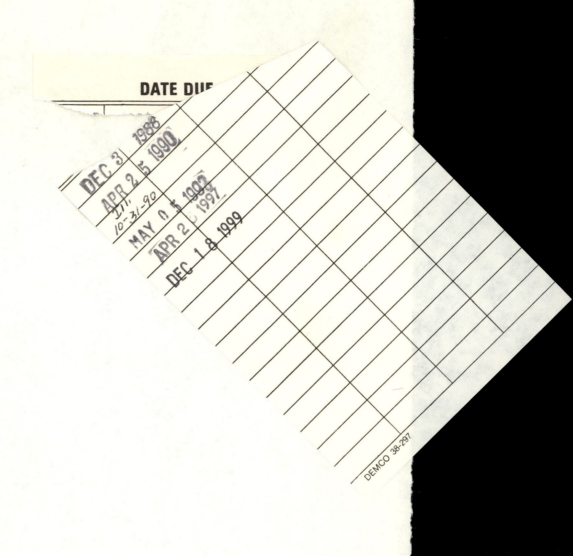